AN INTRODUCTION TO
PARAPSYCHOLOGY
IN THE CONTEXT OF
SCIENCE

Books in the Same Series

by

R. A. McConnell

ENCOUNTERS WITH PARAPSYCHOLOGY
(1982)

**PARAPSYCHOLOGY AND
SELF-DECEPTION IN SCIENCE**
(1983)

An Introduction to

PARAPSYCHOLOGY

IN THE CONTEXT OF

SCIENCE

R. A. McCONNELL

Author & Publisher

BIOLOGICAL SCIENCES DEPARTMENT
UNIVERSITY OF PITTSBURGH

The front cover shows Galaxy M81 as photographed through the 200-inch Mt. Palomar telescope by Milton Humason in 1952 and published in *The Hubble Atlas of Galaxies*. This galaxy, located in Ursa Major, is distant 9 million light-years. The light that made this photograph had traveled most of the way toward Earth before conscious man came into being.

International Standard Book Number: 0-9610232-3-6
Library of Congress Catalog Card Number: 82-99945
© 1983 by R.A. McConnell. All rights reserved.
Manufactured in the United States of America.
Printed on alkaline-buffered archival paper.
Book design by R.A. McConnell.

CONTENTS

II. THE OBSERVATION OF PSI PHENOMENA

III. THE SOCIOLOGY OF PARAPSYCHOLOGY

PREFACE

What is the relation of human consciousness to the physical world? This book presents some first steps toward a scientific answer to that question.

Parapsychological or "psi" phenomena are anomalous in the deepest philosophical sense. To make them acceptable to scientists requires more than a presentation of what is known of their nature. Needed is a re-assessment of the widely scattered areas of belief upon which they impinge. This book reflects my own adjustment to their reality that has taken place over a third of a century. In it I have tried to present psi phenomena in the context of Western science.

For the most part, the book is based on lectures prepared for a course I have given since 1973 to upper-level students at the University of Pittsburgh. Although written at an undergraduate technical level, the material is intended to pass scrutiny by the leaders of the natural sciences. If those leaders reject what I say, I trust they will be forced to attack my facts while grudgingly conceding that my methodological perspective is their own.

No doubt, some parapsychologists also will be dissatisfied with my perception of the facts. I shall not be surprised if I am belabored from both sides.

In this work I make no claim to completeness. The most active areas of present-day parapsychological research are reported in the journals and are therefore treated only briefly herein. I have avoided discussing explanatory theories; for I believe that as yet there are none worthy of attention. I have made no effort to critically survey all past research, nor to specifically resolve "the ESP controversy." The latter is a responsibility that no reader can delegate to an author until the matter has been publicly settled by a consensus of the concerned leaders of science—in this case, the leaders of physics and psychology. However, in my reference list at the end of the book I have marked papers that I think have unusual evidential (or sociological) interest. My attitude toward the student of parapsychology has always been: Whether you as an individual accept ESP as a real phenomenon is your problem and of no concern to me.

This work is divided into three parts, which can be independently studied. Chapters 1–9 present the psychosocial context with which psi phenomena are congruous. Chapters 10–16 are the evidential heart of the book. Chapters 17–26 discuss method, fraud, and prejudice in science and speculate about the future in relation to the present.

This *Introduction to Parapsychology* is the final volume in a series of three. The first volume, *Encounters with Parapsychology* (McConnell, 1981), is a collection of largely nontechnical writings by persons of exceptional intelligence who have associated themselves with this field over the past century. Volume Two, *Parapsychology and Self-Deception in Science* (McConnell, 1982a), is an assembly of original papers too unpalatable to be published through normal channels and too detailed to be included in the present survey. The reader who finds *Encounters* tantalyzingly peripheral and the present volume forbiddingly broad may find in that middle book an easy, step-by-step access to an understanding of parapsychology and its problems.

Since coming to my laboratory in 1967, Thelma Kuzmen Clark has made a profound contribution to my thinking. Throughout the years, first while a student of neuroscience and later as my research associate, she has been the principal critic of my writings. Whatever precision and grace may be found in the present volume are a tribute to her incisive mind and delicate ear. However, I am still not quite certain whether she fully believes in psi phenomena. Certainly, she did not before she began their serious study in 1979.

Part I

THE PSYCHOSOCIAL SUBSTRATE
OF PARAPSYCHOLOGY

1

DEFINITIONS AND QUESTIONS

Behind the Masquerade

What are the boundaries of parapsychology? That depends on whom you ask. There was once a California organization with the wonderful name, "Academy of Parapsychology and Medicine," one of whose directors publicly claimed that parapsychology includes the study of astrology, organic foods, and air pollution. At the University of Pittsburgh parapsychology includes none of these topics.

For our purpose, parapsychology is the study of a class of natural phenomena designated by the Greek letter "psi." From an experiential point of view there are many forms in which psi phenomena might masquerade: mind reading, premonitions, poltergeists, luck at gambling, fortune telling, religious miracles, witchcraft, shamanism, faith healing. These and similar occurrences may, in some instances, involve psi phenomena.

The defining of psi phenomena becomes more manageable if we force them into analytic pigeonholes. So far as is known today, there are just two kinds of psi phenomena: extrasensory perception, or ESP, and psychokinesis, or PK.

Consider any higher organism. Ordinarily it interacts with the world by sensorimotor mechanisms. I have shown this diagrammatically by two arrows associated with the outer circle of Figure 1.1. One arrow represents sensory input to the organism, the other, motor output.

Sensorimotor interaction mechanisms have been studied in biology, psychology, and physics and are well known in principle. They involve heat, light, sound, pressure, gravity, chemical processes, and possibly magnetism. It is generally accepted that for these mechanisms the sensors and effectors are all external to what we call the central nervous system (the inner circle of the figure). Signals into and out of the brain itself, passing in the space between the circles, are sent solely by electrical impulses along neurons and by chemical transmitters in the small gaps between the terminals of one neuron and the receptors of the next.[1]

It is commonly believed by scientists that there are no other

1. Slow chemical signals can, of course, reach the brain via circulating fluids.

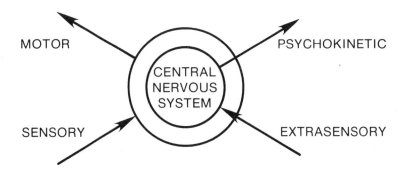

Figure 1.1. Extrasensory and psychokinetic phenomena can be conceptualized as homologous to sensory and motor interactions between a living organism and its environment.

modes of interaction between living organisms and their environment. The opposite opinion is held by a majority of nonscientists. I believe this is one of those rare cases where prevailing lay opinion is right and dominant scientific belief is wrong.

The experiments of parapsychology make it necessary to postulate another, entirely new kind of interaction between the central nervous system and the outside world, a class of interactions that does not involve the known forces and fields of physics. Moreover, the nature of the experimental evidence justifies our calling the new interactions "psychological" as opposed to "physical," although I do not want to pretend that such labeling constitutes an explanation.

These interactions are presumed to occur directly with the central nervous system or some part of it. They are represented in the figure by two arrows terminating on the inner circle.

The ingoing effect is called extrasensory perception. What is ingoing is information—that which is measured in "bits." The outgoing effect is called psychokinesis. What goes out can affect an external physical system. These two reciprocal effects are jointly known as "psi phenomena."

Since physicists agree that we cannot transmit information across a "system envelope" except by means of at least a little energy, and since it may turn out to be only the informational control of external energy that is sent out in psychokinesis, we might at least tentatively regard both psi effects as slight information-energy leakages through normally effective physical barriers. If we are worried about the law of conservation of energy, we can postulate a new "psychic energy," to balance the equation. Poincaré (1903) discussed the precedents for this.

This is a neat model, but it has a limitation. It does not accommodate "precognitive ESP," which is the term for rationally uninferable foreknowledge. By now there is considerable experimental evidence for precognition. If, as I believe, it is a real effect, there will be some revision needed in our conception of causality.

To be certain that there is no misunderstanding of what I mean by psi phenomena, I shall describe prototypical experiments.

Extrasensory perception is a transfer of information from the outside world into a living organism by some means other than the recognized energy modes of physics. This transfer of information is detected by the behavior of the organism. If you were asked to guess the order of a deck of playing cards after it had been shuffled by someone else and laid on a certain table in an isolated room 100 miles away, you might try to use ESP. Any information you got in this way presumably "traveled" between the cards and you and was then exhibited by your behavior in guessing correctly.

ESP is sometimes defined as "a response to an unknown event not presented to any known sense." In card-guessing ESP experiments, the "event" is the position of the card in the deck.

Psychokinesis is the reciprocal effect to ESP in which the behavior of an organism affects a physical system by other than the recognized energy modes of physics. For example, let us suppose that at this moment a dice cage is being turned by a motor in an empty room in another city and that, merely by wishing while seated here, you can cause certain die faces to come up more often than would be expected by chance. This would be an instance of the psychokinetic effect.

These are physically trivial and benign possibilities which, if they occur, are philosophically disturbing because they are totally unexpected from our present scientific outlook. As we shall see, there are other possible forms of psi phenomena that might be of more practical importance.

THE BLIND EYE OF HISTORY

If our purpose is to understand the controversy that beclouds parapsychology, we would be ill-advised to confine our attention narrowly to psi phenomena. We should broaden our investigation to include peripheral aspects of the field and ask a variety of obliquely related questions—questions about scientific method, the meaning of repeatability in a nonrepeating world, the nature of statistical proof, the distinction beteen legal and scientific proof, the structure of scientific revolutions, the history of parapsychology, fraud in science, prejudice among scientists, mental illness among psychics, psychological mechanisms of belief, and the nature of knowing.[2]

This may be too big a task, but I would like to help you make a beginning. In this book I shall try to explain why parapsychological phenomena are not an accepted part of our cultural heritage—why it is that they are not part of the common knowledge of all educated people. There are many reasons why the reality of psi phenomena might be doubted. One is what I call the "historical argument." It takes this form:

Are these phenomena something new in human experience, or are they old? If they are newly discovered, why were they not discovered sooner? If they are old, why are they not in the textbooks of science?

The answer to the first question is that psi phenomena are not newly discovered. They have been known since history began. To understand why they were not discussed until recently in textbooks, we must first recall the nature of human language.

Our representation of reality is by stringing words together. Verbal expression is an artistic abstraction and never represents more than a limited portion of reality. If, as we are taught in psychology, mental perception is selective, then the representation of that perception by words is even more so. This is as true of scientific description as it is of poetry.

Textbooks are systematic selections of experience, organized for the efficient enculturation of students. I want to emphasize the word "selections." Scientific textbooks tell only as much of human experience as is congruent with the culturally prevailing view of nature. What is excluded is not only what falls outside the admitted scope of a given book but also whatever contradicts the basic assumptions upon which that book was written.

This is as it should be. Human comprehension depends upon simplification. If we try to be too accurate or too detailed, the law and order of science disappear and only confusion remains. So

---

2. Beyond these specific concerns lies the peculiar character of our civilization in which the controversy occurs. For the reader who prefers a panoramic approach, I have included "A Background for the Study of Parapsychology" as Appendix A.

instead, we use models in which complex situations are represented by idealized abstractions.

Our theories based on models are always necessarily incomplete. What may be a justified simplification for a limited purpose, is always an oversimplification from some broader perspective. For example, a billiard ball makes a good model of the earth for calculating its orbit around the sun. But a billiard ball has no atmospheric layer and is not a useful model for understanding meteorology.

Because of the limited, ad hoc nature of theories based on models, it is to be expected that new discoveries will not fit old theories. Indeed, existing theories can tell us nothing about what lies outside their scope. How then do we deal with experiments reaching into the unknown?

The first rule of evidence in science is this: If an observation does not fit the accepted theoretical model, that observation must be wrong and should be ignored. This attitude works as long as we are merely fleshing out the familiar framework of science, but eventually it leads us into trouble. To get out of trouble, there is a second rule which goes as follows: If an anomalous observation occurs often enough, investigate it.

How do these ideas apply to psi phenomena? If we go back to the source books, we find that psi phenomena have occurred at least since man began writing, but they occur spontaneously and cannot usually be produced upon demand.

Organized science, from its start only four hundred years ago, was highly successful in dealing with processes involving things of the external physical world, which are independent of the observer and, hence, reproducible. As a result, scientists developed a perspective in which there was no place for the study of consciousness, which, in any case, was a subject already jealously guarded by religion. The rarely apparent, direct intrusions of consciousness phenomena into the physical world, that is, the phenomena of ESP and PK, were regarded as observational errors by scientists.

History books, of course, are selective just like every other form of writing. The selection framework for history is the historian's cultural heritage, a part of which is his understanding of the cosmos. If the natural scientists of the day have great authority, and if they say that ESP is impossible, then all serious references to ESP must be deleted from a textbook of history if it is to be regarded as scholarly. By this dictum, all descriptions of psi phenomena by ancient people were for a long time regarded by modern scholars as superstition, malobservation, or misrepresentation. Historians are no different from the rest of us. Their books tell only what they believe.

It is true, of course, that Western science has a corrective means to avoid being trapped in total stagnation. Rule No. 2, as given above, says: if any observational anomaly occurs persistently, it must be investigated. But scientitsts are busy people and do not like to change their thinking. It usually takes a long time to gain acceptance for a revolutionary truth about nature. Thus it is that psi phenomena, although they have occurred since ancient times, have only recently been described in the textbooks of science.

The following illustration of man's tendency to self-deception appears in the best available English-language history of Netherlands parapsychology (Zorab, 1976, pp. 59–60):

> Toward the end of the last century the investigators of the [British Society for Psychical Research] started to draw the attention of some scholars, students, and writers in the Netherlands. There was, on the other hand, an enormous resistance prevalent in scientific and philosophical circles [that] nearly dealt a fatal blow to the career of the later Dr. Leopold, a classical scholar of repute. He devoted his doctor's thesis to Cicero's treatise, "On divination," and advanced a telepathic hypothesis to explain some of the cases Cicero quoted and which we in modern times regard as belonging to the so-called crisis-ESP type. . . . Leopold's thesis was refused on the ground that telepathy was nonexistent and could therefore not be advanced as a hypothesis in a scholarly paper. Leopold was forced to choose another subject and study a couple of years longer.
>
> The above was told me by a friend of Dr. Leopold, Dr. K.H.E. de Jong, who was also studying classical languages at the University of Leiden. At the time (about 1899) de Jong was preparing a thesis on "The Mysteries of Isis," and he, too, was advancing a telepathic hypothesis. . . . However, when he was informed about the fate that Leopold's thesis had suffered, he quickly covered up the possible telepathic influence in the case . . . in such equivocal phrasing that his professors did not notice it, and de Jong's doctoral thesis was accepted with honours.

SCOPE OF THE UNKNOWN

There are many questions one might ask about psi phenomena. Those that come readily to mind I have sorted into five groups.

● The first is about the characteristics of psi in general:

—Does everyone have at least a little psychic ability?

—In what groups of people is it more prevalent? In men or women? In the young or the old?

—Do certain races of man possess more psychic ability?

—Do primitive cultures have more? Are psi phenomena perhaps suppressed by the self-awareness of civilization?

—Do psi phenomena manifest themselves more strongly in certain periods of history, as in the early Christian era or in the time of witch hunting?

—Are there recognizable personality types associated with psychic ability?

—Does psychic ability correlate with intelligence?

—Is it a sign of insanity?

—When a paranoid schizophrenic says he is being persecuted, is he in some cases using ESP to perceive the true, unfriendly feelings of his family and acquaintances?

—Is psychic ability inherited?

—Can it be increased by training?

—What good is it? Can it be used for gambling?

—Do animals exhibit psi?

• The physical aspects of psi phenomena suggest the following questions:

—Is psychokinesis merely the control of existing energy? That is, with falling dice in a cage, do we affect their final positions merely by applying an infinitesimal force at choice points on otherwise random paths?

—Or does PK imply the injection of gross energy of a kind hitherto unknown to physics?

—Can PK operate on the nucleus of the atom?

—Is levitation of objects possible?

—How strong might PK be? Can faith move mountains, or where do we draw the line between the possible and the absurd?

—Is there any limit to how much we can know by ESP?

—Are scientific discoveries ever made by using ESP?

—Are all scientific discoveries made that way? Is creativity merely another name for ESP?

—Is there any limitation of distance over which psi can operate?

—What relevance, if any, does the so-called inverse-square law of physics have to these effects?

—How far can we reach backward in history using ESP?

—Can we reach forward to predict events still to happen?

● ESP involves people. This suggests another set of questions:

—If we are trying to reach a particular object or individual by ESP, does the thinking of other persons sometimes interfere?

—Is it easier to establish psychic communication with some persons than with others?

—How do we guide our ESP to what we want to know?

—Is it meaningful to speak of a "psychic channel" along which information flows?

—Is there a role for psi in teaching?

—Gaining information from another person's mind implies a person-to-person relationship. Can good or evil inhere in such a relationship?

—Can we read another person's mind even if he does not wish it?

—Does the possibility of psychic communication imply some responsibility on our part for the well-being of other people?

—Can we have psychokinetic relationships with other people? For example, is it possible by PK to transfer from a distance a feeling of happiness and strength to persons we love?

—In so doing, do we exhaust ourselves emotionally as some psychic healers have claimed?

—Is it possible to rob others of energy by PK—to be a psychic leech, so to speak?

—Does the Voo-Doo practice of sticking pins into dolls representing enemies have a basis in fact?

—Could a future system of ethics be based upon the discoveries that might be hoped for in parapsychology?

● Those who are philosophically inclined may be particularly attracted to questions concerning precognition:

—If prediction of the future is experimentally possible, what does this imply about the nature of cause and effect?

—Suppose we saw a train wreck in a precognitive vision. Could we prevent the wreck by warning the engineer?

—If we prevented it, then we must have precognized a possible event that never became a real event. Can we precognize all possible events?

—For every real event there must be an infinite number of possible events. Perhaps we precognize only some smaller class of events that have a high probability of occurring?

—On the other hand, if we can precognize only *real* future events, does that mean that such events are inevitable? Are events predestined?

—To what extent, if any, do we have free will?

● For many persons the most interesting questions of parapsychology concern the essential nature of man—questions about the mind, consciousness, and death:

—What is the relationship of psi to the brain? What part of the brain is involved in receiving or sending psi phenomena?

—Because ESP and PK span space and time in surprising ways, are we justified in asking whether psi is the function of a "mind" or "soul" that is to some extent independent of the brain?

—What might psi research reveal about the nature of consciousness? Does consciousness have experimental attributes not explainable in terms of physiology and communication theory?

—Does each person's consciousness belong only to himself, or does he sometimes share it with others?

—Is it possible for one body to have a double consciousness?

—Sometimes ESP seems to come from dead persons. Is there any survival of individual personality after death?

—Does any part of personality reappear in a new life form? Is there any truth to the Eastern idea of reincarnation?

These are all interesting questions. Scarcely any of them can be answered with certainty today. Many, I believe, will be answered within our lifetimes.

In this book I shall not be able to discuss more than a few of these topics. The rest, the interested scholar will have to investigate for himself. It is not easy to find answers in the library. Most of what has been written about psi phenomena is rife with factual error as well as unwarranted speculation. For every reasonable book there are fifty filled with nonsense. It seems safe to say that, the more important the question, the less we know and the more that has been printed.

One of my objectives is to help provide the reader with a background by which he can judge how much to believe of what he reads. Another is to encourage a willingness not to expect answers to all questions but to know how much is currently knowable and to be resigned in a state of necessary ignorance about the rest.

2

TRANCE MEDIUMSHIP

To gain a perspective for the scientific study of strange phenomena, it is customary to consider accounts of their field occurrence. In the case of parapsychology this leads us down a quasi-religious path that many scientists will find quaint if not distasteful, but which, nevertheless, may provide important insights for guiding later laboratory research.

Spiritualism as a religion or religious sect still exists throughout the Western world, although it no longer attracts much attention. There are several hundred independent congregations in the U.S.A. with a combined membership of less than 50,000.

The central tenet of Spiritualism is the possibility of verbal communication with deceased relatives and friends under suitable conditions. Although supernatural spirits, such as devils, angels, and ghosts of the dead, have manifested themselves throughout history, sometimes directly and sometimes by the so-called invasion or possession of living human bodies, the first widespread belief in the possibility of a friendly dialogue with deceased persons seems to have begun in Hydesville, New York, in 1848.

The Spiritualist movement spread in America and then invaded England and the Continent, achieving its maximum acceptance in the 20 years between 1860 and 1880. Spiritualism, today, is exclusively a religion of the lower socioeconomic classes because its interpretation of its special phenomena conflicts with the world view of educated people.

As a religious sect, Spiritualism should be of professional interest to sociologists, historians, and psychologists. Sociologists may regard Spiritualism as unusual in an advanced civilization because its unifying idea is not a god or a great prophet but a class of psychological phenomena (to be described below). Historians of science will note that widespread public interest in the phenomena of supposed communication with another world led to the founding of the Society for Psychical Research in London in 1882. This is perhaps the only time in history when the scientific investigation of a long-ignored class of natural phenomena was undertaken because those phenomena had become of religious importance. Psychologists will find in the accounts of the practice of Spiritualism many unanswered questions about the nature of human personality as well as hints for experimental investigation.

The phenomena of so-called spirit communication began over a century ago with rapping noises from tables, walls, and other parts of a room while "sitters" sat in darkness, or in near darkness, around a table with their hands on their knees or resting on the table. Sometimes the table would tip, turn, or rise from the floor.

As a rule, there was one person, known as the "medium," usually a woman, who arranged the "seance" or "sitting" and had special rapport with the spirits. The availability of such a spirit expert is not necessary, however. Spiritualist phenomena are sometimes found when interested amateurs hold their own seances.

Originally, most mediums traveled about, giving sittings in Spiritualist churches, and many still do. Later, there arose, especially in England, a large number of private mediums whose services were made available to bereaved individuals rather than to church congregations. Some of the most famous mediums did not work for a fee but were financially supported by their admirers.

In the beginning, the rapping noises were used by the spirits to communicate answers to yes-or-no questions or by an alphabet code. In some cases the medium heard voices or saw visions while in a waking state. Later, the spirits more often took possession of the medium while she was in a trance, and they would talk through her human vocal chords. As a rule, the spirit doing the talking was not the beloved deceased but an intermediary known technically as a "control." The spirit originating the message or conversation was known as the "communicator." The controls might, for example, be deceased American Indians, ancient Egyptians, innocent little girls, or famous persons who had "passed over" some time ago.

As time went on, the competition among mediums sharpened and the spirits grew more powerful. In the dark they might touch the sitter on the face or hands, remove small articles such as watches or handkerchiefs, bring small gifts or "apports" such as flowers, play a muscial instrument that had been placed under the table, or speak through a trumpet floating in the air. So that everyone could see the trumpet rise from the table in the darkness, it was often painted with a phosphorescent pigment.

In still other phases of mediumship the spirit caused the medium to write personal or inspirational messages automatically by pencil and paper while she was in a light trance, or even created messages directly upon writing slates that had been wrapped and sealed beforehand to prevent fraud.

In the heyday of Spiritualism, many truly unusual phenomena were reported. Shapeless white material, known as "ectoplasm," seemed to flow from the medium and turn into the hands, face, or entire body of a dead member of the sitter's family. This re-creation was known as "materialization."

To a convinced Spiritualist it did not matter that occasionally a skeptic would discover fraud by suddenly turning up the gas light or by grabbing the supposed materialization of a spirit, which then proved to be cheesecloth.

Beginning about 1860, mediums specializing in spirit photogra-phy were able to produce pictures of dead people on photographic plates. This was about the time when professional photography first became commonplace in the large cities so that photographic technique was readily available.

The various phenomena produced by mediums can be divided into two classes, those that might involve extrasensory perception and those that look like psychokinesis. Mediums who provide only messages and writings are called "mental mediums". Those who, in addition, produce physical phenomena are known as "physical mediums." Today in Spiritualism, there are many mental mediums but no physical mediums—at least none who are willing to be tested by scientists.

There are perhaps a dozen great names in mediumship with which the student of parapsychology should be familiar. I shall tell about three of them. One was a male, physical medium; the others were female, mental mediums.

D.D. HOME

The most famous physical medium of Spiritualism, Daniel Dun-glas Home (1833–1886), was born near Edinburgh, Scotland, and raised by an aunt in America. He became interested in spirit rap-pings and, in 1850 at the age of 17, left home to travel about, giving sittings in the homes of pious people. As his reputation developed, he went over all of Europe, giving performances for the great and near great, including the Emperor of France and the Czar of Russia.

His repertoire included all the usual phenomena and a few more:

raps, floating lights, voices, playing of musical instruments, levitation of objects, elongation of his own body, the handling of hot coals of fire, and—most magnificent of all—the levitation of himself in the presence of his sitters. All of the documented cases of self-levitation took place in very dim light. For example, by the light of a sliver of the moon Home levitated himself out of an upper-story window in one room and into the window of an adjacent room.

These unusual demonstrations were interspersed with religious exhortations of a general nature. Home enjoyed living among the wealthy, and, without doing any other work, managed comfortably for most of his life by suitable marriages and by gifts from patrons. He was described as child-like and affectionate, inducing complete trust in all who met him. The press treated him with respect. Throughout his entire career he was never detected in fraud. Although his audiences were selected from people friendly to him, they did include a number of skeptical and highly intelligent individuals.

The consensus of opinion among parapsychologists today agrees with that of Frank Podmore (1902), the author of the definitive end-of-century history of Spiritualism, namely, that the most reasonable explanation of Home's demonstrations was that he was a master conjurer with a special capacity for inducing hallucinations in his audiences. For reasons I shall explain in later chapters, I do not agree with the implication that all of his physical phenomena were necessarily fraudulent, although they were certainly produced under such loose conditions that, as scientific evidence, they are worthless.

LEONORA PIPER

Mrs. Leonora Piper (1859–1950), a native-born American, was the first of the two, most thoroughly studied mediums in the history of psychical research. She went into a trance for the first time in 1884 at the age of 25 when she was visiting a professional medium to get advice about her health. Professor William James, the eminent American Psychologist, encountered her a year later and introduced her to Richard Hodgson when the latter came to America from England to become secretary of what later became the American Branch of the British Society for Psychical Research. She was investigated by Richard Hodgson and James Hyslop in the

U.S.A., and by Frederic Myers, Sir Oliver Lodge, and Mrs. Henry Sidgwick in England.

Mrs. Piper used a long list of controls, including a spirit called Sir Walter Scott, a former French physician who called himself Phinuit, and a group of spirits named the Imperator Band.

She ended her trances in 1911 after 27 years because she was sinking deeper each time, so that it was increasingly difficult to bring her out. She continued to produce automatic writing in the waking state for several years thereafter, and then withdrew from systematic psychical research. She died in 1950 at the age of 91 (Piper, 1950).

Throughout her long period of trances she produced ESP prodigiously in the form of personal information about sitters unknown to her. She was followed by detectives and otherwise spied upon to try to discover how she did it. No suggestion of fraud was ever found and she convinced even the skeptical Frank Podmore that telepathy was a real phenomenon (Podmore, 1898). After she had ceased her work, a 650-page volume of the *Proceedings of the SPR* was devoted to a study by Mrs. Henry Sidgwick (1915) of the psychology of her trances as distinct from the evidence they showed for ESP.

The question of whether spirits of the dead might have been involved in Mrs. Piper's mediumship will be considered further under postmortem survival, but professional scientists have been inclined to agree with the anthropologist, Andrew Lang (1900), that ESP is a better explanation.

GLADYS OSBORNE LEONARD

A third medium whose name will live in the history of parapsychology is Mrs. Gladys Osborne Leonard (1882–1968). Her cooperation with the British Society for Psychical Research began in 1915, at just about the end of Mrs. Piper's professional career. Mrs. Leonard continued to work for 41 years, serving both the public and scientific investigators, until her retirement in 1956 (Leonard, 1969). At least 37 papers devoted to the study of her mediumship have appeared in the British and American Journals.[1]

---

1. A major part of the study of Mrs. Leonard was done by a lesbian couple, Miss Radclyffe Hall and (Una) Lady Troubridge. In her sittings Mrs. Leonard revealed secret knowledge of Radclyffe Hall's earlier lover, who had recently died—knowledge that could only have been obtained by what we now call extrasensory perception.

The name, Radclyffe Hall, is of historical importance in the sociology of homo-

In her English childhood Mrs. Leonard showed only minor indications of psychic ability. In her early twenties she had a vision of her distant mother one night at 2 AM, which she learned later was the day and time of her mother's unexpected death. This experience led her to accept Spiritualism and to develop herself as a medium.

Like Mrs. Piper, Mrs. Leonard obtained her messages from spirit communicators while in a deep trance and, to a lesser extent, by automatic writing in a relatively normal state. Unlike Mrs. Piper, she had only one important control, Feda. In many situations her communicators did not use Feda but spoke directly through Mrs. Leonard. Feda was supposed to be the playful spirit of a girl who had died at the age of 13 in childbirth in India more than 100 years earlier.

As in the case of Mrs. Piper, despite the use of a detective agency to find out whether Mrs. Leonard had gotten her trance information about sitters by normal means, no ground for suspicion as to her honesty was ever uncovered.

As a minor part of her work Mrs. Leonard introduced what are known as "book tests," in which the control spirit would state what was to be found on a given page of a distant volume that Mrs. Leonard had never seen. Out of her 532 book tests, 17 percent were wholly successful and another 19 percent approximately correct.

Mrs. Leonard believed in life after death and her purpose in this life was to give others that belief. To help the SPR, she agreed never to read the literature of psychical research—a promise to which she still adhered some 25 years later.

To give some feeling for the nature of the relationship between Mrs. Leonard and her control, Feda, who occupied Mrs. Leonard's

---

sexuality. In 1928 she published a novel titled *The Well of Loneliness*, which is the classic presentation of the case for the humane treatment of homosexuals. Although the heroine was a lesbian of esthetic sensibility and high moral character, the book was suppressed in England and had to be published in the U.S.A. Eventually over a million copies were sold and it was translated into eleven languages. After Radclyffe Hall's death Lady Troubridge (1961) wrote her biography under the title: *The Life of Radclyffe Hall*.

Homosexuals have played a relatively prominent role in the history of psychical research. The reasons are probably scientifically superficial. On the one hand, as a group, they have been shoved through the curtain of cultural pretext and they can easily question orthodoxy's rejection of the evidence for psi phenomena. On the other hand, as biological deviates, they have a special motivation to seek answers about the mystery and meaning of life.

body while she was in a trance state, I quote the following episode, which was reported in her obituary (Leonard, 1969, p. 110) by a recording secretary who became a close personal friend of Mrs. Leonard:

> Mrs. Leonard was a strict vegetarian, fond of fruit and chocolate. I had taken a basket of strawberries to her, but as we never spoke before the sitting, I had placed the fruit on a ledge behind my chair. During the sitting, Feda [in possession of Mrs. Leonard] bent forward, put her arm over my shoulder, and poked a hole through the paper on the basket. She then proceeded to dig a finger in the berries and suck [the finger]. I told her not to do this but to take the whole strawberry and eat it properly. Thereupon Feda declared: "Oh no; Gladys won't let me do that. Since I ate the horse's hair, I mustn't put anything in her mouth." At the conclusion of the sitting I asked the medium about this, and she shuddered: "Don't remind me of that, or I shall be sick." On being pressed to explain, she told me that on one occasion Feda had pushed a finger through a hole in the upholstery of the chair arm, pulled out some horse-hair stuffing, and crammed it into her mouth, trying to eat it. Mrs. Leonard was jerked out of trance to find herself choking, the wire-like horse hair lodged in her throat. She was violently sick. If this incident does not demonstrate separate personality [for the medium and her control] at least it confirms the complete unawareness of the medium.

MEDIUMS AS PEOPLE

In addition to the three mediums I have just discussed, there are well over 100 who achieved some national or international fame and who have been seriously investigated by the Society for Psychical Research. There are countless others of more restricted reputation.

In the light of what we now know about psi, it seems likely that even those mediums who engaged in wholesale fraud had some extraordinary spark of ESP that started them on the road to fame.

I have selected a short list of mediums who, for various reasons, would be especially worth investigating by anyone wanting to look further into this subject. Some of these mediums were highly regarded for their honesty; others were famous as frauds. Not all of those on this list were professional, that is, money-making, mediums. Some of the best were educated persons with other means of support whose interest in mediumship was solely religious or scientific.

Helena P. Blavatsky (1831–1891. Founded Theosophy in 1876).

Rev. Arthur Ford (1896–1971)

The Fox Family (Started Spiritualism in 1848)

Eileen J. Garrett (1893–1970. Founder of the Parapsychology Foundation)

"Mrs. Holland" (1868–1948. Alice Kipling Fleming, sister of Rudyard)

"Mrs. King" (187?–1948. Dame Edith Lyttelton)

"Margery" Crandon (189?–1941. Sponsored by the ASPR Spiritualists)

Rev. William Stainton Moses (1839–1892. One of the founders of the SPR)

Eusapia Palladino (1854–1908. Female, Italian physical medium)

Rudi Schneider (1908–1957. Austrian physical medium) and his brother, Willy (1903–)

Mrs. A.W. Verrall (1859–1916) and her daughter, Helen Verrall Salter (1883–1959)

"Mrs. Willett" (1874–1956. Winifred [Mrs. Charles] Tennant)

I have had personal intercourse with only one of these mediums, and that was very brief. In 1948 I was invited to come to the local Spiritualist church where Arthur Ford was to be the guest medium. When I arrived, along with about two dozen members of the congregation, I made a money contribution that helped pay Ford's travel and living expenses. By extrapolation, I could see that his was not a financially easy life.

He came into the meeting visibly intoxicated, thereby scandalizing some of the faithful. I was later told that he found alcohol helpful in "reaching the transcendental plane." That day, in due course, he went into a trance and gave readings. Some of the audience were well pleased, but none of the messages intended for me was suggestive of psi.

Afterward, Arthur Ford and I went to the bar in a nearby hotel and had a private chat while he had a few drinks. He knew, of course, that I was interested solely in the scientific aspect of his mediumship, and he talked freely. The gist of what he said was that he had no memory of what took place in the trance state and that he had not the slightest idea where his messages came from,

but that he doubted very much that they had anything to do with
the spirits who claimed to be talking.

THE PROBLEM OF FRAUD

What does Spiritualism have to do with parapsychology? We
have found that extrasensory perception and perhaps psychokinesis
sometimes occur when mediums are in trance. That is to say, the
spirit communicator sometimes supplies information that the medium could not have obtained by normal sensory means. Is the
connection between trance phenomena and psi phenomena an intimate one—as was assumed by the British and American Societies
for Psychical Research up to about 1940? Or is the relationship so
remote that, for the study of ESP, we would be better off to ignore
spirit mediumship—as has been done by most parapsychologists
since 1930?

In order to answer this question, we must try to understand
Spiritualism. Who are the spirit communicators? Are they in any
sense the surviving personalities of specific dead persons as they
claim to be? From a psychological point of view, what is happening
when a medium goes into trance?

For many years I was puzzled by the widespread cheating that
one encounters among spirit mediums and even among psychics
who do not believe in spirits. It is generally accepted that psychic
phenomena are sporadic and spontaneous and that, after one has
acquired a reputation as a psychic, there is pressure to produce
false psi to satisfy one's clientele when the real phenomenon is not
forthcoming. I have never found this explanation of fraud altogether convincing—particularly in the case of mediums who give a
religious interpretation to their activities. These people appear
beautifully and undeniably honest. They have that wide-eyed, innocent, relaxed, friendly, trustworthy look that one associates with
all very small children, with some young adults, and with most
successful salesmen. There is no trace of guilt anxiety. How do
these cheating mediums live so comfortably with themselves?

The question can be turned around: If most mediums use fakery
in addition to fantasy, is it not a bit naive to keep searching for
some residuum of real telepathy or real psychokinesis? This question invites an emotional response. The official policy of the British SPR was to refuse to continue to study any medium who had
been caught in fraud. The response of most scientists, when they

have uncovered fraud in a medium, has been to damn the entire subject as unworthy of investigation. Both of these attitudes, I think, are wrong. A reasoned resolution of this dilemma will require ideas that we shall examine in later chapters.

Let me ask, in a new form, a question to which I have already referred. Why have parapsychologists given up the study of mediumship? Is it because there is no close connection between psi and trance mediumship, or because controlled experiments are seen as a better road to scientific understanding? Or is it perhaps because Spiritualism had a bad reputation among scientists, so that Dr. Rhine and his 1930 associates felt that they would be more convincing if they could demonstrate psi without the taint of religious involvement? To a certain extent, all three answers are correct. These ideas will arise several times in the chapters to follow.

3

THE OCCURRENCE
OF MULTIPLE PERSONALITY

IDENTITY DEFINED

The sleeping trance in which the spirit medium most often meets her "controls" and "communicators" would be labelled by psychologists as a dissociated state. In the present chapter I shall explore a somewhat different kind of dissociation, one involving an uncontrolled change of identity or "multiple personality." In the chapter to follow I shall have occasion to compare mediumship and multiple personality.

By the term, multiple personality, I mean one body belonging to two or more persons. I shall initially define multiple personality as existing for a body when either of two questions must be answered *yes*. Does the body exhibit two or more consciousnesses at the same time? Does the body exhibit different personalities from time to time, one of which can be shown to have memories not accessible to the other? In the next chapter, I shall broaden the concept by examining the meaning of "accessible memories."

The evidence for multiple personality is both spontaneous and experimental in nature. Although the spontaneous evidence is more colorful and extensive, I shall start with the experimental evidence because it is easier to understand and believe.

OUR TWO HALF BRAINS

The cerebral cortex, or outer part of the brain, consists of symmetrical left and right halves with well defined interconnections. From animal experiments it was suspected that certain kinds of epileptics could be helped by severing the main connection between the left and right cerebral hemispheres, so that an epileptic seizure starting on one side might not spread to the other. This, in fact, proved to be the case. Consequently, there are a few, otherwise ordinary people who live relatively normal lives although their brain hemispheres have been largely disconnected from each other. How does this affect their behavior?

It is well known that the left half of the brain controls the right half of the body, and vice versa. For example, if the right hand touches an object, most of the associated information exchange between hand and brain is conveyed by nerves connected to the left half of the brain.

In the case of the eyes, however, the situation is more complex. The right half of the field of vision of each eye is sent to the left side of the brain. In other words, the right and left eyes each connect to both sides of the brain. In the split-brain epileptic cases we are discussing, the nerve tract interconnecting the eyes and the brain is left undisturbed, so that the eyes can function normally.

The ears provide another exception to the general rule that each half of the body connects primarily to the other half of the brain. Both ears are connected equivalently to the brain, so that sound into either ear will be more or less equally heard.

What about speech? Does that originate in both halves of the brain? Mostly not. From brain-tumor and brain-injury cases it is known that, for a righthanded person, most of the power of speech is usually in the left half of the cerebral cortex.

As a result, if a split-brain person holds a familiar but unseen object in his right hand, he can *tell* you what it is, but not if he holds it in his left hand. With either hand, however, if he lays the object down, he can *feel and choose* another object like it, sight unseen, if he uses the same hand. In other words, in the bisected brain each half operates with a considerable degree of independence.

In another experiment, if a patient with a surgically split brain is gazing straight ahead and is momentarily shown a large sign spelling the word TARGET so that the letters TAR are flashed to the left field of vision and the letters GET fall to the right of the center of vision, the patient will tell you that he saw only the word GET.

This happens for the following reason. The righthand field of view is optically refracted to the left half of the retinas in both eyes, as shown in Figure 3.1. These halves both connect to the left half of the cortex, which has the power of speech. When all of the direct cross-connections between the two halves of the cortex have been severed, the speech side of the brain receives no information about the letters TAR.

Suppose, however, that instead of being asked to tell what he saw, the word TARGET is flashed before his eyes as described above and then the patient is asked to examine two small cards on which the words TAR and GET appear. As he moves his eyes, both cards are seen by both halves of the eyes. If he is then asked, not to speak, but to point with his left hand to what was originally

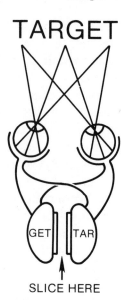

TARGET

GET TAR

SLICE HERE

Figure 3.1. Plan view of projection
of the left and right fields of vision
to the right and left hemispheres of
the brain.

flashed in his field of view, he will point to the word TAR. Similarly, with his right hand he will point to the word GET. One must
conclude that, when the brain has been split, each side is, to a
degree, ignorant of what goes on in the other half and each side
can independently perform at least some mental functions.

Throughout the first half of the twentieth century, in a right-
handed person the left half of the brain was called "dominant" and
it was generally supposed that the right half had little to do with
thinking. It is now known, however, that while the left cerebral
hemisphere is dominant for speech, the right half is stronger for
manipulo-spatial thinking (Gazzaniga & LeDoux, 1978) and perhaps for synthetic and perceptual cognition as well (Sperry, 1982a).
This specialization of function appears early in childhood and
presumably results from the fact that the development of speech by
age 2 pre-empts in the left hemisphere the synaptic capacity of a
portion of the cerebral cortex (namely, the inferior parietal lobule)
that in the lower mammals is devoted on both sides to tactuo-
geometrical thinking. In man, the latter type of thinking, which
does not develop until around age six, is still fully accommodated
in the right hemisphere (Gazzaniga & LeDoux, 1978).

It should be noted that this division of brain function is a tendency rather than an absolute or universal effect. Moreover, from
clinical evidence there is reason to suppose that there is a consid-

erable degree of functional plasticity; so that before puberty, if any part of the cerebral cortex is destroyed, other parts can be trained to take over much of the lost function.

Surgical Twinning

From what has been said so far, it is not evident that bisecting the brain can produce two persons in one body. Most split-brain patients are not aware of their duplexity except by inference, through observation of their own anomalous behavior. The two cerebral hemispheres work independently, as shown by the fact that they can deliver logically incompatible outputs from different private inputs. Through his ears and moving eyes the patient who receives such inputs is equally aware of both outputs but only, ex post facto, of their incompatibility.

In considering this situation, we are faced at the very beginning with a semantic obscurity. Does personhood or self-identity consist of self-awareness, or does it require subjective analysis of that self-awareness? By the word "analysis" in this context I mean linear, logical analysis by means of symbols; which is what we do when we use ordinary language.

If self-awareness alone is enough, then I am convinced that some dogs are persons. But if analytical self-awareness is essential, then only humans possess personhood, and a brain half can be a person only if it has linguistic ability.

Most right hemispheres have no speaking ability and very little linguistic or verbal ability. In the examples given earlier, it was said that each brain half could recognize geometrical similarity, whether of objects or of letters. Language requires additional, more complex logical operations. Suffice to say that, in right-handed persons, not only can right hemispheres not speak, but they cannot comprehend much language and therefore, to that extent, cannot be regarded as separate persons when they are dis-connected from their linguistically sophisticated left mates.

Gazzaniga, LeDoux, Donald H. Wilson, and colleagues have nevertheless demonstrated that in some cases the two halves of a split brain can be two persons with separate, simultaneous, analytic consciousness. Among their split-brain patients they found one who had had a brain lesion in the left temporal region at age two and, possibly as a consequence, had developed strong linguistic ability in both hemispheres even though speaking ability remained exclusively in the left. In adolescence, epilepsy, caused perhaps by scar tissue from the earlier lesion, led to a brain-splitting operation, before and after which the patient was intensively tested by Gazzaniga and colleagues.

This patient could answer questions optically projected to either hemisphere. When using the left hemisphere, he could speak his answers normally. When using the right, he could spell out answers by moving letter blocks with his left hand. In this way, his right hemisphere, unknown to the left, could carry on a conversation, at least to the extent that it could name himself, his favorite friend, his preferred career, and tomorrow's day.

When different pictures were projected simultaneously to the two hemispheres, the patient could make the correct association with each from a battery of test pictures by pointing with the proper hand.

On the basis of these and other tests, the experimenters concluded that each side of the brain of this patient was separately conscious and that each consciousness had no direct awareness of the other (Gazzaniga & LeDoux, 1978). This lack of any co-awareness is an important difference between split-brain dual personalities and some naturally occurring multiple personalities. Co-awareness in the naturally occurring cases suggests that the same cerebral structure can function simultaneously within two personality systems.

Roger Sperry (1982a, p. 1225) reports more recent work in which the disconnected right hemisphere, despite its limited linguistic ability, "generates appropriate emotional reactions and displays a good sense of humor requiring subtle social evaluations" when exposed to pictures of family, pets, personal belongings, historical figures, and television personalities. "Results to date suggest the presence [in the right hemisphere] of a normal and well-developed sense of self and personal relations along with a surprising knowledgeability in general."

SPONTANEOUS SPLITTING

In the first half of the twentieth century there were two famous multiple-personality cases. The first was the Sally Beauchamp case reported by Dr. Morton Prince. The second was the Doris Fischer case investigated by Dr. Walter Franklin Prince (no relation to Morton Prince). In the second half of this century two other cases have attracted public attention. In 1957, the Three-Faces-of-Eve case appeared in a popular book by Thigpen and Cleckley. The Sybil case was described by F. R. Schreiber in a book successfully published in 1973.

I shall touch upon these cases, describing the first one, the Sally Beauchamp case, in enough detail to give a feeling for the clinical aspects of multiple personality.

SALLY BEAUCHAMP

Morton Prince gave a preliminary report of the Sally Beauchamp case in the *Proceedings of the SPR* (M. Prince, 1901). The fullest record of the case appeared in his book, *The Dissociation of a Personality* (M. Prince, 1905). His later theoretical speculation will be found in a book of his selected works (M. Prince, 1929).

The case was reviewed by psychologist William McDougall (1907), who said, "So strange and wildly improbable does the story seem that anyone may well hesitate to accept it. [This case makes it] necessary to admit our complete ignorance of the conditions of psychic individuality." (p. 418) Today, three-quarters of a century later, we are at the beginning of a scientific understanding of this problem.

Morton Prince (1855–1929) was a medical doctor and is best known to psychologists as the founder in 1906 of the *Journal of Abnormal Psychology*. From 1902 to 1912, he was Professor of Nervous Diseases at Tufts Medical School in Boston. Although a life-long member of the Society for Psychical Research, Prince did not share the interests of most of its members. He did not accept any paranormal explanation of supposedly psychic phenomena and was not active in the affairs of the SPR.

In 1898 at Boston, Massachusetts, Miss Beauchamp, a 23-year-old college student came to Dr. Prince for treatment of pain, fatigue, and generally poor physical health of a kind that in those days was called "neurasthenia." In more recent terminology she would have been called a hysterical psychoneurotic. As Dr. Prince was to learn later, five years earlier, in 1893, Miss Beauchamp had suffered a psychological trauma that precipitated a progressive neurotic breakdown of an unusual kind. Ultimately, she exhibited four conscious personalities, which were identified by Dr. Prince as B-I, B-II, B-III, and B-IV. None of these, however, was the original Miss Beauchamp as she existed prior to her 1893 trauma.

B-I, B-III, and B-IV were waking personalities, while B-II appeared only when Miss Beauchamp was in a hypnotic trance.

B-I was the dominant personality in the period immediately following the 1893 trauma. B-III became apparent in 1898 shortly after the patient came under Prince's treatment, and B-IV appeared in 1899 as the result of a second traumatic incident.

Of all of these, B-III was the most colorful. She assumed the name, Sally, and the entire study is known as the "Sally Beauchamp Case."

Before I go on with a description of this case, let me discuss briefly the complexity of multiple-personality relationships. The external observer—Dr. Prince in this case—must get all of his information via two modalities: from the behavior of the patient and from what the patient claims to be thinking concerning the present or the past.

Some of the relational concepts are illustrated by the following questions:

1. Which one or more of the personalities has motor control of the body at any one time? Generally, there is only one personality in control and that personality is said to be "out"—meaning, I suppose, "out on stage" or "out of captivity."

2. Which personalities are receiving sensory input at any one time? When B-III was out, she received no skin and muscle sensations unless her eyes were open and she could watch her body. The other personalities, when out, perceived such stimulations perfectly.

3. Which personalities are aware of the thoughts of another? For example, while B-I was out, B-III could hear and see and be making her own perceptions, and simultaneously be aware of the perceptions and related thinking of B-I.

In Figure 3.2, I have represented very loosely what might be called the "inter-awareness" relationships among these four personalities. I have not tried to represent sensory, motor, or historical relationships.

B-I and B-IV had no memory of each other, or of B-II or B-III, i.e., B-I and B-IV each had no direct awareness of any of the other personalities.

B-II appeared under hypnosis and believed herself to be a combination of B-I and B-IV, sharing the memories of both, even though, as just stated, neither of them shared the memories that B-II acquired while she was out.

B-I, B-III, and B-IV were spontaneously appearing personalities and, under stress, could change from one to another, from minute to minute or day to day.

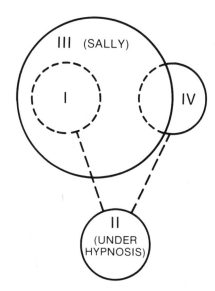

Figure 3.2. Inter-awareness relationships among the four personalities of the Sally Beauchamp case of multiple personality.

B-III (Sally) knew both the actions and thoughts of B-I but only the actions of B-IV. Although B-III was seeing the same objects as B-IV, she did not know B-IV's thoughts about them.

Sally (B-III) claimed never to be asleep while B-I or B-IV was out. That is, Sally had no memory gaps while B-I and B-IV were awake. B-I and B-IV, on the other hand, did have memory gaps whenever they were not out. Thus, it could be said that Sally had coexistent, nonidentical consciousness with B-I and B-IV.

Sally had full motor control when B-I and B-IV were asleep and partial motor control over B-I when B-I was awake, but not over B-IV when B-IV was awake. In other words, Sally could partially control B-I's actions even when B-I supposed herself to be in charge of the body.

Furthermore, although Sally did not gain an independent existence (i.e., the ability to come out) until after Dr. Prince had taken Miss Beauchamp under treatment, Sally claimed that she had always been in existence and that she had complete autobiographical memories from Miss Beauchamp's cradle days onward, when she had lived unhappily imprisoned within Miss Beauchamp as a separate consciousness, without motor control and without Miss Beauchamp's being aware of her.

The personalities of B-I, B-IV, and B-III were distinctively different. B-I, known as the "Saint," was shy, reticent, dependent, honest, idealistic, religious, conscientious, fond of books, and could read French and write shorthand.

B-IV was quick-tempered, willful, insensitive, inclined to tell lies, and generally resented inquiries about herself and interference of any kind. She lacked B-I's acquired skills. Dr. Prince labelled her the "Realist."

Sally (B-III) was childlike, fun-loving, irresponsible, hated books and church, and could not read French or write shorthand. She had none of the usual personality symptoms of neurosis. Unlike B-I, she was full of energy and always felt well. She was never subjectively hungry or fatigued, even when, for physiological reason, she should have been.

After Sally had learned to emerge, she would stay in full control for minutes or even days at a time. She knew almost everything about B-I and B-IV. She was jealous of B-I and afraid of B-IV, with whom she quarreled incessantly.

Sally hated B-I and did her best to make life miserable for her. She once rode six miles into the countryside on a tram and wakened B-I, purposefully leaving her to hike home without money. Another time, Sally collected snakes and spiders on a country trip and mailed them alive in a box to B-I. Sally would often make B-I tell lies and otherwise get her into uncomfortable social situations. Once B-I tried to commit suicide by going to bed with the illuminating gas jet turned on. Sally came on stage, turned off the gas, and opened the window.

After a tremendous battle of personalities, the unwanted Sally finally agreed to disappear and was described as "squeezed out" by the others.

In 1902, after four years of treatment, the supposedly original or real Miss Beauchamp was recovered by putting together B-I and B-IV, that is, by bringing B-II into the waking state. With continued therapy, by 1905, the real Miss Beauchamp was hopefully in sole and permanent control of the body. The disintegrated person, according to Dr. Morton Prince's interpretation, had been reassembled into a healthy whole.

DORIS

If the Sally Beauchamp case stood alone, we would be inclined to question Morton Prince's sanity or honesty, or at least his ability to interpret what he saw. There is, however, no such easy escape from the challenge of multiple personality.

Foremost among a number of similar cases is the one reported by psychologist Walter Franklin Prince. Walter Prince (1863–1934) shares with Richard Hodgson and James H. Hyslop, the distinction of being an early American pioneer in parapsychology. He received a doctoral degree in abnormal psychology at Yale in 1899 and then began his career as an Episcopalian clergyman. Ten years later, while he was a minister in Pittsburgh, Pennsylvania, a young woman, age 20, with serious physical and mental illness, came to his church. His wife took care of her and, subsequently, they adopted her as Theodosia Prince. She suffered from multiple personalities, which so interested Prince that he gave her psychotherapy for several years. Eventually, from this experience, he gave up the ministry and became a full-time psychological investigator.

Dr. Prince was Research Officer of the American Society for Psychical Research in New York City from 1917 to 1920 and of the Boston Society for Psychic Research from its creation in 1925 until his death in 1934. (See Chapter 9, titled "History.")

Theodosia Prince, as a patient, was reported upon under the pseudonym, Doris Fischer. The study of Doris extended over three years from 1911 to 1914. The resulting material came to 1400 pages in the *Proceedings of the American SPR* (Volumes 9 and 10, 1915 and 1916). For a discerning review, see F.C.S. Schiller (1918).

The patient exhibited five personalities: She was born in 1889 as "Real Doris." "Margaret," the childlike mischief maker, comparable to Sally in Morton Prince's case, appeared at age 3 when Doris was picked up and thrown to the floor by her drunken father. "Sleeping Margaret," a mature and cooperative person who eventually claimed to be a guardian spirit, appeared also at age 3 at the same time as Margaret. "Sick Doris," who showed the most symptoms of hysteria, appeared at age 17 upon the death of Doris' mother. "Sleeping Real Doris," a partial personality without apparent self-awareness but with an uncanny memory, appeared at age 18 when Doris fell, striking her head violently.

Doris Fischer began therapy at age 22 and continued to age 25. Walter Prince viewed his therapy, not as a re-integration of personalities in the manner of Morton Prince, but rather as a process of encouraging the unwanted personalities to disappear. After five months, Sick Doris disintegrated and her memories were taken over by Real Doris. Over a period of 15 months Sleeping Real Doris simply faded away and finally disappeared. It took more than two years before Margaret was regressed mentally, deprived of her sight, and eventually left without power to emerge. At the end, Sleeping Margaret offered to go away, but she seemed a useful creature and was allowed to stay. She came out only when Real Doris was in normal sleep and showed herself only by engaging in conversation with Dr. Prince.

Walter Prince reported that Doris exhibited some minor psychic phenomena while she was in therapy (W. Prince, 1915, pp. 56–59) and in the years that followed (W. Prince, 1926, pp. 26–27). The relation of dissociation and psi phenomena will be discussed in later chapters.

There are several features about the Doris case that, taken together, make it of more scientific value than the Sally Beauchamp or any subsequent case. First is the fact that the patient was taken into the home of Dr. Prince for therapy. After she was cured, she lived there for 20 years until Dr. Prince died. His note taking was extremely detailed.

A second important feature of this case is that Walter Prince's report on Doris is just that. Although Morton Prince had interpreted the Sally Beauchamp case in terms of Pierre Janet's theory of hysteria, Walter Prince soon gave up all attempts at theorizing and contented himself with observation.

Another feature of interest is that, while Morton Prince used hypnotic suggestion and this may have tended to accentuate, if not create, the individuality of the personalities, Walter Prince chose not to use hypnotic procedures and thus minimized contamination of his observations.

In his report on the Doris case Walter Prince has left us a great mass of data waiting for our understanding. In a memorial volume to Walter Prince, Gardner Murphy (1935, p. 81) said: "Perhaps as Kepler used Tycho Brahe's data in founding modern astronomy, some student of the future will see the full meaning of the [Doris case] and complete the building, the foundations of which Prince so solidly laid."

FACES OF EVE

For a generation spanning World War II, the phenomenon of multiple personality almost disappeared from the literature of psychiatry and psychology, only to re-emerge with the writings of Thigpen and Cleckley (1954).

These psychiatrists published *The Three Faces of Eve* (Thigpen

& Cleckley, 1957), a work successfully constructed to become a best seller among popular books. With the publication of Eve's own account of her illness (Sizemore & Pittillo, 1977), it became evident that Thigpen and Cleckley's report was seriously deficient. It must be acknowledged, however, that these doctors of medicine, by reaching the mass market, did help spread the knowledge that multiple personality is more than the Dr. Jekyll–Mr. Hyde literary creation of Robert Louis Stevenson.

SYBIL

A professional science writer, F.R. Schreiber (1973), was invited by psychiatrist, Dr. Cornelia Wilbur of New York City, to write a book about one of Dr. Wilbur's patients. Sybil Dorsett, as she was known in the book, was afflicted with multiple personalities—16 by later count. Sybil began psychotherapy at age 31 and was not cured until 1965, after 11 years of treatment, requiring 2300 office visits.

Sybil knew that she suffered from memory gaps in which she did things that were uncharacteristic of her waking self, but she was unaware of the existence of her other personalities until told of them by her psychiatrist.

The secondary personalities would appear, singly or in pairs, pretending to the world to be Sybil but pretending to themselves to be someone else. In addition to their own memories they had some memories belonging to one another and to Sybil, and one of the secondary personalities seemed to possess complete memory and understanding of all the others, including Sybil.

Since Schreiber wrote a popular book, how much can one believe as to the historical correctness of the account? I am inclined to think that it is almost entirely true, except for the author's creation or embellishment of conversation and behavioral details to make it a more saleable story.

It must be remembered that the opinions expressed by the personalities were not necessarily true. They believed, for example, that among themselves there were differences in physical appearance— complexion and hair color—that were, of course, nonexistent.

One might ask, to what extent were the personalities in this case induced in the course of psychotherapy. Probably not at all. Hypnotic suggestion was not used until the therapy had been under way for five years.

Sybil was grievously abused in her early childhood by her schizophrenic mother. Although such mistreatment is likely to precipitate a psychoneurotic breakdown and the formation of multiple personalities in a hysterically predisposed person, I doubt whether such extreme mistreatment is a necessary condition for this phenomenon to appear. I suspect that, in its milder forms, multiple personality is very common, but that it is seldom recognized merely because psychiatrists are trained to believe that it is rare.

4

AN INTERPRETATION OF MULTIPLE PERSONALITY

How Psychology Responds

I have referred to four outstanding cases of multiple personality.[1] What are we to make of them? At some stage, after hearing a certain amount of this seeming nonsense, we begin to wonder what is going on. Is the patient merely pretending? Who is deceiving whom?

But that is the impression one often gets when dealing with mental illness. If you are interested in this aspect of psychopathology, you may wish to read *The Myth of Mental Illness* (Szasz, 1961). However, I do not endorse this book. I think Szasz treats a difficult subject from a naively flippant point of view. Multiple personality phenomena provide a strong argument against Szasz's game-playing interpretation of mental illness.[2]

The mystery we face is human consciousness. What is consciousness? What is its relation to the brain? And what are we, beyond our consciousness? These are frightening questions, and, until recently, the tendency of psychologists has been to assume that it is foolish to consider them.

I asked a clinical psychologist how the subject of multiple personality is handled in the classroom. His answer was that today we are more concerned with the nearly normal people whom we treat every day than we are with extreme psychoneurotics. I next asked: "That is a good clinical answer, but is there no theoretical interest in multiple personality?" His reply was: "Perhaps there is in physiological psychology." I assume he was referring to split-brain experiments.

In other words, that large part of psychology that concerns itself

---

1. Additional cases are summarized by E.R. Hilgard (1977). However, he ignores the two-volume Doris Fischer Case by W.F. Prince—perhaps because it was reported in a parapsychological journal (W.F. Prince, 1915; 1916).

2. Szasz is the most visible representative of a countercultural school of social psychiatry whose adherents argue that the so-called "mentally ill" are, at worst, mildly deviant individuals who have been taught to "play the role" of insanity by the disapproval of society, and especially by being labeled and institutionalized (Murphy, 1976). One difficulty with Szasz's proposition is that it leaves unexplained the not-infrequent cases of hallucinatory paranoid schizophrenia that are recognized by the family physician but left unlabeled for legal reasons until after an act of criminal violence has been committed.

with human personality prefers to ignore this subject. To the student psychologist and to the layman it must often appear that psychology as a profession is ignoring many interesting and important questions.

Before you make a hasty judgment of psychologists for this behavior, I ask you to wait for my later chapters in which I discuss the broader question: How does science work? How, for example, are questions for research chosen? Why are some questions ignored even though they may be interesting and important? How does such selective interest eventually lead to scientific revolution?

EXTENT OF PATHOLOGY

Are multiple personalities pathological? Sufficient criteria for multiple personality are a sudden discontinuity in sense of identity while in the waking state, or the persistent, intermittent unavailability of a group of memories. Both of these conditions are maladaptive in the long run and, hence, pathological.

Within the scope of this book I can do no more than outline this question of psychopathology. In a technical sense, multiple personality is a form of hysteria. Hysteria, in turn, is a form of neurosis. The neuroses are a class of mental illness less serious than the psychoses. In hysteria, the patient has pains, hyperaesthesias (pathologically acute sensory sensitivity), local anesthesias and paralyses. These seem to have no physical cause. They come and go, often without apparent reason, and are organized along body-image rather than neurological lines. The hysterical patient may also suffer tremors, total or partial blindness, and amnesia, as well as extreme emotional lability.

In all of the multiple-personality cases we have considered, some of the personalities showed pronounced symptoms of hysteria. For instance, there were areas of the body without touch sensation for one personality but not for the others, and these areas changed from time to time. Beyond that, some of the hallucinations that these personalities experienced would ordinarily be classified as psychotic, and more specifically, as schizophrenic.

One might ask whether multiple personality is not "just a form of schizophrenia." That is not an easy question because schizophrenia is not a simple clinical entity. There are several kinds of "schizophrenic reaction"; just as there are several classifications of neurosis. Some clinical cases are so distinctive that there is no doubt as to exactly what label to use. Many others are not. Schizophrenia is now known to be largely hereditary (Heston, 1970). There is some evidence suggesting that hysterical neurosis may not be (Shields, 1973).

How might one respond to the question: Is multiple personality a form of schizophrenia? A simplistic answer is: No, because cases of multiple personality are classified, instead, as "dissociative reactions" under "neurotic disorders" according to the second edition of the *Diagnostic and Statistical Manual of Mental Disorders* of the American Psychiatric Association (1968).[3]

Regardless of this fact, there may be cases in which the label "schizophrenia" seems to fit. I suspect that Eve in *Three Faces of Eve* would be one such. But I would hesitate to use that term for Sally, Doris, or Sybil.

The basic difference between neurosis and schizophrenia is this. In schizophrenia the patient is making poor contact with reality. In neurosis the patient has a good grip on reality, perceptually speaking, but responds to it in an illogical or extreme fashion as though part of the needed information or logic mechanism were unavailable. This distinction sounds reasonable, but in practice it cannot always be maintained. However, in the Sally, Doris, and Sybil cases the application of the rule seems clear. The several personalities, to the extent they were complete, were reasonably well oriented toward external reality—as much, let us say, as the average person on the street.

Regardless of the precise diagnosis of the mental illness, are cures of multiple personality permanent?

---

3. The authors of the *third* edition of the *Diagnostic and Statistical Manual* (American Psychiatric Association, 1980) adopted the policy of classifying mental illness of unknown cause (i.e., most mental illness) on the basis of clinical manifestations and without regard to existing theories. Also, because it was recognized (p. 9) that "there is no consensus in our field as to how to define 'neurosis'," it was decided to give up that word.

These decisions have the curious effect of placing in separate categories neurotic symptoms that are undoubtedly closely associated in etiology. For example, conversion hysteria becomes a "somatoform disorder," while multiple personality is a "dissociation disorder."

This relabeling has the added advantage (from the psychiatrist's point of view) that the public, which had come to understand and use the older terms for various kinds of neurotic illness, can now more readily be excluded from the diagnostic process.

The question of the meaning and validity of psychiatric diagnosis arises in various ways in parapsychology. The matter is discussed in Appendix B.

Morton Prince (1929, p. 268) reported in 1920, 15 years after the end of therapy, that Miss Beauchamp was married and living a normal life.

The sequel to the Doris Fischer case is the most fully known. After Doris was cured and became Theodosia Prince, she went on under Dr. Walter Prince's direction to develop psychic ability (W.F. Prince, 1926) and remained in sound health until Dr. Prince died 20 years later. Mrs. Prince had died some years earlier, and being left alone after Dr. Prince's death was unendurable for Theodosia. She had a psychotic breakdown in which some supposed spirit communicators came to torment her, and she attempted to commit suicide by poisoning. A friend of Dr. Prince gave her psychotherapy and, after several months, with the cooperation of "Sleeping Margaret," Theodosia was returned to apparently good health (Worcester, 1935).

Thigpen and Cleckley (1957) left the impression that Eve had achieved healthy, single selfhood. Twenty years and many personalities later, Eve herself believed that she was much improved but not necessarily cured (Sizemore & Pittillo, 1977).

Sybil Dorsett was reported as totally cured and living a happy life when her book went to press, seven years after the completion of therapy.

In all of these cases it seems reasonable to infer that the patient's tendency to hysterical neurosis was not changed by treatment and could be expected to emerge under emotional stress.

In an earlier chapter I described briefly the trance mediumship of Spiritualism. Now we have looked at multiple personality. Both phenomena show diversity of consciousness. How do they differ and how are they alike?

A sleeping trance, voluntarily entered by a medium and terminated on schedule, may be very odd but it is not necessarily pathological. The "spirit controls" and the so-called "direct communicators" that take over the speech organs or the writing hand of the medium may have well-developed personalities but they also have a separate sense of identity that acknowledges the personality of the medium and her ownership of the body. One is left with the impression that the medium retains her own integrity, even though she is in abeyance while she allows some part of her mind to engage in role playing.

Multiple personalities, on the other hand, take over all or part of the body (leaving the rest nonfunctional), and they may persist indefinitely so that there is no uniquely normal state. This clearly justifies the label "pathological." It does not, however, suggest to me any theoretical distinction between a multiple personality and the controlling spirit of a trance medium. I think it likely that they are essentially the same.

CLUES TO CONSCIOUSNESS

What is the significance of multiple personality? In cases of multiple personality are there really two or more persons living in one body, or are we seeing merely different aspects of a single person? Here is Morton Prince's answer (1905, p.3):

> Cases of this kind are commonly known as "double" or "multiple personality," according to the number of persons represented, but a more correct term is *disintegrated personality*; for each secondary personality is a part only, of a normal whole self. . . . The disintegration resulting in multiple personality is only a functional dissociation of that complex organization which constitutes a normal self. The elementary psychical processes, in themselves normal, are capable of being reassociated into a normal whole.

According to Morton Prince, in these cases there is one person who has disintegrated and who, with proper treatment, can be put back together again into a "normal whole." From a philosophic point of view, this is a reassuring answer, reflecting the earlier studies of hysteria by Richet and Janet, but is it an adequate answer? Walter Prince in 1916 was careful not to draw any such theoretical conclusion. Opinion today, based upon both split-brain research and multiple-personality clinical experience, leans strongly to a multi-person interpretation. Multiple personalities are often so mutually incompatible that they cannot be integrated into a functionally effective whole. In therapy, one or more personalities must be permanently suppressed if good health is to be attained. Is such suppression by the therapist a form of murder?

Of what can we be certain? On the one hand, there is only one brain per head. On the other, there may be more than one self-consciousness, and sometimes these exist simultaneously. Each consciousness displays a distinct personality. These personalities in some cases appear to be complete for most practical purposes, but in other cases they are clearly fragmentary. In some instances the personalities struggle desperately against one another for immediate dominance and for long-term survival. Sometimes two of the personalities fuse together and become one. Sometimes multiple personalities regress mentally or can otherwise be caused to disappear.

These facts point to basic questions: What is consciousness? What is the relation of consciousness to brain structure? How can a single brain support two or more consciousnesses simultaneously? What is the "unconscious"? Can the unconscious get motor control of the body? Can the so-called unconscious become a conscious personality? (Morton Prince thought that Sally was Miss Beauchamp's unconscious.)

We are not yet able to give final answers to these questions. However, as a result of split-brain research, we can begin to make guesses that may be rather close to the truth. In their book, *The Integrated Mind*, to which I referred in Chapter 3, Gazzaniga and LeDoux (1978) offer a number of observations and speculations about the nature of consciousness.

These authors believe that "the brain has a variety of ways to encode and store information and that a given information storage system is not necessarily accessible to every other network of stored information" (p. 125).

They suggest that the same experience may be encoded in memory by several modalities simultaneously. If these do not include the verbal modality, such experience cannot usually be reached by analytic consciousness later (p. 132), although it may be effective in determining behavior.

Different aspects of the same experience are stored separately. With regard to a carnation, the ideas that it is a flower, that it is called "carnation," its shape, its smell, that it is red, and that it grows in a particular part of one's garden would all be stored in different memory banks, having varying degrees of cross-referencing capability.

The variety of storage systems is surprising. Left- and right-hand skills are stored separately. Various elements of language are differently recorded. (A brain-damaged person might be able to recall verbs but not nouns.) The same element of language may be stored differently in different contexts. (Remembering "red" as it applies to fruits might be impaired by brain damage, but not "red" for fire engines.)

The neural mechanisms mediating visual imagery are distinct from those mediating visual perception, i.e., mental life is neurologically separated from sensorimotor experience. "It is as if mental life is transacted in codes that transcend perceptual experience on the neural level" (p. 123).

Favorable or unfavorable emotional response to a stimulation can be stored and later emitted without analytic (i.e., verbal) awareness of the stimulus. It seems undeniable that the implications of this for free will and social responsibility are enormous.

The mind is a social entity consisting of many mental subsystems. "The uniqueness of man, in this regard, is his ability to verbalize and, in so doing, create a personal sense of conscious reality out of the multiple mental systems present" (p. 151).

These authors suggest that verbal memory is the key to thinking and that it organizes and coordinates other memory banks to the extent that it has access to them. It functions to create a sense of personal identity—by distortion of reality to whatever degree may be necessary.[4]

HANDLING CONFLICT

The foregoing ideas presented by Gazzaniga and LeDoux (1978), which are revolutionary in their own right, seem to me to need only a little extension to encompass the facts of multiple personality.

Human personality is built by each individual out of genetic potentialities and the experience of living. Ideally, there is only one personality per body, which changes and develops throughout life, forgetting nothing and integrating all new experience.

Actually, it never happens that way. The brain is highly selective in its perceptions and gathers only that which comfortably conforms to what it already knows. From time to time, despite the perceptual vigilance of the brain, anomalous experience forces itself upon the individual. Preferably, this results in an enriched, more encompassing world view. This modification process is what we call "education."

However, if the new experience is extraordinarily threatening and the person is genetically predisposed to that kind of neurosis, the memory systems of the brain may disable some of their unifying cross connections. As a result, various non-verbal systems of the brain can aggregate independently, and even simultaneously,

---

4. An appreciation of the progress represented by the work of Gazzaniga and LeDoux in our understanding of consciousness may be gained from other recent attempts to deal with this topic (*See*, Natsoulas, 1978).

with all or part of the verbal system of the brain; thus giving rise to multiple personalities.

Gazzaniga and LeDoux have suggested that any experience that is not analytically perceived will be stored, if at all, without retrieval connections to the verbal system. While all retained infant experience may thus be stored, there seems no reason to doubt that, in children and adults, analytically perceived unpleasant experience can sometimes be stored exclusively in nonverbal systems (i.e., nonanalytically) without the usual retrieval connections thereto.

To summarize, while most individuals store unpleasant experience so that it is simply inaccessible to the language system, hysterical neurotics use, instead, an unstable disabling of the integrating mechanism of the verbal system and sometimes a splitting of consciousness.

MECHANISMS OF REALITY AVOIDANCE

In the classical Freudian view, neurosis is undue anxiety that is triggered by environmental stress but that has its origin in forgotten childhood incidents. The cure, supposedly, is to recall and re-evaluate those incidents with the help of a psychoanalyst.

Without such help, the patient builds more or less successful defenses (self-deceptions) against the anxiety-triggering environment. If these break down, they are replaced by others of increasing pathology, which, typically, take the form of phobias (for specific situations), obsessions (with ideas), compulsions (to perform ritualistic acts), or, as previously described, hysterical conversion (paralysis, anesthesia, paraesthesia, blindness, tic, tremor, catalepsy). Eventually, there may be total functional collapse.

Since Freud's time we have learned that: (a) The form and extent of neurosis depends partly upon genetic predispostion. (b) Sometimes there are no specific childhood incidents but merely extended periods of stress. (c) Some of the somatic characteristics of the so-called "neurotic personality" (e.g., lack of stamina) are not a part of the mental pathology but are simply independent, associated features of a genetically caused syndrome.

To these ideas I would add: (d) Neurotic defenses are only a small segment of a larger, generally unrecognized family of mental mechanisms for avoiding reality, some of which I shall now briefly discuss.

Persons of below-average intelligence tend to be mentally improvident and therefore encounter reality only as it is thrust upon them. At that point their most common defense is to deny reality by the outright violation of logic. Limited mental competence allows them to use propositions such as $A < B < A$.

Persons of superior linear-thinking ability most commonly avoid reality by refusing to consider unpleasant matters not likely to affect them directly. Successful scientists are predominantly linear thinkers. Most of them maintain their equanamity by refusing to concern themselves with anything but their research. If some anxiety-causing social issue penetrates this defense, they may dispose of it by joining the appropriate do-good organization. Persisting questions of value are often relegated to a sanitary mental compartment labelled "religion," in which a magical solution can be employed.

Unlike linear thinkers, strongly intuitive thinkers are not occupied by protective trains of thought and must resort to more complex reality-avoidance tactics. One class of the latter is "memory management."

Memory management occurs most blatantly in multiple personality. We recall that, while in the classical case, a hysterical neurotic loses part of his sensorimotor function, the multiple-personality variant loses unity of consciousness as defined by memories of past sensorimotor events. In clinical multiple personality there will be sudden transitions between personalities, i.e., dramatic shifts in the constellation of consciously accessible memories, and, as we have seen, in some cases multiple consciousness may exist simultaneously within a single brain.

The essential element of multiple personality is the disconnection of parts of memory from unitary conscious control. This may be no different in principle from going to sleep, but in the case of sleep the disconnection is dependably organized "for the purpose of providing rest."

Why should we assume that brain disconnection possibilities are limited to the foregoing? Why not, for example, expect gross variations in intelligence because of disconnection of some of the reasoning apparatus? Among students, I have seen cases of fluctuating IQ that could be neatly explained as "multiple intelligence."

It is well known that in normal persons there are frequent, back-and-forth shiftings in the relative accessibility of groups of memories determining affect. If these shifts of mood reach clinical proportions, the patient is described as "emotionally labile." Perhaps affective set is often biochemically determined without involving memories. It seems more probable, however, that mood change ordinarily includes memory management in which there is a temporary loss of certain memories, but not noticeably of memories for past sensorimotor events.

What becomes disconnected on such occasions are emotional memories. The resulting mood changes may be recognizably pathological, i.e., maladaptive. For example, while in one mood a person may entangle himself with an environmental situation that is found to be unendurable in later moods. From a practical point of view this is little different from the escapades of multiple personalities. There is reason to believe that clinical shifting of moods in adulthood can result from excessive childhood stress.

Just as moods can vary by the temporary connection and disconnection of emotional memories, so various personality changes can result from permanent memory suppression. Such changes are sometimes called "development" or "maturation" when, in fact, "selective forgetting" might be a more accurate term.

Since temporary mood shifts and permanent memory suppression are universal phenomena, perhaps all of us are mentally ill to one degree or another. The justification for this statement is the fact that none of us can grasp, much less accept, more than a small part of the reality to which we have been sensorily exposed. Reality is overwhelming. We must reject most of it in order to function.

This raises interesting questions about the distinction between mental normality and pathology. What is the healthiest mental behavior? Is it wise to limit perception to what is pleasant (e.g., by choice of duties)? Why *not* suppress unpleasant memories? Should we allow our moods to come and go as they will—the more, the better? It can be argued that none of these stratagems has long-term survival value for the individual or for society.

In some obscure, currently incomprehensible way, the best procedure may be to cast our perceptual net widely and then control our resulting moods by using some otherwise uninvolved part of the brain. Moods should be constantly screened, both for immediate social appropriateness and for compatibility with long-term goals.

The foregoing conceptions are too narrow, of course. Memory management is only one defense against reality. As previously mentioned, another is logic violation—which can be quite subtle, as in the tacit distortion of the scope of a referent. Universally used by persons of low intelligence, logic violation is also often systematically employed by persons of intellectual prominence. Among quantitatively trained scientists, however, it is usually a last-ditch defense reserved for dangerous threats to ideological security.

Like memory management, logic violation by the intellectually competent can result from childhood stress. Unlike memory management, logic violation is always pathological.

The topic of multiple personality will arise again, as "multiplicity of mind" in Chapter 5, under "unconscious deception" in Chapter 6, and in Chapter 19 on "Fraud in Parapsychology".

5

CONSCIOUSNESS AND SOCIETY

To Whom Does Our Thinking Belong?

In the last chapter I examined consciousness in terms of brain function and psychopathology. Now I shall consider consciousness in relation to psi phenomena and society.

I define *consciousness* as the state of thinking attentively, whether analytically or intuitively. Conscious and unconscious thinking represent a spectrum. Conscious thought is whatever is within the span of attention at the moment. This is a matter of degree; only conceptions of limited scope are fully at the center of attention. At the same time, depending on the situation, more—usually much more—is peripherally within awareness. Outside of awareness, unconscious memories range from those easily recalled for analytic consideration to those that are effectively unavailable for examination at any time.

Depending upon our definition of it, consciousness ceases intermittently or totally while we are asleep. Contrariwise, unconscious thinking, i.e., unconscious memory-data processing, presumably proceeds to some degree at all times from birth to death.

Consciousness is a personal attribute. It originates within each of us, and its immediate content is ours alone unless we convey it to others by word or action or in some other way.

To whom does our unconscious thinking belong? Some parts of it we can discover and examine with difficulty or not at all. Meanwhile, other persons may conceivably have access to parts of it by ESP without our knowledge or permission. What is the extent of this possible sharing process?

Some of our unconscious thinking clearly originates in our prior conscious thinking. Some of it doubtless derives from sensorimotor experience of which we were never verbally aware. Are there perhaps other external sources of unconscious ideas?

Although conscious and unconscious thinking together determine the history of mankind, we have no specific knowledge of the social importance of the unconscious realm of thought. Still less do we know of the possible social role of psi phenomena, operating upon the unconscious thinking of all of us.

Following the Second World War, I saw documentary films

covering the gamut of wartime violence and cruelty. The one impression, above all others, that I retain from those films is the ecstatic madness in the faces of the shouting masses in the city of Berlin after Hitler's early victories. In my imagination I have travelled backward and forward from that time in history, from one mob to another, always haunted by the question: What unconscious logic creates such irrational frenzy? Is there perhaps some psychic factor waiting to be understood by parapsychology? Because of this and much else that is unexplained in the rise and fall of civilizations, I suspect that the science of sociology will not be born except as the child of parapsychology.

MAN'S CONSCIOUS GRASP OF REALITY

What distinguishes man from other animals is his innate ability to organize and preserve his past by means of language. This genetic development has made man the most conscious of all animals, and, indeed, justifies a definitional dichotomy between man and other mammals.

To achieve his present civilization, man first had to become aware of himself as an entity in relation to his environment. Thereafter he had to gain knowledge of other things not presented directly to his senses, knowledge of such things as distant places, atomic particles, and his own unconscious mental processes. He did all this by extrapolation, starting with the immediately-given, nonverbal, sensory experience of the infant human—which we may believe is not significantly different from that of the infant chimpanzee. Language was the instrument for this extrapolation.

Analytic consciousness is not given to us, but is constructed by each of us by manipulating words whose meaning each of us has invented for himself. Therefore, what we call understanding, is both culturally based and individual. No two persons can have the same understanding. It follows that all understanding remains incomplete. (This idea is developed further in Chapters 17, 18, and 21.)

We construct our own consciousness. This was said very well by William James nearly a century ago. The following excerpt is from his textbook, *Principles of Psychology*, in the chapter on "The Stream of Thought." (James, 1890, 288–289):

> The mind, in short, works on the data it receives very much as a sculptor works on his block of stone. In a sense the statue stood there from eternity. But there were a thousand different ones beside

it, and the sculptor alone is to thank for having extricated this one from the rest. Just so, the world of each of us, howsoever different our several views of it may be, all lay embedded in the primordial chaos of sensations, which gave the mere *matter* to the thought of all of us indifferently. We may, if we like, by our reasonings unwind things back to that black and jointless continuity of space and moving clouds of swarming atoms which science calls the only real world. But all the while the world *we* feel and live in will be that which our ancestors and we, by slowly cumulative strokes of choice, have extricated out of this, like sculptors, by simply rejecting certain portions of the given stuff. Other sculptors, other statues from the same stone! Other minds, other worlds from the same monotonous and inexpressive chaos! My world is but one in a million, alike embedded, alike real to those who may abstract them.

The recognition of personal consciousness as something that is different for each of us, raises interesting questions. Do we all experience the same real world in which we live and die, or do we make our own worlds? Are there inherently unpleasant stimuli, or, by a lifetime devoted to "the power of positive thinking," can we create our world as we wish it to be? Are there real differences among our neighbors in such dimensions as kindness, intelligence, and will power, or are these all arbitrary perceptions of our consciousness for which we, not they, must assume responsibility?

At least in broad outline, the answers to these questions are obvious. Our ordinary personal awareness is not necessarily arbitrary or spurious, but is constrained by physical reality, past and present, external and internal, and is oriented toward biological survival.

We select what we will perceive from what is available in present outer reality, and we select the framework from past experience within which we will do our perceiving. Indeed, it is necessary for survival that we be selective.

But it is also possible to be selective in a way that is clearly pathological. We call this kind of selection "reality denial," although in principle, it is not different from the selectivity necessary for good health. It is only in extreme cases that healthy selection and pathological denial are easily distinguishable activities. This is one of the paradoxes of life. The philosopher, social scientist, or psychotherapist who denies this paradox is either confused or dishonest.

MULTIPLICITY OF MIND AS A REVOLUTIONARY CONCEPT

Most scientists and laymen, when asked to discuss the possible importance of psi, start by trying to imagine what it would be like to live in a world where one can read other person's minds and cause objects to jump by will power alone. As I shall now explain, a consideration of the social aspects of unconscious thought will suggest to us more subtle and powerful implications of psi phenomena than such mere Mickey Mouse applications. These deeper implications will hold, whether or not nature will ever allow each of us to learn to perform miracles by means of PK and ESP.

Three conceptions of the nature of man's existence dominated philosophy in seventeenth-century Europe: idealism, materialism, and Cartesian dualism. Idealists claimed that thought is the ultimate reality and that matter is a mirage. Materialists believed that physics encompasses all of reality and that consciousness is an inconsequential aspect of the biological process of thinking. Descartes held that there are two independent realms, mental and material, totally different but capable of intimate interaction. By the device of declaring mind, i.e., mental processes, to be in the province of religion and beyond the scope of science, dualism temporarily won the debate and became the basis of science and social order. A detente was possible in which science and religion could each play the role for which it seemed best fitted at the time.

Revolutions of whatever kind come about because of expanded consciousness. In the eighteenth century, with increased education and growing leisure, the common man became aware of his political power and of inconsistencies between prevailing religious doctrine and social reality. The result was the revolt of the masses— the end of which is not in sight. Political revolt was accompanied by a widespread abandonment of religious dogma, thereby jeopardizing one leg of Cartesian dualism.

The scientific revolution which distinguishes our civilization, gathered speed in the seventeenth century with a recognition among educated people that nature in its physical aspects was unknown but discoverable. A little later, philosophers began to suspect that mental aspects of nature were likewise unknown but perhaps discoverable. This was the beginning of psychology, which led to the abandonment of Cartesian dualism and to the later substitution of materialistic monism—as I shall now briefly relate.

Unconscious thinking is a revolutionary psychological concept whose power, first recognized by Frederic Myers and Sigmund Freud, is just now beginning to be fully appreciated. To understand the situation, we begin by noting that the word *unconscious* is misleading. It is description by negation or exclusion. A more apt expression would be "multiplicity of mind of which we are only indirectly aware."

We have already discussed the multiplicity of consciousness that occurs in multiple personality. Moreover, each of us, whether clinically ill or not, has within ourselves an unconscious diversity of mind over which we have no direct control but which affects our conscious thinking and distorts our linguistic grasp of reality. This has been known for a long time.

Multiplicity of mind within a single organism was soon recognized to imply a functional dependence of the thinking process upon brain structure. This contradicted Descartes' assumption that mind is an independent thinking entity. Thus, the prevailing metaphysics of science vis-a-vis social order crumbled.

If the quality of man's thought largely depends upon the brain structure he has inherited, and if his behavior is influenced by parts of his mind of which he is unaware, he is not the intellectual captain of his destiny in the way believed in the Age of Reason. He is not the wholly accountable moral entity supposed in the Judeo-Christian tradition of yesterday. Moreover, because of the self-constructed nature of the content of his consciousness, he must accept the fact that ultimate reality is forever beyond his apprehension. All he can hope to know are constantly unfolding vistas of experience.

The response of scientists to this impasse was two-fold. The less compulsively logical refused to abandon religion. Instead, they separated their thinking into two spheres: humanistic and scientific. As regards man's destiny and duty, they believed what they wished. In their own area of science, they insisted upon doubt, logical rigor, and unitary theorizing.

The majority of scientists, however, felt driven toward philosophic consistency and rejected religion in favor of materialistic monism. They declared that mind does not exist and that consciousness is but an impotent epiphenomenon of the working brain.

Materialistic monism is an impractical philosophy because it must deny all purpose in life save the individual's own pleasure. Given the kind of world in which we find ourselves, the materialists have been forced to devise diverse, socially liberal strategems to deceive themselves that theirs is a self-consistent way of life. If rationality is to be admired, there would seem to be little basis for preferring the agnostic monist to the believing dualist.

Meanwhile, the populace, hearing no single voice of authority in matters of man's nature as it determines morality, continues to drift. It has been claimed, with some justification, that it is largely through the recognition of man's diversity of mind that our value system has been destroyed and that our civilization is in danger. We have discovered that the mind is not an independent, unitary soul in the traditional theological sense. Our old explanations of our place in the universe are incompatible with reality. We have not yet discovered what it is that reality demands of us.

It is here, I think, that parapsychology enters the picture. Psi phenomena at the present time are almost entirely beyond our conscious control. They are repressed by conscious consideration, and when they do break into awareness, it is with typically Freudian distortions—as I shall discuss in Chapter 13. More importantly, they can occur as objective, external phenomena of the material world and therefore could be directly relevant to real-world morality. As we shall see, psi phenomena suggest space-and-time-independent, person-to-person and person-to-thing connections occurring for the most part without our awareness. Our unconscious thought interacts directly with the external physical world. It requires neither prescience nor faith to say that it is probable that an understanding of psi phenomena will eventually lead us to a social value system conforming more closely to reality than does any system now known.

In his Nobel Prize lecture Roger Sperry (1982a) elaborated some of the above ideas concerning multiplicity of mind. On the basis of his split-brain research he affirmed that consciousness is an emergent property having causal efficacy.

> The events of inner experience, as emergent properties of brain processes, become themselves explanatory causal constructs in their own right, interacting at their own level with their own laws and dynamics. The whole world of inner experience (the world of the humanities), long rejected by 20th-century scientific materialism, thus becomes recognized and included within the domain of science. . . . It follows that physical science no longer perceives the world to be reducible to quantum mechanics or to any other unifying ultra element or field force. The qualitative, holistic properties at all different levels become causally real in their own form and have to be included in the causal account. . . .
>
> The results add up to a fundamental change in what science has long stood for throughout the materialist-behaviorist era (Sperry, 1981). The former scope of science, its limitations, world perspectives, views of human nature, and its societal role as an intellectual, cultural, and moral force all undergo profound change. Where there

used to be conflict and an irreconcilable chasm between the scientific and the traditional humanistic views of man and the world (Snow, 1959; Jones, 1965), we now perceive a continuum. A unifying new interpretative framework emerges (Sperry, 1982b) with far reaching impact, not only for science but for those ultimate value-belief guidelines by which mankind has tried to live and find meaning.

This is a magnificent statement that parapsychologists will endorse without reservation. In his writings elsewhere Sperry prefers "causally emergent monism" over "interactionist dualism" and rejects the possibility of psi phenomena a priori (1980, p. 201) in the apparent belief that they imply dualism. However, most parapsychologists today regard psi phenomena, like consciousness, as an emergent manifestation of brain processes. Philosophic predilections notwithstanding, neuroscientists would do well to focus their critical attention upon the question of the empirical reality of psi phenomena and to render their judgment accordingly.

Unconscious Traditions in History

Lancelot Law Whyte (1896–1972) advanced a hypothesis (Whyte, 1974) of the role of the unconscious in history that may prove seminal in our developing understanding of self-awareness in man.

He postulated the existence of unconscious traditions (*Zeitgeisten*) in history possessing the following attributes:

1. They evolve cumulatively over several generations.
2. They are carried by sometimes-isolated chains of individual minds, often in a substantial fraction of the population.
3. They are transferred from person to person by unconscious mechanisms (imitation, and non-verbal communication generally).
4. They may extinguish under various stateable circumstances.
5. They may culminate or emerge into consciousness in verbal or material form, often through the agency of men of genius whose own contributions may be important.
6. They may be at the same time partly conscious and partly unconscious.
7. They include both complementary and competing traditions.
8. They govern the future of man, just as conscious traditions preserve the status quo.

Some of these (partially) unconscious traditions, according to Whyte, are: nationalisms, the method of Western science, humanism, living styles, technology.

Whyte postulates that unconscious sensory transmission is what gives life and continuity to every great cultural fluctuation. From what we know about the nature of ESP, it is perhaps more likely that these so-called "traditions" are, in part, a kind of psychic collaboration. If this should prove true, sociology and history will take on a new aspect.

6

ALTERED STATES OF CONSCIOUSNESS

NORMAL DISSOCIATION

The early chapters of this book are devoted to states of consciousness that are of special interest to parapsychology. I have already discussed trance mediumship and multiple personality as well as miscellaneous aspects of conscious and unconscious thinking. The present chapter will discuss hypnosis, unconscious deception, and what I shall call the passive-alert state of awareness.

I want to begin, however, with the idea of *dissociation*. I shall vaguely define dissociation as what occurs when a person loosens or loses his normal sense of identity or sense of command over his cognitive processes. This subjective definition has objective criteria. For example, a dissociated person is less responsive than normally to sensory stimuli and may engage in motor activity of which he will later admit he was unaware. Other criteria will be given in the discussion of hypnosis.

Dissociation is probably necessary, but certainly not sufficient, for the production of psi phenomena. It is also a prelude to what is called mystical experience. Dissociation is, in fact, a major aspect of all "altered states of consciousness" and occurs to varying degrees in the normal waking state. For example, each night, for all of us, progressive dissociation leads to sleep, which itself is a dissociated state.

To the question: Is waking dissociation necessarily pathological? I give you the following answer from Walter Prince (1926, pp. 30–31).

> Some learned specialists [hold that waking] dissociation . . . is always pathological. This generalization I regard as a mistaken one. . . . The cases of disintegrated personality most powerfully focus the attention and next those of the borderline of hysteria and hypnosis. We are apt to forget the useful part that dissociation plays in our ordinary normal lives. There is dissociation in reverie, giving us restful states, in day-dreaming not far removed from sleep-dreaming, in flights of imagination which stimulate to creative effort, in busily talking while the unregarded hands still play the piano, in taking out a key and unlocking a door while one's attention remains busy with a newspaper, in walking rapidly and avoiding rough places in the path while

one is deeply engrossed in a scientific problem, in a million instances of multiple activity.

No amount of twaddle about unconscious cerebration . . . can obliterate the fact that to perform an intelligent feat, intelligence must be called into play, and that, if that part of our intelligence of which we are aware is not responsible, some other part must be. So far as we do unconscious thinking, it is dissociated thinking. This dissociation may consist, as it normally does, simply in a subliminal thought stream, or the subliminal stream may become conscious and acquire the status of a personality, or, in extreme cases, [may] assume temporary solitary dominion—there is every possible gradation in between. . . .

It is in the very nature of the [human] machine that we should be subconsciously thinking, and that the products of this dissociated mental activity should constantly be bubbling up and enriching the supraliminal stream. If one dreamed but a few times in his lifetime, he might think himself temporarily deranged; but dreams, the products of a consciousness dissociated from that of our waking hours, are normal activities.

Rarely when one is awake . . . one can trace a subconscious mental act. . . . Once . . . I happened to remark to a lady in the office that a friend of mine had [erroneously] referred to Professor John Dynely Prince as the man who studied monkey language. I added that, of course [instead, he] meant Professor Garner. This was all that I had any intention of saying, but I found my lips going on mechanically while they curved into a broad smile and said: "I suppose the connection is that Prince is instructor of Semitic languages." And then the smile faded out and I looked out of the window puzzled to account for my involuntary grin or to make any sense in what I had just said. I was as ignorant of my meaning, for the moment, as the most obtuse observer could be. The idea was just coming up above the threshold, in another moment I should have given expression to it, when the lady said, "Oh, I see, simian." A poor pun, but such as it was it had been achieved in a dissociated part of my consciousness, which had actually enjoyed its humor and expressed it in my face while my conscious self was without comprehension of either the pun or the smile.

This quotation from Walter Prince makes it evident that some degree of dissociation and multiple mental activity, even to the point of initiating and controlling motor behavior, is not only benign but essential to our functioning.

HYPNOSIS, ITS NATURE

Can the laboratory production of ESP be enhanced by the use of hypnosis? We shall come to that question in the next chapter. At present, I would like to describe briefly the phenomena commonly associated with hypnosis.

I shall not, however, attempt to summarize various available explanatory theories. Even those who write books on this subject are not in agreement. There are by now at least six, well-elaborated theories of hypnosis. Of one thing we can be sure. If so many theories are needed, none of them is satisfactory.

One of the requirements of a good scientific theory is that it drive out and destroy all competing theories. If there is more than one theory covering the same set of operations at any one level of organization, that is an indication of our ignorance. We shall examine this and other characteristics of scientific theory in Chapters 17 and 18.

As for hypnosis, it would make little sense to take time to examine weak theories that will surely disappear.[1] We could, however, find use for the following descriptive comment on which to base preliminary discussion: *Hypnosis occurs in a dissociated state apparently induced largely by the purpose of another person as expressed by conversation or other symbolic behavior.* You will notice that I have arbitrarily excluded self-hypnosis. I believe that, as we learn more about hypnotic dissociation, we shall discover that the hypnotic operator can play a crucial role that may set hypnosis apart from states of self-induced dissociation.

Nearly everyone is familiar with the specifically observable phenomena of hypnosis, which include:

—Catalepsy

—Temporary paralysis

—Hypersensory sensitivity

—The suppression of pain

—Hallucinations

—Age regression

—Post-hypnotic amnesia

—Post-hypnotic suggestion

---

1. For those who would like to pursue the current conceptual meanings of hypnosis in the psychological literature, I suggest two short journal articles by Ernest Hilgard (1973a; 1973b), one of the foremost authorities in the field. For a brief treatment of all scientific aspects of hypnosis, see *Divided Consciousness* by Hilgard (1977).

The foregoing are generalized by Hilgard (1965, pp. 8–10; 1968, pp. 6–10) into the following seven characteristics of the hypnotic state:

1. Weakening of the planning function. The hypnotized subject loses initiative and lacks the desire to make and carry out plans of his own.
2. Redistribution of attention. Attention to many of the sensory stimuli of the environment decreases.
3. Availability of visual memories from the past, and heightened ability for fantasy production.
4. Reduction in reality testing, and tolerance for persistent reality distortion.
5. Increased suggestibility.
6. Role-playing behavior.
7. Amnesia for what happened in the hypnotic trance.

The reader may wish to investigate the question: To what extent do these phenomena occur in dissociated states other than hypnosis?

Aside from the above phenomena, per se, hypnosis displays three important process characteristics:

1. Hypnosis can be induced by the hypnotic operator using an almost endless variety of symbolic behaviors, the underlying intent of which is to dominate and to dissociate the hypnotic subject. Mental dissociation of the subject can be encouraged by the application of finger pressure to the carotid artery of the neck. Stage hypnotists often do this, and it can be dangerous.

2. The nature of hypnotic response will depend in large measure upon expectation, experience, and innate subject differences. For example, if the subject has been led to believe that he should exhibit cataleptic rigidity, he is more likely to do so.

3. There are all degrees of hypnotic response, ranging from a scarcely perceptible weakening of one's grasp of reality to a trance so deep that it may result in death. Only rarely, however, is there difficulty in bringing a subject out of hypnotic trance. It is probable that death will not occur in the trance state unless there is a recognizable pre-existing pathological condition.[2]

---

2. The possibility of death by hypnosis will be angrily denied by those whose professional livelihood depends upon hypnosis. The following considerations may

There is one question concerning hypnosis that is impolite to discuss, namely: Does the subject surrender his or her will to the hypnotic operator? In real life, could Trilby be subjugated by Svengali as in Du Maurier's nineteenth-century novel?

Most psychologists teach, and most clinical practitioners believe, that the answer to this question is *no*. But there are others who say that, while total control is not ordinarily possible, nevertheless, under some conditions a subject in a hypnotic trance can be made to commit an immoral or criminal act that the same subject would not otherwise do.

One line of reasoning behind this statement runs as follows: Immoral acts are not, as a rule, wholly bad. For example, the young woman who resists sexual seduction may at the same time desire it for any of several reasons. Her virtue consists in weighing the immediate advantages against the more remote disadvantages and deciding that the latter should be given preference. In this view, any factor that alters the balance of her judgment is a force for good or for evil. In such a situation, hypnosis may have an effect in shifting the balance of ambivalence.

If one accepts this argument, the question of interest is not whether—but to what extent—the hypnotic subject loses command of himself. That depends upon the susceptibility of the subject and upon the "power" of the hypnotist. I have found in the modern literature only one candid and responsible treatment of this problem (Young, 1952).

When one comes to realize that hypnosis is not a discrete state but a continuous spectrum of possibilities that might occur in any social encounter, other questions, such as the following, come to mind.

To what extent is the repentant sinner the hypnotic captive of the pentecostal preacher? How often is the doorstep buyer of an encyclopedia the hypnotic victim of the salesman? Should we not regard political oratory as a clinical skill? Is courtship ever the development of a hypnotic relationship?

If these are meaningful questions, what happens to the myth of

---

encourage you to reserve judgment on this question. Most academic investigators avoid the use of psychotic or seriously hysterical subjects and thus minimize the danger of losing control. Their benign experience could be misleading. Laboratory tests of self-induced trance by professional yogis have demonstrated the near cessation of vital functions for extended periods of time. I see no reason to doubt that the same condition of near death could be induced by hypnosis and could result in death, either by accident or design.

personal responsibility? Could civilization, as we know it, survive the acceptance of hypnosis as an ubiquitous phenomenon?

These questions are so unwelcome that we are tempted to avoid them by denying their significance. There is a theory of hypnosis, advocated by T.X. Barber and based upon Skinnerian principles, that does just that. According to Barber (Barber, 1965, 1969; Barber, Spanos, & Chaves, 1974), hypnosis is not a state and the hypnotic trance is nonexistent. The experimental program of his theory is to assign most of the statistical variance of so-called hypnotic behavior to manipulatable, antecedent variables, such as mere verbal suggestion, so that the whole topic loses its conceptual novelty and become nonthreatening.

I have pursued the "mind control" aspect of hypnosis a little further than otherwise might seem appropriate for a book on parapsychology because I want to suggest that a similar set of frightening questions will become apposite if and when we accept extrasensory perception and psychokinesis as everyday social phenomena. To go one step further, perhaps psychokinesis will be found to be the essence of hypnosis. Perhaps the hypnotic operator applies PK to the brain of the subject. The work of Vasiliev, Tomashevsky, and Dubrovsky (Vasiliev, 1962, Chap. 7) would seem to allow no other conclusion. I shall examine this question in detail in Chapters 15 and 16.

For the intelligent, far-sighted scientist, the first line of defense against all such embarrassments is to deny the reality of psi phenomena. I suspect it is for this reason that some of the most brilliant scientists I have known are resolutely adamant in their refusal to examine the experimental evidence for ESP and PK.

UNCONSCIOUS DECEPTION

Earlier, I raised a question about the frequent incidence of fraud in Spiritualism, particularly among so-called physical mediums. You will recall that I asked whether it was worthwhile trying to conduct research with a cheating psychic.

We can now discuss this question in a new perspective. Dissociation is necessary for the production of psi phenomena—that seems to be true even if we do not know why. Dissociation, even at its mildest, is a process of selective perception, a form of self-deception, a kind of reality avoidance. The person who makes a good spirit medium has learned to abandon immediate reality and to give himself up to wish-fulfilling fantasy. By a detached effort of the will he (or she) performs the seeming miracle of ESP. But this devotion to purpose may lead to a total abandonment of moral inhibitions that stand in the way of the desired accomplishment.

If a psychic is a mental medium, along with true psychic knowledge, he may create and offer meaningless fantasies. In other words, he may tell lies (Mrs. Sidgwick, 1900; Lang, 1900). We do not say he is a fraud, but merely that his information is incorrect.

If he is a physical medium, he may have abandoned responsibility for his motor control. He will produce PK if he can, but he will also simulate PK by every available fraudulent means. For this we are quite willing to blame him. As between the physical medium and the mental medium, it could be argued that we are using a double standard of morality.

We know from the studies of Freud that the unconscious mind is a bad logician and will satisfy itself with the most transparent deceptions. Perhaps we should not be surprised that those who have become adept at dissociation are not to be trusted. They can smile the sweet smile of innocence while they deceive us with another consciousness.

If this idea that dissociation implies ethical irresponsibility has some truth to it, there might be important applications in everyday life. Perhaps criminality correlates with a tendency to mental dissociation, with or without a clinically recognizable multiple personality. This idea conceivably could open a new era in social psychology.

THE PASSIVE-ALERT STATE

We are familiar with our normal state of consciousness and its daily fluctuations. Are there other, quite different states? There is sleep, of course. Sleep is a nonconscious state in which episodes of dream consciousness may occur. Might there be remote states of consciousness other than dreaming? How could we enter them? Perhaps if we could first give up normal consciousness we might be able to reach some other state.

There are various physiological ways of giving up normal consciusness, such as by ritual dancing, fasting, taking drugs, or receiving a blow on the head. We shall examine a more conservative, and in some ways more interesting method, namely, by direct volition in the manner of the Eastern studies, Zen and Yoga.

Each of us voluntarily gives up normal consciousness every night as we fall asleep. Evidently something more than that is required if we are to reach some other state of consciousness that is both interesting and exotic. Total relaxation will not do. There must be a selective relaxation of the powers of the brain. In some sense, volition and awareness must be retained in order to reach the desired state. We might try to become both passive and alert.

To achieve a passive-alert state of consciousness, we must clear ourselves of trains of thought involving the past and the future, for these are the essence of normal consciousness. What will be left is a passive awareness of the present. This means direct, nonverbal awareness of ourselves and our environment.

For the beginner, passive awareness is most readily achieved by directing attention to what might be called a "psychological point"—something without psychological size or shape. This point in psychological space could be a single word, an object, or an activity so simple that it will not readily support rational thought. To be able to give attention continuously to an idea that has no detail requires effortful practice.

The advanced devotee of meditation, however, does not need a point of concentration. He is able to achieve a state of alert thoughtlessness merely by wishing to do so. He commands his mind to clear, and it does. When so engaged, he perceives all data that are presented to his senses, rejecting none but responding to none.

After the state of passive-alert consciousness is attained, what happens next? Sometimes, what happens is a "mystical experience," a self-rewarding, ineffable state of enriched perception, of weakened will, and of felt unity with the universe. Whether or not a full-blown mystical experience occurs, upon returning to normal consciousness, the meditator may feel refreshed, inspired, and better able to cope with the discouragements of ordinary living.

In the U.S.A. the benefits of this technique have given rise to a popular, nonreligious movement called Transcendental Meditation. From a psychological point of view, the hocus-pocus of the "mantra" (prayer word) now can be seen as valid technique—including the secrecy that preserves the mantra free of contaminating mental associations.

Our primary concern here is not with mystical states but with the fact that ESP and PK are more likely to occur when a person is in a state of passive-alert consciousness. The reasons for this are un-

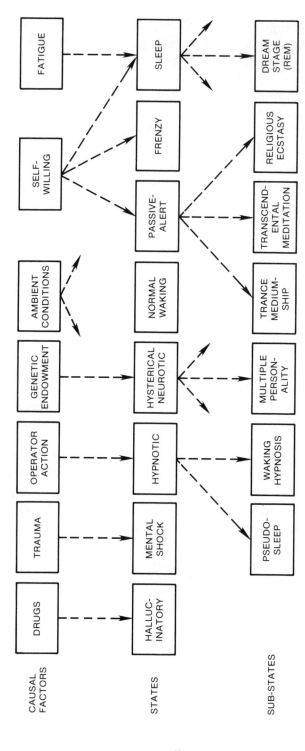

Figure 6.1. Some commonly labelled states of consciousness. Dashed lines show frequent connections. All states are to some extent dissociated. Unconscious mental activity occurs in all states. Psi effects can presumably occur in all states.

known, as is likewise any direct connection between psi phenomena and mystical experience. The importance of dissociation to the production of psi will be discussed in the next chapter.

CATEGORIES OF CONSCIOUSNESS

Risking the charge of pontification, I present in Figure 6.1 a categorization of the states of consciousness to which I have referred in this and earlier chapters. This figure is a measure of our ignorance. It is a symptomatic listing of dissociated states with some of their precipitating factors.

It is the task of the brain scientist to discover the neurophysiological features that differentiate these states. The task of the parapsychologist is to unravel the relation of dissociation to the production of psi. Not much progress has yet been made at either task.

7

FACTORS FAVORING PSI

THE ROLE OF DISSOCIATION

In a survey of parapsychology why should we spend much time on the subject of mental dissociation? It can be argued that, while dissociated states played a dominant role in the first half-century of parapsychology, they passed into obscurity when experimentation entered the laboratory.

Beginning with J.B. Rhine in 1930, and until about 1960, parapsychologists concentrated on producing psi under controlled, laboratory conditions so that they could prove to themselves and to skeptics that ESP and PK actually occur and are not the result of self-deception. Parapsychologists have recognized that dissociation, by any name, is a dirty word—whether it is called hypnosis, trance mediumship, hysteria, selective perception, or just daydreaming. In our culture, when one says that a person is daydreaming, the flavor is usually one of disparagement. Psychologists may not understand dissociation, but they recognize that it is somehow the antithesis of the objective, publicly compared perception of reality that is the hallmark of good science. Parapsychologists share this distaste for dissociation. For a long time they tried to separate their laboratory research from it, both for their own satisfaction and to appease the skeptics.

There are two reasons why parapsychologists did not entirely succeed in this separation. As shown by the Walter Prince quotation in the preceding chapter, dissociation, in one form or another, is a part of everyday life. And as discussed in the remainder of this chapter, dissociation is proving to be as important for the laboratory production of psi phenomena as it was in the trance mediumship of yesteryear.

As philosophers, how are we to understand psychic ability in relation to mental dissociation? Here is a partial and admittedly speculative answer, which must have appeared many times in the literature, although I do not remember having read it myself. Perhaps it will suggest experimental investigation.

Dissociation has to do with the structure of individual consciousness. Psi phenomena are an interaction between the individual and the rest of the universe. What we find is that there must be a partial breakdown of the unity of individual consciousness before a parapsychological interaction between the individual and the outside world can appear. It is as though the unity of the individual is antithetic to unity with the universe.

Hypnosis and ESP

To determine by experiment the effect of hypnosis on ESP, one must first be able to tell whether the test subject is in the hypnotic state or in his normal state. That is, one must be able to define operationally the difference between these states.

This is difficult because there are no known physiological concomitants of hypnotic dissociation—no way of telling, as by electroencephalograph, heart rate, or autonomic activity, whether the subject is "hypnotized." The only objective criteria of hypnosis are its behavioral effects, but these can all be produced to some degree without a formal hypnotic induction procedure and may therefore be argued to be characteristic of the nonhypnotic state.

To meet this predicament, there are two, more or less distinct options open to the experimenter, either of which would be valid for many uses of hypnosis in parapsychological research.

In the first option, the experimenter largely ignores behavioral criteria. He selects subjects by means of a susceptibility test and then submits them to a standardized induction procedure. After that, unless there are indications to the contrary, the subjects are *presumed* to be in a hypnotic state and are given whatever parapsychological tests may be called for by the protocol of the experiment.

In the second option, the experimenter regards hypnosis as a quantitative rather than a qualitative state. He uses such induction procedures as may be necessary for the individual subject (with or without susceptibility pre-selection) and then judges by behavioral criteria whether that subject is *adequately* dissociated (hypnotized?) before proceeding with the parapsychological experiment.

In comparing hypnotic and nonhypnotic conditions in an experiment, one might use the same subjects at two different times, or one might use different groups of subjects. The same-subject procedure avoids the difficulty of enormous individual differences in hypnotic susceptibility but runs the risk of contamination by subject expectation developed from previous experience—a problem not altogether circumvented by the usual procedure of using balanced groups with differing orders of presentation.

Concerning ESP and hypnosis, two questions have been asked in the laboratory: (a) Do subjects perform better at an ESP task when under hypnosis as compared to when in a normal state? (b) Can subjects be trained by hypnosis to become good ESP performers?

The answer to the first question is almost certainly *yes*. As described by Honorton (1977, p. 447), 12 out of 19 studies involving direct comparisons of multiple-choice ESP performance in hypnosis versus the waking state yielded significant treatment differences. He says (ibid., p. 450): "I believe that the conclusion is now inescapable that hypnotic induction procedures enhance psi receptivity."

The answer to the second question may be *yes*. Quite possibly, those who have marked native ability can be trained to improve it, but the training procedures, which may include hypnosis (Ryzl, 1962), are lengthy and not fully specifiable (Sinclair, 1930, pp. 116–128).

These are empirical answers, whose interpretation is of doubtful validity. If hypnosis is, in fact, a process in which the operator exerts a psychokinetic influence upon a dissociated subject, our conceptualization of its role in parapsychological research will need revision. (See Chapters 15 and 16.)

OTHER PSI ELICITING TECHNIQUES

The common methods for inducing hypnosis in an untrained subject all employ instructions to the subject to relax physically and mentally. If the induction process is stopped before the subject is detectably dissociated, one can discuss the situation in terms of relaxation instead of hypnosis.

Relaxation is considered to have both muscular and neural components. Moderately successful attempts have been made to define relaxation by electroencephalography, by basal metabolism measurements, and by autonomic activity indicators.

In a series of experiments at the University of Houston and at Texas Southern University, Braud and Braud (1974) found significant positive dependence of ESP response upon induced relaxation as determined by self-report and by electromyography on the forehead. Their work suggests that a relaxed state is favorable to the occurrence of ESP. Later confirmations are described by Stanford and Mayer (1974) and by Honorton (1977).

Relaxation can be regarded as lowered arousal rather than as increased dissociation. The brain may be supposed either to remain normally integrated but less active, or to shed control of some of its parts. The choice between the concepts of low arousal and dissociation as facilitating ESP opens interesting questions for debate and experimentation.

Another technique used to attain a state of passive consciousness in parapsychological research is by information deprivation. This can be accomplished by isolating the subject physically from the environment so that he receives little sensory stimulation. A more practical way is to expose the subject to a *Ganzfeld*, a field of uniform sensory stimulation, containing no information. Typically, the subject reclines in a comfortable chair with a half ping-pong ball taped over each eye and with his face dimly illuminated. At the same time, random noise or a recording of waves on a seashore is fed to his ears. The subject is told to clear his mind and remain as far from sleep as possible while he is given a parapsychological test. There are by now a number of studies demonstrating the effectiveness of the Ganzfeld technique in producing psi phenomena. It is widely believed that the Ganzfeld procedure is a major step toward an ESP experiment reproducible by prescription (Braud, Wood, & Braud, 1975; Sargent, 1980; Terry & Honorton, 1976). Again, one can go to Honorton (1977) for an excellent and readily available summary. But what I find lacking in the literature generally is a willingness to use the unifying concept of dissociation.[1]

Dreaming sleep is another brain state that has been investigated for its psi-facilitating properties. The evidence for the occurrence of ESP while dreaming is both spontaneous and experimental. The laboratory evidence is now regarded as conclusively affirmative (Krippner, Honorton, & Ullman, 1972; Ullman & Krippner, 1970; Van de Castle, 1977).

Psychoactive drugs have been used informally with some success in parapsychological research, but the limited evidence suggests that one can do as well with nonphysiological treatments.

Attempts at detecting cerebral hemispheric specialization in rela-

---

1. In the annual indexes of the *Journal of Parapsychology* and the *Journal of the ASPR,* as of 1981 the last entry under "dissociation" appeared in 1971 and referred to a lecture by Gardner Murphy in which he listed dissociation after motivation, target affect, and belief as factors affecting ESP.

tion to psi have yielded only mildly encouraging results (Broughton, 1976; 1977).

WHO CAN BE PSYCHIC?

Dissociation is not a sufficient condition to produce psi. Achieving a passive-alert state of consciousness does not ordinarily elicit parapsychological phenomena, even if that is one's purpose. Very few people in hypnosis show ESP, even when it is demanded of them. Multiple personalities are not known to be necessarily psychic. (Of Doris's several personalities, only the playful child, who in the end had to be put to death, showed flashes of ESP. If any paranormal effects occurred to Sally Beauchamp, to Eve-of-three-faces, or to Sybil Dorsett, they were not reported.) In trance mediumship, spirit communicators do not always produce paranormal information. Most of what they offer is gossip or maudlin philosophy. It is a tiresome chore to sift for evidence of ESP in the records of a trance sitting.

Although dissociation seems to be a necessary condition, one need not be a trance medium or exhibit multiple personality to repeatedly experience outstanding ESP. Genetic endowment is presumably of key importance.

Nowadays we find psychics existing in all kinds of economic niches in our society. They may be stage mentalists, fortune tellers of East European ethnic groups, devoted members of conventional sects who read the Bible and decide they have a gift from God, public seers who make predictions and write best-selling books, medical psychics, such as Edgar Cayce who, long after his death, still holds an enormous quasi-religious following, and in ordinary life we find people such as Bill Delmore, a Yale law student, and Felicia Parise, a leukemia research technician in a New York City hospital. (The last two names appear as test subjects in the experimental literature.)

Although psychics are not characterized by a particular occupation, many drift into a financially remunerative use of their special abilities. The oddity of those abilities in an unsophisticated culture may force an outstanding psychic to consider himself to be a prophet or even an incarnation of God.

If we cannot tell a psychic by his occupation, can we do so by his personality? Perhaps partly. It is widely believed that "sensitives" have three personality traits:

1. They dissociate readily.
2. They are intuitive rather than rational; that is, they are "feeling," rather than "thinking," persons.
3. They are open rather than defensive in their attitude toward the world.

NORMAL-STATE PSI

The test subjects whom we use in parapsychology experiments, particularly those drawn from a casual population such as college students, are often able to demonstrate psi effects without being subjected to any preparatory procedure and while remaining in what is evidently a normal state of consciousness. However, to the extent that normal-state subjects are successful, they tend to show two characteristics suggestive of the passive-alert dissociated state: They are relaxed and they are interested.

Psi is sometimes described as a motivated, spontaneous process. Is this not self-contradictory? How can a spontaneous process be affected by wishing? What the phrase means is that, while waiting for psi to happen, one must wish for it but not think directly about it. One must want it with part of one's mind but not at the focus of one's attention.

It seems safe to say that in the normal-state production of psi phenomena some appreciable degree of dissociation is essential. When we try to produce these effects in full consciousness, they simply do not happen. We must momentarily trick ourselves, or our subjects, into inattention.

Subjects performing in the normal state of consciousness are believed most likely to succeed if they are in a comfortable, non-anxious, noncritical, spontaneous mood. They are required to have a delicately favorable attitude toward the experiment. The proper nature of their interest may be described by such phrases as "pleasantly stimulated" and "nonapathetic," rather than as "intensely curious" or "eager to succeed."

It is generally agreed that the handling of laboratory subjects must always be such as to encourage interest and relaxation. The atmosphere should be one of social affection rather than scientific curiosity.

AWARENESS OF PSI

Does the psychic percipient ever know when he has used, or is using, ESP, or is ESP completely unconscious?

There are many well-authenticated cases of spontaneous ESP in which the percipient was so convinced of the truth of a premonition that he took immediate action as a result. It is evident from these cases that the fact of the occurrence of psi as a special information-gaining event is sometimes directly known to the person who spontaneously experiences it.

With regard to experimental ESP, the picture has been less clear. In the literature there are a number of studies that consistently suggest glimmerings of awareness of success in card-guessing with unselected subjects. These effects have been so weak, and the resistance of psi to conscious control so painfully evident, that it has been a common belief among parapsychologists that any knowledge of success in tests of intentional ESP should be considered to be secondary extrasensory perception of the coincidences between target and response and should not be regarded as direct awareness of the ESP process.

However, the work of Kanthamani and Kelly (1974b) would seem to allow the following conclusion: At least one high-scoring subject has been able to identify with near-perfect accuracy at the time of card guess, or subsequently but before check-up, most of those trials in which he would be found successful in guessing correctly both suit and face of an ordinary playing-card deck.

The trials believed successful were labeled "confidence calls." The rate of success in confidence calling was so high, compared to rate of success on nonconfidence trials, as to reasonably exclude the hypothesis that confidence calling is merely a secondary ESP task. Rather, it appears that the subject "must, in fact, [have been] detecting some aspects of the processing of psi information in himself." (ibid., p. 378)

This finding has theoretical importance. For the long view, it is now reasonable to expect that psi can some day be practiced with accuracy—after genetic or physiological control has been attained. The immediate effect should be to encourage research on psychological and physiological psi-mediating processes. What kinds of internal cues are available to the percipient? Do they depend upon the nature of the targets? What internal states allow the production of these cues?

EXPERIMENTER INFLUENCE

It is well established that some experimenters can elicit ESP and others cannot (Eleanor Sidgwick, 1900, p. 36; Pratt & Price, 1938;

Honorton, Ramsey & Cabibbo, 1975). While there is no reason to doubt that friendly, casual, supportive behavior by the experimenter will favor psi production as compared to abrupt, formal, unfriendly behavior, the problem is generally believed to involve the personality of the experimenter in more subtle ways. In the absence of any dependable information on the matter, I shall indulge in the following deliberately provocative speculation.

Perhaps the occurrence of psi phenomena is facilitated, not only by dissociation in the subject who is supposedly engaged in producing psi, but also by a dissociating type of personality in others who are psychologically connected with the experiment. It may be that the best experimenters are not those who are most tightly oriented. I do not mean that self-deception or unconscious fraud are necessary in the successful experimenter, but perhaps merely a greater tendency toward benign dissociation than is proper for a stereotypical scientist.

This is dangerous ground I am treading. Successful parapsychologists may not care to entertain this speculation. Hardheaded skeptics may say that this is what they have always sensed about the parapsychologists they have met, namely, that they tend to be easy-going in their relationship to physical reality.

In a wholly subjective integration over a tiny population of successful parapsychologists, I have come up with several other personality traits which I offer as points of incitement for needed research on this topic. It is my impression that those who have produced the most in the way of experimental results, tend to be manipulative in their social relationships, self-assured in their judgments, strong in their ego defenses, self-aware but not self-analytical, and intellectually earnest rather than playful. Of course, these may be merely traits that are necessary for anyone who stays with a controversial and socially unrewarding field. I shall discuss the matter of the personality attributes of successful experimenters under the subheading "Parapsychology as Science" in Chapter 17 in connection with the problem of isolating the experimental system.

8

POSTMORTEM SURVIVAL

DEATH AS TABOO

The title of this lecture, Postmortem Survival, is a gentle expression and perhaps the only gentle language I shall be using while on this topic. Death is a brutal fact. If we hope to deal with it scientifically, we shall have to be somewhat callous in our approach.

What would it mean to survive after death? Perhaps first we should ask: What is death? What, for example, does it mean to us who remain alive when someone else dies? That person ceases to communicate with us. The body becomes motionless and cold. It disintegrates into simpler molecules and eventually ceases to have recognizable shape. It is gone.

What does death mean to the person who dies? There may or may not be pain immediately before death. There is undoubtedly loss of consciousness. But is that loss of consciousness permanent? Does there cease forever to be any awareness and sense of individuality?

Before trying to discuss this question, it might be helpful to return to the living and to their attitudes toward dying. There are some rational reasons for wanting to stay alive. Perhaps we are enjoying life so much that we do not want to leave it. Perhaps we feel an obligation to finish some important, creative work. Perhaps we do not wish to bring sorrow to those whom we love by depriving them of our company.

There may also be good reasons for hoping for death. These might be summed up in the idea that, if the present and prospective unpleasantness of living outweighs present and expected satisfactions, we ought to commit suicide. Since most of mankind are starving, ill-clothed, inadequately housed, have chronic illness, are lacking in satisfying love relationships, and have no realistic prospect for improving these conditions, why are there not more suicides?

Why do most persons, regardless of present unhappiness, want to postpone death? Do they fear pain that might be a part of dying? Probably not; for drugs can suppress pain or even consciousness until death arrives. Do people fear that after death they may be in pain or otherwise uncomfortable? Pain is an excitation of the nervous system. After death the body disintegrates so that pain, as we know it, could not be felt.

But perhaps there is a new kind of discomfort that a surviving entity might suffer? "To sleep; perchance to dream." We have no way of knowing. Then what is it we fear? Is it simply fear of the unknown?

Why should we fear the unknown? Curiosity is a normal trait of the higher animals. One would expect people who are bored by life to be eager for the new experience of death and curious as to what, if anything, comes after it. Some years ago I was personally acquainted with a high-school student who said goodbye in a note explaining that he was committing suicide as an experiment. Why are there not many more like him?

Some who reject suicide say that they fear in death the loss of companionship and identity. Why should one fear the loneliness of nonexistence?

Perhaps the only answer to all such questions is that we must accept our given nature without understanding it. Living things exist in the first place only because they are genetically constituted with a tendency to persist. Those individuals who deviate from the norm by lacking this tendency soon die and rarely propagate their kind. Their deviant genes are lost from the population pool.

As a description of reality, biological predestination may engender humility and resignation, but it neither satisfies our curiosity nor exhausts the philosophic problem of death.

Why are we reluctant, if not unwilling, to discuss death? Why, in a Freudian sense, is this subject taboo?

Why does society prevent a condemned man from taking his own life before the appointed hour for his execution? Is it vindictiveness, a wish to see the criminal suffer on our terms for what he has done to us? Or is it something more subtle?

Why has it often been considered a crime to commit suicide—a crime for which the suicide's heirs may be made to pay? Does society need to force the individual to meet his economic commitments, or are the living somehow offended by suicide?

Why does it matter to us if a stranger tries to commit suicide in our presence? When some beggar, whose wretched condition we could not imagine as endurable for ourselves, climbs to a high place and threatens to jump, why do we mobilize the police and firemen and interrupt traffic? Why do we spend thousands of dollars trying to prevent the death of someone to whom we would not previously have offered a bowl of soup?

Why, instead, do we not say: "If you have thought it over and wish to die, you have our sympathy. We will not stop you."? The answer, I think, is clear enough. We are not concerned with saving a life, but with preserving our own peace of mind. If this man jumps to his death, he will have shown by his example that life is not always worth living and will have suggested that perhaps our own life may not be worth the trouble it entails—for us and for others.

If we are challenged in this way by the prospect of someone else's suicide, our anxiety rises and we are uncomfortable. We try to explain away his action. We say he is insane; although there may be no other evidence of irrationality. We cannot accept any idea that seems to threaten our own existence.

I hope I have said enough to convince you that the question of death is emotion laden. So much so, that merely to think about it engenders irrationality. It is in this context that I wish to approach the question of postmortem survival.

It will be difficult for us to deal with "PMS" scientifically because we fear death. We will postpone our own death by every means at our command. We will avoid planning for it as long as possible. And we will use magic to deny that it is coming for all of us or that it has recently come to someone whom we loved.

What is magic? And how do we use it? Magic is the employment of symbols for the direct modification of reality. In primitive cultures it is customary to use amulets and rituals. In literate cultures the symbols most used are words. A little reflection shows that, aside from giving instruction, the most common use of words is magical and that the use of "word magic" against death is no different from the use of magic for other purposes, every day, throughout our lives.

Words by which we try to deceive someone else are not magical for us but for the person who believes us. The salesman who misrepresents his product is using words to work magic upon his victim. Words are magical for us, only when we use them or allow them to be used to deceive ourselves about reality.

It could be argued, for example, that the social sciences are almost entirely devoted to word magic because the words used in those sciences do not make sufficiently close connection with empirical reality. The point I am making is that using word magic is not simply a vice of unintelligent people. Quite the contrary. The more intelligent one is, the more one needs magic as protection against reality.

Why do people hope for postmortem survival? Some undoubtedly expect to be compensated for failure in this life. Most simply fear death, and the idea of another life appeals as a partial denial of death—a kind of word magic. Mankind's irrational feelings toward death do not mean that there is no such thing as PMS but merely that it is very difficult to be objective when examining the matter.

With this much of an introduction, we are ready to begin a discussion of two questions: What is the possible meaning of postmortem survival, and is there evidence favoring or disfavoring any kind of PMS? I shall consider the second question first.

REVELATIONS OF DYING

The psychological evidence suggesting the existence of life after death can be divided into two parts: that associated with dying and that which supposedly reveals the next life as an ongoing adventure. Under the first heading we shall discuss apparitions seen *of* the dead or dying by others at a distance and also apparitions seen *by* the dying as well as other death-bed experiences. Under the second heading, i.e., evidence possibly revealing the nature of the next life, we might include Spiritualist phenomena and claims of reincarnation.

By "apparition" I mean here a visual hallucination of a human form. Apparitions near time of death have been reported from all parts of the world and from all epochs of history. In the most common cases of this class, the apparition is identified as a friend or relative who is dying or has just died. When, as sometimes happens, the percipient has no knowledge of the impending death, he is left with a feeling of mystification.

Sometimes the apparition conveys unknown information of a mundane kind, as in the case of the will of James L. Chaffin (Johnson, 1927) in which the phantom of a father who had died four years earlier appeared repeatedly in dreams to a son and revealed the existence and hiding place of a will under which that son eventually became a beneficiary.

In those cases where the apparition gives previously unknown information, the viewer may refuse to believe that it is all the work of his imagination. And when the apparition is of someone already dead at the time of the vision, the viewer may be inclined to regard the experience as evidence of postmortem survival.

This was a not-unreasonable interpretation until sometime in the late 19th century when experiments were begun which showed that very ordinary information could be transferred in the laboratory without the use of the senses but by what we now call extrasensory perception. If there is no inclination to invoke spirits to account for these laboratory experiments, then there can be no prima facie justification for ascribing an apparition to a departed soul. It is simpler to suppose that a veridical or truth-revealing apparition is a hallucination generated in the percipient's brain as a means for expressing extrasensory information that was unconsiously received.

Another kind of veridical apparition, less common but nevertheless well documented, is that seen by the dying. In some cases, for example, the dying person sees waiting for him "on the other side" a relative or friend whose prior death was, until then, unknown to him. Again, however, the simplest explanation is that the dying person, in a condition of heightened sensitivity, perceives by ESP the information of the prior death of someone else and dramatizes it in a culturally appropriate form.

I find scientifically more tantalizing the subjective experience of exaltation sometimes observed by persons who are nearing death. In a popular book, Moody (1975) reported that for some people the approach of death brings "out-of-body" sensory experiences coupled with ineffable feelings of joy, love, and peace. In a scientific survey of deathbed observations by physicians and nurses, Osis (1961) found that hallucinatory experiences of a comforting nature are quite common near death. Such anecdotal material leaves one with the feeling that by more suitable methods something of importance might be learned in this area.

MEDIATED MESSAGES

The history of Spiritualism is a futile dialectic between believer and skeptic. In the beginning, spirit mediums often gave information presumably unknown to the medium but confirmable by the sitter. When telepathy or person-to-person ESP was offered as a counter-explanation to the spirit hypothesis, the Spiritualists, undaunted, went on to show that sometimes the medium produced information unknown to either the medium or the sitter. But then it was realized that this did not rule out telepathy from distant persons. The next step was to demonstrate spirit information that could only have come in pieces from two or more living persons but that could have come from a single, dead person. The skeptics were unconvinced. This, they said, could be multiple telepathy. The believers produced information unknown to any living person but verifiable from documents. But in the laboratory the same thing was demonstrated by guessing unknown, machine-produced targets. It was found that there was no need for a telepathic sender. The receiver could reach out by ESP to inanimate objects.

At this point, the spiritistically inclined claimed still more ingenious proofs. They found that the departed spirits would intrude into seances when not wanted and identify themselves to mediums and sitters who had never known them. Sometimes the same communicating spirit would send identical messages to several mediums who were strangers to one another but who were all reporting to the Society for Psychical Research.

During the years 1905–1925 there were a long series of what were known as "cross-correspondences," which involved two or more mediums working in a cooperative rather than a repetitive fashion, and which were intended to reflect the knowledge or the personality of a person who had died.

In a simple cross-correspondence, several mediums at separated places and times might receive—ostensibly from the same dead scholar—several supplementing clues about Greek or Roman literature even where neither medium nor sitter had a classical education. When these clues were pieced together by experts, they seemed to reflect the personality, or at least the earthly knowledge, of the deceased.

In a still more complicated arrangement, known as the "Ear of Dionysius Case," spirit communicators ostensibly representing two recently dead Cambridge scholars, A.W. Verrall and S.H. Butcher, combined their efforts to send messages reflecting their previous earthly relationship by using classical references that were puzzling to all those living until the final clues were given through a spirit medium at a later time.

Still another class of medium test for survival was the so-called "proxy sittings," which were strongly pursued in the twenty years from 1925 to 1945. In this kind of sitting, after accepting a personal trinket of the deceased sent by a distant bereaved "sitter," who was unknown to both the medium and to her trance-recording secretary (called a "proxy sitter"), the medium would sometimes produce various kinds of true personal details about the deceased, which in some instances were unknown even to the bereaved, distant sitter.

In medium studies of the present century, there has been a trend away from dissociated speaking and toward automatic writing by the medium. (Automatic writing is a common, motor automatism that occurs in a dissociated state.) This provides a less personal contact with the other world but has the advantage of leaving an objective record. From the investigator's viewpoint this was important because tape recorders did not become available until after World War II.

As we can dimly see, it must have been an exciting time while the living scholars of the SPR were searching for evidence of the survival of their recently dead colleagues. This activity seems futile to parapsychologists today, now that we have fully accepted the fact that telepathy, clairvoyance, and even prediction of the future have been demonstrated in the laboratory and can be called upon to explain in principle any evidence for "spirits," no matter how complicated or intuitively impressive that evidence may seem at first glance.

Despite the failure of several generations of ardent investigators to prove that any fragment of human personality survives bodily death, there are still some respected parapsychologists who concentrate their attention on this problem.

OUR BIOLOGICAL AND CULTURAL DEPENDENCE

Let us now consider the arguments *against* postmortem survival. When the average person in Western civilization thinks of life after death, he thinks of survival of personality and consciousness in some discarnate form. How can that kind of survival be consistent with what we know about the dependence of our individuality upon our bodies?

Life began with single-celled organisms having only a limited response to external stimuli. Multi-cell creatures developed a nervous system that served to integrate behavior and to mediate afferent and efferent transactions with the environment.

At increasing levels of phylogenetic complexity we discover discrimination, awareness, and, finally, self-awareness (both intuitive and analytic). Although I would not insist that these are the same thing, I see no basis for sharp distinctions among them (Griffen, 1976). No one would hesitate to say that a mouse has awareness, and I do not think that anyone who has known many dogs will deny that some dogs show a primitive degree of self-awareness. Only man has any significant degree of analytic self-awareness. The experimental biological evidence shows that these characteristics depend upon the nervous system and, specifically, upon the brain.

Likewise, the personality of animals and men resides primarily in the brain as determined by genetic endowment and environment. Our memories are stored therein. Damage to the brain can permanently alter personality in ways that are predictable from the physical location of the damage. It is hard to conceive of personality persisting after death without the anatomical substrate upon which it was so intimately dependent in life.

This argument was put very well by the distinguished Cambridge philosopher, C.D. Broad (1938, p. 158):

> The physical data supplied by normal sense perception and the mental data supplied by the introspection and observation of normal waking persons are the bases on which the whole system of natural science, including psychology, is built. In this vast coherent system there is not a single fact to suggest that consciousness ever occurs except in intimate connexion with certain highly specialized, complex, and delicate material systems, viz. the brains and nervous systems of living organisms. There are innumerable facts which show that, during the life of an organism, the nature and degree of consciousness associated with it vary concomitantly with the general health and the special physiological processes of that organism. If we confine our attention to this aspect of the case, we receive an overwhelming impression that consciousness is utterly and one-sidedly dependent, both for its existence and for its detailed manifestations, on brains and nervous systems and on processes in them.

These ideas can be developed further, particularly as regards long-term survival and transmigration or re-incarnation. Unless we have an identical twin, it is all but impossible that there was ever a person with our genetic endowment. Our total personality, which changes constantly throughout our life, is the product of our genetic make-up and of our late-twentieth-century culture. If we survived as individuals, we would be as alien to the distant future as we would be if transferred alive back to the Jurassic Period among the dinosaurs and pterydactils. In the perspective of history we make no sense as individuals except in our own tiny niche of time.

Still another counter-argument to spirit messages as evidence for PMS is the fact that, although psi phenomena have been known in all historical periods, for the most part they have been interpreted as representing the agency of supernatural spirits of many kinds. Only beginning in the nineteenth century were these phenomena supposedly used to communicate with deceased human beings for the purpose of proving life after death. This suggests that the apparent forms of Spiritualist phenomena are an interpretation shaped by contemporary cultural forces rather than by an unchanging reality.

What Might Survive?

Turning now to the question of the possible nature of postmortem survival, I would like to quote a passage from a classic paper on this subject by Gardner Murphy (1945, pp. 90–91) titled: "Difficulties Confronting the Survival Hypothesis."

> [Suppose we could agree that the evidence we have discussed as favoring survival was not destroyed by the counter-arguments.] The question would still remain whether the thing within us which survives is in fact a personality in the sense in which we ordinarily use the term. . . . Any demonstration of the survival of personality would have to show that all the essentials are in fact capable of enduring and remaining together. A memory, by itself, is not a personality, nor is a feeling, nor an act of will, however poignant and intense such experiences may be. Even if the cross-correspondences and the proxy cases be taken as making very probable the continuation beyond death of certain elements of individuality, it is possible that these, like the iron filings around a magnet, are brought into function by virtue of the needs of the living. . . .
>
> Hauntings . . . might arise from fragmentary psychological processes transcending the operation of the percipient's mind, but associated with his perception of particular buildings or places. In the same way, it is quite possible that . . . memories associated with [some specific dead person] come naturally into place when [an imitation of that] personality is induced in the trance consciousness [of a medium].
>
> It might be better to state all this in terms of some such analogy as the following: . . . For a time after a stone is dropped into water, the orderly commotion of spreading rings can be seen. . . . It is quite possible that the processes of the brain initiate changes in some sort of matrix of which we have no direct knowledge and that these changes survive in the matrix for some time, regardless of the continuation . . . of the original physiological activity. . . . [This would leave us uncertain] as to whether the entity that survives is really a whole personality, and [uncertain] as to the length of time during which such survival might continue.

In certain cultures the reincarnation of some aspect of individual human personality into another human or into an animal at some time after death, is a common article of faith. To give an operational meaning to this kind of survival, memories might be carried over from one life to the next. However, even if such memories could be positively identified by their informational content as belonging to times past, there would seem to be no way of deciding whether anything more had survived and no sure way of determining whether they had come from a particular person.

The most thoroughgoing treatment of the question of postmortem survival, whether in discarnate or reincarnated form, will be found in a work by C.J. Ducasse (1961), who until his recent death was a professor of philosophy at Brown University, Providence, Rhode Island. Those who are especially interested in reincarnation will wish to read a scholarly report of 20 suggestive cases by Stevenson (1966).

As It Stands Now

What is *my* opinion on the matter of postmortem survival? First, I must confess that I have not studied the subject deeply. I have not carefully evaluated the evidence from the classical period of psychical research. I have no patience with the question of PMS; even though I welcome the interest of other experimenters in this problem. I think it is an unrewarding question, but I cannot forget that, often in the history of science, progress has resulted from the persistent asking of a question that most investigators had already passed by. All that I require of any experimenter who wants my endorsement for research on PMS is that he be historically sophisticated, technically competent, and intellectually honest.

You may ask, why, specifically, do I think PMS, as such, is a scientifically sterile line of research? The best answer I can give is that I feel certain that our present phrasing of the problem is inconsistent with what we already know and that we can not yet hope to rephrase the problem correctly.

What we already know from parapsychological research is that the unit of life that seems to be isolated and individual as soon as we progress beyond crystalline virus, is in fact not always isolated even when we shield it from all the force fields known to physics. There is a remaining relationship, presumably between centers of consciousness and the rest of the universe, that is of a psychological nature.

This relationship has been observed both in terms of the behavior of the living organism (as when a person guesses cards) and in terms of the effect of the behavior of the organism on inanimate systems (such as on falling dice). The relationship is informational in one direction and forceful in the other, and it can reach forward and presumably backward in time. In its informational aspect the relationship can express itself in both the perceptions and the complex symbolic manipulations of consciousness, that is, by both images and words.

To know that much, in the context in which we know it, is enough to be sure, in my judgment, that parapsychology is the most important area for psychological research today, but still it is not enough to allow us to talk about postmortem survival of personality.

For those who, nevertheless, want to pursue this topic, may I offer a clarification regarding what is, or is not, PMS research. There is an unexamined tendency for some people to think research on spontaneous psi phenomena to be somehow in the category of PMS research and, conversely, to think that experimental psi research is in some sense opposed to PMS. These are incorrect associations. It is quite likely that the answer to PMS will eventually come out of the laboratory. On the other hand, I regard the investigation of spontaneous psi phenomena, such as poltergeists and premonitions, as both exciting and important, even though I see these phenomena as psychological rather than spiritistic.

What Can We Hope To Learn?

Without postmortem survival the challenge posed by the future remains unmet. To die with a total lack of understanding of death is an affront to our dignity so great that throughout history, until recently, man has sought solace in mythical and revealed explanations. Now these explanations are rejected by educated persons, and we dimly perceive that as a result our will to exist is in jeopardy.

The scientific study of death has become a sociological necessity. If it is foolish to expect postmortem survival within the customary meaning of the word "survival," what else might be hoped for with regard to the end of each life? I believe that we cannot expect to justify any specific hopes for the time after death. If for no other reason, we are lacking the language in which to conceptualize such hopes. But in my estimation, we can expect to attain an expanded understanding of the meaning of death in terms of the ending of unitary consciousness.

This understanding, when it comes, may abate the fear of the unknown that many now feel. It may give death a role in a psychic economy just as we now see the role of death in the evolutionary scheme. Death may thereby attain a new dimension of inevitability that may make it, if not acceptable, at least less onerous to each of us.

9

HISTORY OF PARAPSYCHOLOGY

This short history concerns the scientific era of parapsychology, which may fairly be said to have begun with the founding of the British Society for Psychical Research in 1882. I regret that I am unable to describe research outside the United Kingdom and the U.S.A., although there have been significant contributions to the scientific literature from Argentina, Australia, Canada, France, Germany, India, Israel, Italy, Japan, The Netherlands, Poland, Scandinavia, South Africa, and the Soviet Union. Often these contributions have been the courageous, single-handed, long-term efforts of scientists, engineers, or scholars of considerable stature within their own professions. Only one great country is missing from this list, and now there is more than a hint that the People's Republic of China may become active in parapsychological research (Jen, 1982).

After a chronologically ordered description of outstanding people and organizations, first in the United Kingdom and then in the U.S.A., I shall discuss the research activities occurring in three periods of time, as follows:[1]

The first twenty years, 1882 to 1901, reach from the beginning of the SPR to the death of its two most important founders, Henry Sidgwick in 1900 and Frederic Myers in 1901. I shall cover this period by describing three classic books that, along with the *Proceedings* and *Journal* of the SPR, furnish the record of what was accomplished.

The second period of psychical research extends from 1901 to about 1930. These were three decades of transition from "applied" to fundamental research on the nature of the human psyche, from a hope of solving the riddle of the universe in our time to a realization that the answers were still a long way off, from speculative theory back to empiricism, and from sophisticated introspection to objectivity and quantification. This period marked the culmination of the investigation of psychic sensitives who thought they were in

---

1. Lists of some historically prominant parapsychologists and of U.S.A. centers of research are given in appendixes C and D, respectively.

touch with a spirit world and the rise of the laboratory testing of anyone who had psychic ability or thought he might have it.

The third and current period of parapsychology opened about 1930 when J.B. Rhine began his card-guessing experiments at Duke University in Durham, North Carolina. It started with an intensive but largely unsuccessful search for independent variables of personality and environment that might control the appearance of psi phenomena. The conception of those phenomena was systematized along operational lines (for example, by the introduction of the term "extrasensory perception"). The *Journal of Parapsychology* was founded for the reporting of exclusively experimental research. A major objective of this period has been to establish psychical research as a recognized field of science.

After covering the activities of these three periods, I shall discuss scientific organizations in parapsychology from a sociological point of view. Why are they born, and what determines their growth, decline, and demise? I shall end with comments on prescientific parapsychology.

Other subdivisions of historical time might be chosen for study. Ellenberger (1970, see below) reaches back to primitive societies. Gauld (1968) is concerned primarily with the interval 1870–1900. Mauskopf and McVaugh (1980) concentrate on the period 1915–1940. These are three, scholarly, booklength histories of parapsychology. More briefly, J.B. Rhine (1967) has described parapsychology in the years 1892 to 1951, with special reference to its interaction with American psychology.

United Kingdom

The Society for Psychical Research was founded in London in 1882 to investigate "that large group of debatable phenomena designated by such terms as mesmeric, psychical, and Spiritualistic."

Since then, "mesmeric" or hypnotic phenomena, as they are now called, have been accepted by orthodox psychology as an area for investigation, and parapsychologists have (mistakenly?) come to regard hypnosis as of only incidental interest. The phenomena of Spiritualism have been filed under the heading "other dissociation phenomena," where they are generally ignored by both psychology and parapsychology. That leaves only psychical phenomena, now called "psi phenomena," as the present-day concern of the Society for Psychical Research.

It is an important historical fact, to which I shall return later, that the roots of the SPR lay in the problem of postmortem survival. The SPR was founded largely by persons whose ultimate concern was toward communication with the dead (Gauld, 1968).

Psychical research in the beginning did not lack for eminent sponsors in England. There were the physicists, Sir William Crookes, Professor William Barrett, Sir J.J. Thomson, and Lord Rayleigh. Among the early officers of the Society were men of political prominence, such as Arthur Balfour, later Prime Minister of Great Britain. Honorary members included the writer, John Ruskin, and the poet, Lord Tennyson. There were Alfred Wallace, who shares with Charles Darwin credit for the natural selection theory of evolution, and the British statesman, William E. Gladstone. Gladstone called psychical research "the most important work being done in the world."

The intellectual leader and founding president of the Society for Psychical Research was Henry Sidgwick (1838–1900), Professor of Moral Philosophy at Cambridge University.

His sister married the future Archbishop of Canterbury. He married Eleanor Balfour, the sister of the future Prime Minister. Mrs. Sidgwick's sister was married to Lord Rayleigh, the Nobel prize-winning physicist. The Sidgwicks were thus closely connected to the fields of religion, politics, and science.

Henry Sidgwick is reputed to have been one of the ablest and most versatile scholars of his time. It is difficult to picture a man when all those around him described him in superlatives. It was said that his intellectual and moral courage was so great that merely to know him gave meaning to life.

The most unfavorable comment that I have found was that he was a poor teacher and a poor administrator. He could always see a problem in such complexity that he could not discuss it with the self-assured conviction that satisfies students and resolves administrative conflicts. He never found the answers to the fundamental ethical problems that he spent his life examining. With regard to psychical research, he never convinced himself that there was a life after death; although he did finally conclude from the evidence that there might be.

Eleanor Sidgwick (1845–1936) was interested in mathematics and wrote papers jointly with Lord Rayleigh. She and her husband were among those chiefly responsible for the admission of women to Cambridge University. She was the Principal of Newnham Women's College at Cambridge from 1892 to 1910.

After the death of her husband and Frederic Myers at the turn of the century, Eleanor Sidgwick was the main strength and guide of the SPR for the next 25 years. Although her husband is usually mentioned first in the history of psychical research, her contributions may have been greater than his.

Since 1900 there have been many notable names in British parapsychology, but I can think of only one experimenter, G.N.M. Tyrrell (1879–1952), a mathematician and physicist, whose contributions to the literature of parapsychology will surely be studied in the twenty-first century. His writings, both experimental and philosophical, carried forward the SPR's tradition of intellectual distinction.

UNITED STATES OF AMERICA

The first American society for psychical research was founded in Boston in 1885, three years after its British counterpart. Its officers included psychologists William James (1842–1910), Joseph Jastrow, G. Stanley Hall, and Morton Prince. These names are still remembered with respect by the psychological profession. The first president of the American SPR was Simon Newcomb, Director of the United States Naval Observatory. The most illustrious president was Samuel Pierpont Langley (1834–1906), a University of Pittsburgh astronomer and, later, Secretary of the Smithsonian Institution. He is best known for the fact that he built and successfully flew an unmanned steam-driven aeroplane in 1896, seven years before the Wright brothers made the first manned flight.

In 1890, after only five years of life, the American SPR was reorganized as a branch of the British SPR—probably because the distinguished officers and members of the American council felt that, to be worthwhile, a psychical research society needed the invigoration and guidance of persons totally committed to it, which they, of course, were not. Perhaps also, they were uneasy about their enthusiastic secretary, Richard Hodgson (1855–1905), and thought he could work more comfortably in association with his British friends. The American branch of the SPR continued actively under Hodgson until his death.

Richard Hodgson, the first fully dedicated American parapsychologist (Sidgwick, et al., 1907), is best known for his exposure of the fraudulent activities of Mme. Blavatsky, the founder of Theosophy, and for his investigation of the American medium, Mrs. Piper.

Hodgson's last 18 years were spent in the U.S.A. When not engaged in psychic research, he would relax as a popular member of a Boston social club. Many of his summers were spent in the Adirondack Mountains, where he especially enjoyed the company of children. Aside from psychical research, his major intellectual interests were puzzles and poetry. He said that he came to America because he could not stand the stuffy English ways. Somewhat insensitive to others, he has been described as full of fun but lacking a sense of humor. It is reported that he was difficult as a collaborator and that he did not like to be beaten in competition. His personality showed a touch of paranoia and, occasionally, vindictiveness.

While engaged in a game of handball, Hodgson suffered a heart attack and died in 1905 at the age of 50. The notes for much of his later work with Mrs. Piper were in such condition that they could not be untangled. A man of intense conviction, he was loved and respected because of his totally uncompromising intellectual honesty.

In 1902, Professor James H. Hyslop (1854–1920) of Columbia University gave up his philosophy chair and went to work with Hodgson. Two years later, while thinking gloriously of the future, Hyslop set up a shadow corporation which he called the American Institute for Scientific Research. Its announced purpose was to do research in both abnormal psychology and psychic phenomena, keeping the two fields separate but controlling the funding of both.

After the death of Hodgson in 1905, Hyslop created an American Society for Psychical Research under his Institute. Nothing more was done about research on psychopathology, although the Institute for Scientific Research did not disappear as a legal entity until about 1923. James Hyslop was an energetic organizer and a competent investigator who, driven by a strong belief in spirit communication, worked himself to an early death. During his time, by public lectures he raised $185,000 as an endowment for the ASPR. He was the second notable figure in American parapsychology.

Hyslop took on Walter Franklin Prince (1863–1934) as his assistant in 1916, and the scientific continuation of the ASPR should have been assured after Hyslop's death in 1920. Unfortunately, by 1923, legal control of the organization had been captured by Spiritualists. These men were interested in religion to the exclusion of science, and quickly brought disrepute upon the ASPR.

Walter Prince could not work under these conditions, and in

1925, under the sponsorship of two eminent psychologists, William McDougall (1871–1938) and Gardner Murphy (1895–1979), a new organization called the Boston Society for Psychic Research was established to give Prince a financial and professional base of operations. Prince occupied the post of Research Officer of that Society until his death in 1934. I have already discussed Prince's early work in the chapter on the occurrence of multiple personality. For a well balanced biography see T.R. Tietze (1976).

By 1941, the notorious "Margery" case of mediumship had run its course and the ardor of spiritism had considerably subsided, allowing Gardner Murphy and George Hyslop, the son of James, to recapture the American SPR. Since then, the ASPR has prospered scientifically. Its *Journal* and Rhine's *Journal of Parapsychology* are currently the leading publications of the field.

Shortly after the ASPR fell into disrepute, J.B. Rhine (1895–1980) and L.E. Rhine (1891–) met the psychologist William McDougall at Harvard, trailed him to the Psychology Department at Duke University in 1927, and three years later began card-guessing experiments. In 1934, J.B. Rhine's first book, *Extrasensory Perception*, attracted so much public attention that the other faculty members of the Psychology Department decided that he should continue on his own. With the help of a friendly university president an independent Parapsychology Laboratory was set up in 1935. With McDougall as co-editor, J.B. Rhine founded the *Journal of Parapsychology* in 1937.

Later, when Rhine was approaching retirement, the faculty at Duke did not wish to sponsor a continuation of his work. A new organization, the Foundation for Research on the Nature of Man, was established in 1962 and moved just outside the Duke campus in 1965, where its operation continues as one of the currently most active centers of psi research and education.

Plans for founding this organization led to a quarrel between J. B. Rhine and J. Gaither Pratt (1910–1979), who had been associated with Dr. Rhine as a prodigious investigator for more than a quarter century. In 1964, Dr. Pratt was invited to the University of Virginia at Charlottesville to a post under Dr. Ian Stevenson in the Department of Psychiatry. The University of Virginia arrangement was formalized and expanded in 1968, and Charlottesville remained an active center of experimental research until Dr. Pratt's retirement in 1976.

Somewhat earlier, in 1962, a parapsychological laboratory was established by Dr. Montague Ullman in the Department of Psychiatry at the Maimonides Medical Center in Brooklyn, New York. Initially, work there centered upon the demonstration of ESP in dreams of subjects while in normal sleep. Subsequently, under the leadership of Charles Honorton, Maimonides became the foremost center of research on psi in altered states of consciousness. After Dr. Ullman's retirement, Honorton, in 1979, established a research laboratory at the Princeton (New Jersey) Forrestal Center. Other American laboratories are listed in Appendix D.

In both the British and American Societies for Psychical Research membership had been open to anyone. The members provided the money, and the scientists ran the organization. This symbiosis, as we shall see later in this chapter, was both helpful and harmful to scientific progress. In 1957, Dr. Rhine and his staff decided that it was time to try to set up an international professional organization open only to those whose interest in parapsychology was principally scientific. The resulting Parapsychological Association, with a present total membership of several hundred, has held annual conventions in the U.S.A. or abroad since its beginning. Full members are those who have made a significant scientific contribution to the literature. Associate membership is given to scientists who have not actively entered the field. The formal purposes of the Parapsychological Association are: "to advance parapsychology as a science, to disseminate knowledge of the field, and to integrate the findings with those of other branches of science." This organization now publishes its proceedings under the title *Research in Parapsychology*.

A recent survey of the Association (McConnell & Clark, 1980) showed that 78% of its Members and 56% of its Associates hold doctoral degrees from among at least 15 different disciplines, and that, interestingly enough, 32% of the membership still harbors some degree of doubt concerning the reality of ESP.

NINETEENTH-CENTURY RESEARCH

In 1886, four years after its founding, the SPR published a two-volume work, *Phantasms of the Living*, by Gurney, Myers, and Podmore. This is the first of the three great books of the first twenty years of that organization. It deals exhaustively with the available evidence for telepathy between living persons—what we would now call a form of ESP. In some 1400 pages the authors cover: (1) Spontaneous ESP: methods for evaluating its evidence and the evidence itself. (2) Experimental ESP: methods of conducting experiments and the results obtained. (3) Theoretical speculations as to the scientific and philosophic implications of the observational findings.

The second of the three great works of the early period of the SPR is Frank Podmore's *Modern Spiritualism: A History and a Criticism*, published in 1902. Podmore (1856–1910) was originally a believer in spirit agency, but became a resolute skeptic after several well known mediums were exposed as frauds. His two-volume work, 700 pages long, covers the following topics from a critical-historical point of view: possession and witchcraft, poltergeists; seventeenth-century faith-healing; hypnosis in England, France, Germany, and America; and Spiritualism in all of its ramifications, together with separate chapters on several of the more prominent spirit mediums of the nineteenth century. For anyone seriously interested in Spiritualism, this work is an essential first source.

Human Personality and Its Survival of Bodily Death, by Frederic W. H. Myers (1843–1901), published posthumously in 1903, is the last and most important of the early SPR publications. The influence of this work has spread beyond psychical research. The title is misleading. The book is not primarily about survival of bodily death. It is rather a survey of human personality written by a poetic scientist with a view to convincing himself and the reader that the survival of bodily death is probable.

The scientific merit of this book for us today lies in the thoroughness of its summary of what was then known about man as a psychological entity. If you ever feel that modern psychology has lost its way as it has traveled along its specialized paths, you may gain a refreshing perspective by returning to Myers two-volume 1300-page masterpiece. The chapter titles indicate the scope of the work: Introduction. Disintegrations of personality. Genius. Sleep. Hypnotism. Sensory automatism. Phantasms of the dead. Motor automatism. Trance, possession, and ecstacy. Epilogue.

The achievements of the first 20 years of the SPR can be summed up in three sentences. (1) Just about every possible speculation on the psychological nature of man using the concepts available at the end of the nineteenth century will be found in *Human Personality*, *Phantasms of the Living*, or the *Proceedings of the SPR*. If anyone conceives a supposedly new idea of what man is or might be, it will probably be found discussed at length in these sources. (2) The techniques and evidential standards for the investigation and evaluation of spontaneous ESP established in that era have been generally conceded to be beyond criticism. (3) All of the ESP phenomena reported in *Phantasms of the Living* have since been observed many times and may be regarded as established. These are the extrasensory transfer of information in the form of (a) emotion, (b) compulsions to act, and (c) images or verbal thoughts, whether the transfer occurs in dreams or in the waking state.

THE THIRTY-YEAR TRANSITION

For convenience I have divided parapsychology into three historical periods fixed by the appearance or disappearance of the brighter stars in the field of its literature.

The transition period began in 1901 with the deaths of Henry Sidgwick and Frederic Myers and ended about 1930 when J.B. Rhine started his card-guessing experiments.

Within that period, and perhaps around 1925, the balance of interest shifted from psychical research, which was concerned with life after death, to "parapsychology," whose purpose was to learn more about the living. Since then, the prospects for postmortem survival have seemed increasingly dim and the need for understanding human nature, ever more urgent.

What happened in those 30 years was not, however, a simple transition from old to new, but a culmination of the old and a fumbling development of the new. As already described, this period saw an elaboration and refinement of earlier methods of "spirit communication" using automatic writing, cross-correspondences, and proxy sittings. After 1900, it became increasingly apparent that research with spirit mediums was going nowhere. Although this work continued long after 1930, enthusiasm for it largely disappeared shortly after the end of World War I.

What happened in this second historical period was more than a shift of attention from the next life to this one. There was a change in research methods, in the kind of experimenters, and even in the organizations devoted to this work. I shall discuss these in reverse order.

Whereas previously, psychical research societies were oriented toward their members' experiences, now the investigators turned toward the laboratory; so that the unity of membership interest weakened. This posed serious problems which have not yet been resolved.

A new breed of parapsychologist arose. With the passing of the educated leisure class in England, the dedicated amateurs who created much of the golden age of British science no longer existed. Not even the genteel poverty of Richard Hodgson was possible. Professionalism became the hallmark of leadership.

The greatest change of all was in the methods and techniques of research. In keeping with the trend in psychology and the social sciences generally, the new professionals aimed to be experimental and quantitative.

Quantitative experiments in telepathy and clairvoyance had been tried with some success from the early days of the SPR. Worldwide, between 1880 and 1899, there were 52 published experimental reports of ESP, 34 of which were carried out by people from the professions (Pratt, Rhine, Smith, Stuart, & Greenwood, 1940, Chapter 4). Why was this kind of research not given more attention then, and why did it become of dominating importance after 1930?

For this evolving situation there were many reasons, some of which we have already mentioned: the change in research objectives, a realization of the difficulty of the research problem and of the futility of a passively observational approach, and a changing social and scientific milieu. Most specifically, however, after 1930, the hope for a repeatable experiment that would allow the manipulation of well defined variables was the justification for emphasis on quantitative experimental method. That hope was not soon to be fulfilled.

Research Since 1930

Without attempting to examine individual experiments or experimenters, what can be said about parapsychological research since 1930? What has been tried? What has been learned?

In a sense, there are no new psychic phenomena. All of the new, as well as the old, can be classified under either extrasensory perception or psychokinesis. Nevertheless, the experiments with dice and other falling objects in the 1930s under J.B. Rhine's leadership, opened a new line of research and raised the subject of psychokinesis to scientific respectability after many uncertain encounters with physical mediums. Discoveries of fraud had been commonplace, particularly in the 1870s at the peak of the Spiritualist movement and again in the 1920s when many mediums tried by trickery to whip up interest in their dying trade.

At the beginning of the present period, mechanical apparatus did not play a major role in parapsychological research. The year 1936 saw the first use of a rotating die cage in a PK experiment. More recently, the use of electronic target randomizers has become widespread in forced-choice ESP experiments. Much of today's research, however, is concerned with the psychological conditions associated with psi and does not lend itself readily to automation.

As in the last century, parapsychologists in the modern period have used especially psychic subjects when they could find them. No longer, however, are these subjects likely to regard their abilities as a gift from God. Those who do, generally have little patience with scientific research. In addition, there has been an extensive use of relatively unselected subjects—such as those found in classrooms, or volunteers drawn by a general solicitation.

Since about 1930, when the professionalization of parapsychology began, there has been a hierarchy of experimenters. Most numerous were beginners who did one or two experiments, with or without success, but without bothering to study the literature beforehand. At the other extreme, there has been a small number of professionally oriented persons who have undertaken systematic experimentation—sometimes successful—more often, not. The accomplishments of these two groups contrast markedly. Except that they kept the journals alive, the dilettante experimenters have contributed little in our search for understanding. On the other hand, even the unsuccessful systematic work has often told us something of value for the future.

What are the new findings in parapsychology since 1930? As J.B. Rhine has said, ESP was fully established long before he came on the scene. The important new findings, as they seem to me, are five in number: (1) Psi ability is widespread and perhaps universal among humans. (2) Psi has a strong genetic component, so that some people show much greater psi ability than do others. (3) There are certain preparatory states of consciousness that facilitate the observation of psi. (4) Psychokinesis as the gross movement of inanimate objects is an experimental reality. (5) Hypnosis may be the use of psychokinesis by one person to influence the mind of another. Some of these topics will be dealt with in chapters to come.

ORGANIZATIONAL PERSPECTIVE

Why has the Society for Psychical Research continued to exist from 1882 until today, whereas the first American SPR lasted only five years and then had to be absorbed and financially supported by the British? Does this relate to the fact that the first American SPR was formed and governed by scientists who disdained interpretation; while in the British SPR, two-thirds of the first governing council were spiritistically oriented (Gauld, 1968)?

A successful social organization must have motivational homogeneity, but in the case of the British SPR there were some rather extraordinary internal divisions of purpose as well as background. In the founding group there were both scientists and spiritists, and some of the scientists were spiritists. There were both professional scientists and amateurs, and some of the best research was done by the amateurs. As members, there were both experimenters and their experimental subjects, with some of the subjects participating in the management of the organization. It was a diverse set of relationships that for a long time seemed to satisfy most of the dues-paying members.

Two things are needed to start a large, membership-funded scientific research organization operating outside of orthodox science. There must be a reservoir of public enthusiasm for the task, and there must be eminent sponsors who will lend dignity to the enterprise.

To keep such an organization going, one more ingredient is necessary. There must be emotional commitment by persons with intelligence and energy—the kind of commitment in which people give of themselves and their money. That is what the British SPR had and what the American apparently lacked.

The American sponsors, some of whom I named earlier, were comparable in eminence to their British counterparts, but their commitment was intellectual rather than emotional, or perhaps one should say that their emotions were already committed elsewhere.

As you may know, scientists, as scientists, are rarely devoted to scientific truth. Scientists are puzzle solvers who amuse themselves and gain the applause of others by winning at the game of peek-a-boo with nature. The emotional commitment of scientists may be to profession, money, family, church, country, politics— but scarcely at all to abstract truth.[2]

---

2. For a development of this idea, see Chapter 18 on "Progress in Science."

Spiritism, although widespread in America, had not penetrated the intellectual leadership as it did in Great Britain. The British sponsors were excited by the idea of postmortem survival. Moreover, there was the tradition there of an educated leisure class, a tradition that encouraged a man of ability and wealth to devote himself primarily to whatever he believed most worthwhile.

In consequence, the SPR had young, diligent workers—perhaps ten of them—and the best were at the near-genius level of ability. Their leader, Henry Sidgwick, was only 43 when the SPR was founded, and the average age of the five outstanding workers listed in Appendix C was 36.

Like the first American SPR under Hodgson, the second, founded in 1906 following Hodgson's death, was essentially the instrument of one man. First, there was James Hyslop, and thereafter, until his unavoidable resignation, Walter Prince. (It will be recalled that the American SPR was controlled by Spiritualists from 1923 to 1941).

By contrast, the workers in the early British SPR were many in number and pursued science so vigorously that those whose interest was solely in religion dropped out in discontent or anger. Over the years, there were many squabbles within the SPR, but the scientists always held the upper hand. As late as 1930, Sir Arthur Conan Doyle, the creator of Sherlock Holmes, resigned in protest over the SPR's criticism of an Italian medium.

As professionalism in psychic research has grown, especially since World War II, the SPR, which is largely an amateur organization, has produced very little. Hopefully, this will change as university interest in parapsychology expands in the United Kingdom.

The revived American SPR has avoided some of the difficulties of its British sister by emphasizing research fed to it from the outside by professional parapsychologists. But because its primary activities are no longer oriented toward the personal psychic experiences of its members, there are internal dissensions that could seriously threaten the organization's existence.

There is today a strong popular interest in the occult. Among the uneducated this leads to astrology, witchcraft, and other left-wing manifestations of superstition (McConnell, 1973; McConnell & McConnell, 1971). For those with more education, so-called parapsychological societies, clubs, and "foundations" spring up everywhere. These rarely last. As a rule, they are started by persons who are unfamiliar with the history of parapsychology, who do not understand science, whose training has been in symbol manipulation, and who think that research is done by talking, writing, urging, thinking, and raising money. In truth, of course, one thing is needed to advance science: experimental work by intelligent, sophisticated scientists. Without that, there is no progress. Elsewhere (McConnell, 1974a), I have offered more specific ideas on how parapsychological research might be efficiently furthered.

PRESCIENTIFIC PARAPSYCHOLOGY

As the present book was being polished for publication, I chanced upon Ellenberger (1970), *The Discovery of the Unconscious*. Although subtitled "The History and Evolution of Dynamic Psychiatry," it is, in fact, a sociological treatise on the dangers of popularizing and practicing preparadigmatic science and on the folly of premature theory building.

Ellenberger's survey reaches from primitive societies to the mid-twentieth century. The scope of the work is such that his treatment of Freud does not begin until page 418. Parapsychological interest centers on the period, 1775 to 1900, in which, starting with Mesmer, hypnosis became the dominant tool for the study and treatment of mental illness! Great amounts of empirical information about mental dissociation were gathered in that period that could have value for present-day research. Much of what I have covered in the preceding chapters is described in Ellenberger—from multiple personality to rampant psi (although the latter is either lightly passed over or labelled as something else). I was chagrined to find the casual mention of insights that I had re-created at some cost from modern, sanitized sources.

From Ellenberger, I also discovered the historical inadequacy of Part I of the present book. What I have written may be helpful to a beginner, but the professional parapsychologist will find it worthwhile to start earlier and to dig more deeply.[3]

After a triumphant ascent to psychiatric respectability, hypnosis was abandoned around 1900 because of the great experimental difficulties it presented and not because it was evaluated and found sterile. Psychiatry turned, instead, to the nonexperimental study of psychological mechanisms for the understanding and treatment of

---

3. For a scholarly but inadequately documented nonevaluative history of the seemingly miraculous, see Inglis (1977).

mental illness. Because concepts such as "ego" are a long step removed from observation, psychiatric theorizing could be free of operational definitions—and, indeed, it has been ever since. The result has been bad science and questionable medicine.

One lesson to be learned from the disappearance of nineteenth-century hypnosis is that, despite the reality of psi phenomena, all scientific interest in these phenomena could be swept away in some future decade of social turmoil unless we fasten the roots of parapsychology to the elemental facts of nature—which is what we have attempted without much success since 1882.

It is my hope that the reader who has faithfully studied the preceding nine chapters can safely sample the scientific literature of parapsychology in the chapters to follow without getting lost in statistical technique and physicalistic preconceptions.

Part II

THE OBSERVATION
OF PSI PHENOMENA

10

MECHANIZED METHODS

Target Selecting Devices

Psi phenomena can be viewed as a relation between a person and an object. The object may contain information that is to be acquired by the person (ESP) or may serve as an indicator of psychic force originating in the person (PK). To separate chance effects from weak, sporadic psychic effects, it is customary to use the calculus of probabilities. This is most simply done by means of forced-choice tests in which the person being tested confronts a certain number of possibilities having equal chance probability, e.g., the faces of a gaming die or the cards of a playing deck. To illustrate this experimental paradigm, I have chosen for detailed examination a paper titled, "Precognition of a Quantum Process" by Helmut Schmidt (1969a).

Before World War II, the public had become familiar with forced-choice ESP experiments in which the subject under test tried to guess a deck of cards in which there were five different kinds of faces, all occurring with equal frequency, so that the probability of success in any one trial was one-fifth. In the Schmidt experiments an electronic device was substituted for the card deck and the number of possible choices was set to four, so that the probability of success per trial, or p-value, was one-fourth.

In J.B. Rhine's ESP deck of 25 cards, because there were ordinarily five of each kind, the experimenter had to be careful not to reveal the cards until all 25 guesses were completed. Otherwise, as the test subject neared the end of the deck, if he had a good memory, he could know exactly what cards remained and could improve his chance of success accordingly. With an electronic card deck there can be an infinite number of trials, each of which is independent of all the others, so that the probability remains constant even though the subject is told of his success or failure after each trial.

Another important difference between an ESP machine and an ordinary card deck is ease of automation. To avoid recording errors with card targets requires much effort: the use of serially-numbered data sheets; independent, double recording; and a tight experimental protocol. In Schmidt's experiments the entire procedure was automated, using mechanical counters for immediate read-out and punched-tape for later computer analysis.

In any multiple-choice ESP machine there must be a randomizing process. The needed random numbers might be (1) taken from a published book of random numbers and programmed into the machine, (2) generated using the roulette-wheel principle, in which the wheel is brought to rest slowly by friction, or (3) generated by a roulette wheel, using a discrete, naturally-random event to determine when the wheel will suddenly stop.

The last is the method in Schmidt's apparatus. A radioactive sample consisting of strontium-90 with a 28-year half-life is used to trigger an "ion-avalanche counter." In the instant in which that happens, an electronic roulette wheel is stopped, thereby choosing one target out of the possible four.

A Precognitive Matching Machine

Before I describe Schmidt's apparatus, how it was used, and what results it gave, I should say something about the experimenter. Helmut Schmidt did this work in 1967 while he was a senior research physicist at the Boeing Scientific Research Laboratories in Seattle, Washington. In 1969, when the aerospace industry suffered a setback, Dr. Schmidt moved to the Institute for Parapsychology, part of J.B. Rhine's Foundation for Research on the Nature of Man, in Durham, North Carolina, where he became a full-time parapsychologist. More recently, he has been at the Mind Science Foundation in San Antonio, Texas.

Schmidt was born in Germany and received the doctor of philosophy degree from Cologne University in 1954. He was a U.S. National Academy of Sciences Fellow at the Berkeley Campus of the University of California in the year 1956–57. As listed in *American Men and Women of Science*, his areas of interest are the foundations of quantum mechanics, cosmology, solid-state physics, and parapsychology.

The paper I am discussing was Schmidt's first in parapsychology. His apparatus, although electronically complex, is simple to use. Figure 10.1 is its functional, block diagram. The box at the top, labelled "square-wave generator," operates continuously throughout the experimental session, generating an up-and-down step voltage which completes one up-down cycle in one-millionth of a second.

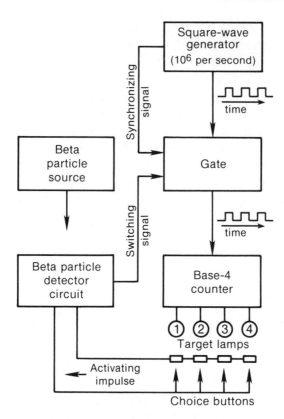

Figure 10.1. Helmut Schmidt's precognitive matching device with probability of trial success equal one-fourth. Features not shown: punched-tape recorder, nonresettable trial and hit counters for verifying punched-tape record, resettable trial and hit counters for display to the subject, and interlocking controls described in text.

This step voltage is fed through an open "gate," whose function I shall describe, and goes to an electronic counter operating on the number-base, four. The square wave makes the counter count in the sequence: 1, 2, 3, 4, 1, 2, 3, 4, and so on, at one-million counts per second. When the gate is suddenly closed, the counter stops on 1, 2, 3, or 4 and a correspondingly numbered target lamp comes on.

The gate can be closed and a lamp lit by pushing any one of four "choice buttons" that are located next to the four target lamps. The task of the subject is to push the choice button in front of the lamp that is going to light. If he guesses right, he has a hit. If some other lamp lights, he has a miss. The chance of a miss is evidently three times as great as the chance of a hit.

The important question, of course, is exactly what determines which lamp will light after a button is pushed. In a simplified version of this machine the pushing of any button closes the gate immediately. Thus, the subject's task is to "guess" the numerical position of the base-4 counter to within one-millionth of a second. Since the counter is constructed with circular symmetry, there is no electrical difference in passing from 4 to 1, as compared to going from 1 to 2, etc. Hence, if the subject guesses correctly, it must be either by chance or by ESP, since neural response time (and temporal resolution) is of the order of milliseconds and not microseconds.

In the apparatus used in this experiment another complication has been added so that the time of closing of the gate is determined by a beta particle coming from a radioactive strontium sample after the subject pushes any button. In other words, pushing a button merely sensitizes the detector so that it is ready for the next beta particle. Since the average radioactive counting rate can be set to ten per second or more by selecting sample size and counter geometry, there need be no appreciable delay between the pushing of a choice button and the lighting of a target lamp.

Although the *average* rate of radioactive counting can be easily adjusted, the exact instant at which any one nuclear decay occurs has always been regarded by physicists as strictly random and immune to control by any known means. As we shall see, this fact lends a special philosophic interest to the experiments I shall discuss.

There are several refinements that improve the precision of the machine. If the gate-switching signal arrives at the gate in that small fraction of one-millionth of a second when the square wave is changing the counter, the gating signal is automatically delayed by a synchronizing pulse from the square-wave generator until there can be no uncertainty in the base-4 count.

The apparatus has another delay feature, not shown on the diagram, that prevents its operation faster than twice a second. After any button is pushed, the machine cannot be operated again until one-half second after the lamp is lit and all buttoms are released. If the subject pushes two or more buttons at exactly the same time, the recording devices are blocked for one-half second and the trial is not counted.

The recording devices are not shown on the block diagram. The first of these is a paper-tape recorder that punches holes on every trial to show which button was pushed and which lamp lit. By use of different punching codes, the tape shows whether the subject was instructed to try for as many hits as possible or for as many misses as possible. When the test session is over, the punched tape is processed by a digital computer.

Second, a pair of nonresettable electro-mechanical counters records the number of trials and the number of successes. These counters are read regularly as a check on the computer analysis and also serve to show that no punched tapes have been lost.

Third, a pair of resettable electro-mechanical counters shows trials and successes. These are reset to zero at the beginning of each session so that the subject can watch how well he is doing.

How can one be sure that this complicated machine will work properly? Schmidt says that the design is essentially fail-safe, so that there can be no nonrandomness unless there is an obvious gross malfunction. In addition, the machine has been carefully tested for the of kinds nonrandomness that might help the subject to get a high score. This was done by operating the machine by pushing one of the buttons mechanically at a rate of about one a second, over a period of 100 days, usually immediately after the experimental sessions, until five million random numbers had been generated.

These numbers representing four lamps were computer-analyzed to find out two things: (1) whether any one of the lamps tended to come on more often than the rest, and (2) whether any one lamp tended to follow any other lamp more often than expected by chance. The analyses showed no evidence of nonrandomness. For example, it was concluded with a confidence of 10^{17}-to-one that for the population from which the random test numbers were drawn, none of the four lamps had a relative frequency greater than 0.252, where 0.250 is the chance-expected frequency.

BINOMIAL THEORY

Before presenting Schmidt's experimental results, I shall describe what one might expect from this equipment under the laws of chance and how one might decide if ESP is occurring.

The probability of success, p, in any one response or trial is one-fourth, while the probability of failure, q, is three-fourths. Also, as shown by randomness tests, every target is independent of the preceding targets.

But what about the subject's guesses? Are they independent of one another? The answer is *no*. In fact, we are sure that no person can generate a highly random series of guesses in a task of this

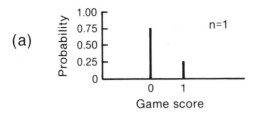

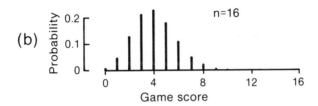

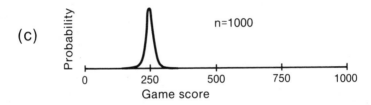

Figure 10.2. Binomial distributions of probabilities of game scores for various numbers (n) of trials per game when the probability of success in each trial is one-fourth.

kind. But in a matching experiment such as this one, it does not matter whether both targets and responses are random. The only requirement is that at least one of the two matched series be random. When statistical trials are thus mutually independent with a fixed probability of success, both the trials and the resulting distribution of scores are called "binomial."

The idea of a "distribution of scores" can be understood from Figure 10.2a, which shows the frequency distribution of scores for single trials. If one is counting successes, a hit corresponds to a score of one; while a miss means a score of zero. The graph says merely that we expect three times as many misses as hits.

If we group 16 trials together and call them a "game," the most probable distribution of game scores, if chance governs, is that shown in Figure 10.2b.

The most probable number of successes, corresponding to the highest bar on the graph, is given by the formula: $np = 16\,(1/4) = 4$. This is also the average score, i.e., the "expectation." Scores of 3 and 5 are a little less probable. The pattern is roughly symmetrical on either side of 4. There is a small probability of getting no successes, $P = (3/4)^{16}$ (which equals about 0.01), and a still smaller chance of getting 16 hits, $P = (1/4)^{16}$ (which equals about 10^{-9}).

The height of each of the bars on this graph is given by the "binomial expansion":

$$(q + p)^n = q^n + nq^{n-1}p + [n(n-1)/2]q^{n-2}p^2 + \ldots$$
$$+ [n!/\{(n-r)!(r)!\}][q^{n-r}p^r],$$

where $p = 1/4$; $q = 3/4$; $n = 16$; r = number of successes (i.e., the game score); and "!" means the product of the preceding and all smaller integers.

Therefore, the height of the most probable bar score is :

$$[(16 \cdot 15 \cdot 14 \cdot 13)/(1 \cdot 2 \cdot 3 \cdot 4)](3/4)^{12}(1/4)^4 = 0.23$$

Thus, if you made 16 guesses with the Schmidt machine, you would be 23 times as likely to get a total score of four as a score of zero.

Suppose in one game, consisting of 16 trials, you obtain a score of 12 hits. How often would you expect to get so large a score by chance alone? To find the answer, you must add together the heights of the five bars corresponding to scores of 12, 13, 14, 15, and 16 (which are all too small to see in the figure). The answer is about 10^{-4}.

If, instead, the total number of trials is 1000, the minimum possible score is still zero, but the maximum score is 1000, and the mean and most likely score is $np = 1000(1/4) = 250$. The lines on the graph are so close together (for example, between a score of 249 and 250) that we draw only the "envelope" of the bars, as shown in Figure 10.2c.

This envelope is almost exactly what mathematicians call the normal curve of error. That is why they say that, for large values of n, the binomial distribution approximates the normal distribution.

The width of the peak at 250, as measured between the inflection points where the curvature reverses, is twice the standard deviation, σ, which is a number given by the expression:

$$\sigma = \mathrm{SQRT}(npq) = \mathrm{SQRT}[1000(1/4)(3/4)] = 13.7$$

This is roughly how the curve is drawn in the figure.

In any normal curve the chance of getting a score more than three times the standard deviation away from the mean is very small. Therefore, in the present case for $n = 1000$, nearly all scores will lie between 200 and 300, if chance alone is operating. For example, in 1000 experiments of 1000 trials each, the probability of getting even one score outside the 200–300 range would be less than one half. In fact, one score of 350 in 1000 games of 1000 trials each, would, for all practical purposes, show that something other than chance was at work.

We are now in a position to understand exactly what is meant when it is claimed that an experiment yielded a probability value of 0.01.

In an ESP statistical experiment, usually the first thing we want to know is: Did ESP occur? However, we cannot ask that question directly. Instead, we may ask the following: In an infinite series of hypothetical experiments such as the one performed, how often would one get a score equal to, or larger than, the score actually obtained, assuming that chance alone was operating?

To find the answer, we integrate (sum) the proper area under the envelope of the theoretical distribution of chance scores. Since the total area under the curve is set equal to unity, the area under the tail beyond the obtained score represents the desired probability. On the basis of this probability we can accept or reject the null hypothesis (H_o) that no causal difference exists between our score and the chance-expected score. Typical criterion levels for rejecting the null hypothesis in the life sciences are 0.05 and 0.01. A probability less than 0.05 is often said to be "suggestive"; while a probability less than 0.01 is often called "statistically significant."

An exceptionally small score relative to the expected mean in a chance-governed experiment would be just as surprising as a very large score. Because in many psychological experiments it is impossible to predict with confidence the direction of score deviaton from the mean that might be caused by the procedure under investigation, one may choose to add the areas under both tails of the distribution beyond the observed absolute deviation. The resulting "two-tailed" probability is then compared with the chosen criterion level.

The two questions, "Was chance alone operating in the experiment, and, if more than chance, was it ESP?" are not mathematical questions, but must be answered by engineering judgement.

Unfortunately, many competent scientists have so little contact with the world outside their specialty that they are nonplussed by these questions.

PRECOGNITIVE MATCHING DATA

The data in the Schmidt paper are from two experiments, which followed one another by several months and are related in a manner that I shall describe later.

About 100 volunteers were screened in a preliminary test, and of these, three who did well were chosen for the first experiment. As it happened, two of these were professional mediums and the third was an amateur psychic.

The apparatus was carried into each subject's home and used only when the subject felt he could do his best. Since the apparatus was foolproof, it could have been used without the presence of the experimenter. However, except for a small part of the tests with one subject in the first experiment, the experimenter was always present. (During that small part when the experimenter was absent, the scoring rate did not increase.)

The subjects were allowed to play with the machine as much as they wanted with all recording devices disconnected.

In all of this work the subject chose his own pace, which was generally in the range of one trial every two seconds.

The permissible length of each experiment was set in advance and the probability values were calculated accordingly. The length of each session, however, was adjusted to the whim of the subject since, under the chance hypothesis, this could in no way affect the overall result.

The first experiment was done in the months of February through May of 1967 and the second was done in September through November of the same year. In the first experiment the subjects were told to get as many hits as possible. The results are given in the top half of Table 10.1.

N is the number of trials or guesses made with the machine. The "observed deviation" is the number of successes greater than the chance-expected number. In other words, the deviation is the displacement of the actual score from the peak of the chance probability curve. The "critical ratio" is the number of standard deviations corresponding to the observed deviation in the preceding column. The probability corresponds to the expected frequency of

Table 10.1
PRECOGNITIVE MATCHING DATA GATHERED BY H. SCHMIDT (1969a)
USING HIS PRECOGNITIVE MATCHING MACHINE
The probabilities have been corrected for prespecified variations in the number
of trials

Subject	Sessions	Goal	Trials N	Observed Deviation	Critical Ratio	Proba- bility
Experiment 1						
OC	11	+	22,569	+285.75	4.39	10^{-4}
JB	5	+	16,250	+ 90.5	1.64	.15
KR	2	+	24,247	+315.25	4.68	10^{-4}
Total	18		63,066	691.5	6.36	10^{-8}
Experiment 2						
OC	4	+	5,000	+ 66	2.15	.03
JB	11	+	5.672	+123	3.77	10^{-3}
JB		−	4.328	−126	4.42	10^{-4}
SC	6	−	5,000	− 86	2.81	10^{-2}
Total	21		20,000	401	6.55	10^{-11}

getting a deviation with an absolute value as great as, or greater than, that actually obtained, if one were to do an endless series of similar experiments in which chance alone were operating. You will notice that the first and third subjects did well but that the number of successes of the middle subject, JB, was not far from the peak of the probability curve.

In the second experiment, in some of the sessions, the subject, JB, tried to get hits, and in other sessions he tried to get misses. As described earlier, depending upon the purpose, the trials were coded differently on the punch tape so that the digital computer would recognize the difference. For the second experiment one subject from the first experiment was no longer available and was replaced by the 16-year-old daughter of one of the other subjects. The data for the second experiment are given in the bottom half of Table 10.1

In comparing the two experiments, it is evident that subject, JB, did much better in the second experiment than in the first. Schmidt speculated on this in a footnote, saying that between experiments he had a chance to get acquainted with JB, who was a professional medium, and that the medium gave a demonstration of ESP using "token objects" that Schmidt found impressive. Schmidt thought that this might have created psychologically more favorable working conditons.

As a further test of the randomness of the machine, the paper tapes from OC's response in the second experiment were run through a reading machine which pushed the choice buttons correspondingly. This was done ten times at various speeds (to check for nonrandomness as a function of speed), and the resulting total deviations were found to be all well within the chance-expected range.

The chronological accumulation of the results of the second experiment are shown in Figure 10.3 (Schmidt, 1969b). Unless one questions the sanity or honesty of the experimenter, these are highly convincing experiments. Personally, I do not see how otherwise to avoid the conclusion that a psi effect of some kind was operating.

As Schmidt himself recognized, there is no way to be sure whether the deviations from chance in these experiments represented precognitive ESP or psychokinesis. Was the subject predicting what was going to happen or was he causing it to happen? In particular, by pushing one of four buttons, was he precognizing to within one-millionth of a second when the next radioactive decay would occur, or was he, instead, causing that decay to occur at a slightly irregular time, or—a third possibility—was he using psychokinesis to control electron movement somewhere else in the apparatus in such a way that the scoring was favorable?

CONTROLLING A RANDOM WALK

Subsequent work by Schmidt (1970) reaffirmed by a different procedure the possibility of the psychokinetic control of radioactive decay. In this later experiment a binary counter, delivering a random succession of plus and minus outputs, was connected to a display consisting of nine lamps in a circle with only one lit at a time. Every time a radioactive decay occurred, the lighting would shift clockwise or counter-clockwise one lamp, depending to within one-millionth of a second upon whether the random number generator had stopped on a plus or a minus pulse.

In performing an experiment, the machine was turned on and allowed to go for 128 jumps, after which it would stop automatically. This took about two minutes. The result was what a mathematician would call a 128-step random walk in a circle. The subject was told to try to force the light to travel clockwise or counter-clock-

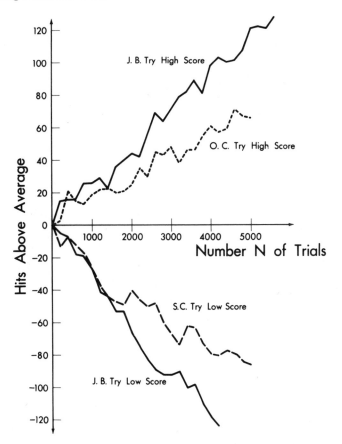

Figure 10.3. Chronological accumulation of total score deviations above and below the chance-expected average in Schmidt's second experiment using his precognitive matching device (Schmidt, 1969b). Computed after every 200 trials. The final deviations are those shown in Table 10.1.

wise as he preferred. Depending on the subject's choice, a recording switch was thrown so that a step in the desired direction always registered as +1. The results were independently recorded by electromechanical counters and punched paper tape.

In a preliminary test Schmidt found that he had a group of subjects from among the staff at the Institute for Parapsychology for whom the circle tended to move in the direction opposite to their wishes. In a separate, confirming series using the best negative scorers, Schmidt found, after 256 walks, that his subjects had a negative deviation of 302, yielding a two-tailed probability of less than 0.001 for the confirmation alone.

Schmidt did not speculate as to whether the negative deviation was due to a dislike of the experiment, to a generally negativistic attitude of these Institute staff members, or whether the negativism may have been primarily within the experimenter himself.

The randomness of this machine was checked by a four-million number sequence which was analyzed, as in the earlier experiment, for plus and minus balance, as well as for the frequency with which either sign was followed by the same or opposite sign. No evidence of nonrandomness was found.

While this experiment suggests that psychokinesis was controlling directly either the time of a nuclear decay in the radioactive sample or the flow of electrons in the binary counter, it could also be regarded as a matter of starting the test walks at times when negative deviations were destined to happen. In general, a tight distinction between PK and precognitive ESP is hard to make unless one is dealing with a gross, nonstatistical phenomenon, such as levitation.

11

SPONTANEOUS PSYCHOKINESIS

CLASSIFICATION OF THE PHENOMENA

Parapsychologists in attempting to systematize their field have usually pigeonholed all psi phenomena into "extrasensory perception" and "psychokinesis". Conceptually, ESP is an inward flow of information to a person, while PK is an outward flow of energy. Because PK, unlike ESP, is not recognized by a behavioral response (such as guessing a card), it is, in general, not possible to identify the source of psychokinetic energy. In some cases of spontaneous PK the circumstances may even suggest the presence of an invisible being, although this interpretation is gratuitous on the basis of what we know at present.

Spontaneous PK has been classified as "recurrent" or "nonrecurrent." Recurrent spontaneous PK (RSPK) is popularly supposed to be caused by "poltergeists"—boisterous spirits who throw things about and otherwise make a nuisance of themselves. A poltergeist infestation of a house may last, off and on, sometimes for several months. In many cases a living adolescent is involved—suggesting either mischievous fraud or the psychic turbulence of growing up.

Hauntings of places are presumed to continue for years and would be classified under RSPK if there were a reason for invoking psychokinesis. However, the common manifestations of haunting are hallucinatory rather than physical. Things are seen or heard, but there is no other reason to believe that anything physical has happened. If psi is involved, it would seem more likely to be ESP than PK.

Nonrecurrent spontaneous PK is thought to occur most often at times of emotional crisis. An example might be the mysterious breaking of a glass dish at the moment of death of a distant member of the family (L.E. Rhine, 1963).

On more ordinary occasions, objects are reported to have jumped or slid when imperiously, but jokingly, commanded to do so. While not strictly spontaneous, such movements are not really expected and, for the most part, are nonrepeatable (L.E. Rhine, 1970, p. 338).

Under such circumstances it is impossible to know whether an unusual happening was caused by chance physical factors or by an unknown psychological force. The principle of parsimony requires that we assume the former, while leaving open the possibility of the latter.

Unexpected PK effects defy evaluation and would not have been seriously regarded by parapsychologists were it not for the occurrence of analagous effects in laboratory experiments.

A Pittsburgh Poltergeist

The flavor and challenge of spontaneous psychokinetic phenomena will be found in the following condensation of a study of a poltergeist (Pierce, 1973). I have chosen this paper for several reasons: The case presents a variety of claimed phenomena. It involves independent observations by four adult persons in two unrelated families. The investigator is well known to me, and, in fact, I joined him in a site visit in which three of the four observers in the case were re-questioned in detail concerning the stories they had previously given.

The investigator, Mr. Henry Pierce, is the science writer for a Pittsburgh, Pennsylvania, daily newspaper and is publicly known for his longstanding concern for the orderly development of parapsychology. My admiration for his professional judgement and common sense has grown over the years.

When his investigation was completed, his attitude (and mine) might have been summed up this way: There it is. What do we do with it? We cannot believe it, but we cannot legitimately suppress it. We are not pleased by what the case would seem to suggest about the possible scope of psychic phenomena. If what the participants saw and heard is accurately set down, how can we hope to tame parapsychology so that it becomes an acceptable subject for study by conventionally minded scientists?

To begin, I present the journal abstract of this paper:

> Recurrent spontaneous PK effects were reported independently by members of two families living in a three-year-old house in suburban Pittsburgh during a seven-month period in 1971–1972. Members of both families also reported seeing a child-sized, mist- or wave-like form on several occasions. Sounds described as "childlike laughter" were reported by both families. The phenomena did not occur in association with any single living agent. Investigation disclosed the violent death of a child associated with a former resident rather than with the house itself. Psychological records on the dead child revealed

personality characteristics consistent with those suggested for RSPK agents in general and for the phenomena in this case in particular.

Hauntings of a place are popularly associated with earlier violent death at the same location. Poltergeists are believed to be most often caused by a psychologically disturbed adolescent. This case sounds like a haunting poltergeist, which may be unique in the literature of poltergeists.

It appears more probable, however, that if genuinely psychokinetic effects were involved in this case, the focal person was the wife living on the second floor. Although by itself not singularly impressive, this case has caused me to attend seriously to the literature of poltergeists, which I had previously viewed with a carefully distant interest.

What follows is scarcely more than a listing of the major phenomena. The journal paper, on the other hand, is given in such detail as might be expected from an experienced news reporter

The locus of this real or imaginary drama was a free-standing, two-story brick dwelling in a middle-class Pittsburgh neighborhood. At the beginning of the events here reported, the two apartments of the house had just been rented through a local realtor to two families previously unknown to one another. The owner resided in New York City.

Mr. Pierce entered the case at the request of the groundfloor wife. Anonymity was requested by both families. Pseudonyms have been used in the reporting.

Ellsworth and Naomi Cramer lived on the second floor with their infant daughter and a dog. Ellsworth, age 24, with a bachelor degree in physics and mathematics, was employed as an industrial engineer by a local steel plant. His wife, Naomi, had completed two years of hospital experience as a registered nurse shortly before resigning to give birth to their child.

Peter and Clair Henry occupied the downstairs apartment with sons, age 18 months and four years. Peter, age 28, was a nuclear-reactor training engineer for a large corporation. His wife had less formal schooling than the other three but evidently shared their critical attitude toward the subject matter.

Both wives said they were frightened by the events reported here; while the husbands could perhaps better be described as distressed by this interruption of the rhythm of their lives. All were anxious that the phenomena be terminated. In exploring their problem with the investigator they preferred ordinary explanations to psychic. None admitted to an interest in, or much knowledge about, psychic phenomena.

The phenomena began mildly in late August, 1971, grew in intensity until the investigator's first visit in late February, 1972, and died away by mid-April of the same year.

Only the more dramatic or inexplicable happenings are described below. There were other suggestive but nonevidential events, such as lights switched on repeatedly in the absence of the renters, and noises from the other apartment when no one was known to be there.

The phenomena observed will be grouped by observer, beginning with Naomi Cramer, the former nurse who lived upstairs with her husband, the steel-plant engineer, and their infant daughter.

February 15, 1972. The eight pieces of a disassembled plastic salt and pepper set flew to the floor at Naomi's feet from the kitchen counter, a distance of three meters, when her back was turned to make a telephone call.

About February 20. While rocking her infant in her downstairs neighbor's apartment, Naomi felt the chair rocking of its own accord with sufficient force to prompt her to jump up so that the baby might not fall from her arms.

February 23. About 5:30 AM, while changing the baby's diaper, Naomi heard childlike laughter although the baby was not laughing.

April 22. While her husband was away, at about 11:30 PM, Naomi followed her barking dog into the living room and saw a dancing cloud for about two minutes in full light in the middle of the room. There was childlike laughter and the dog was frightened.

If the story stopped here, the easy explanation would be that Naomi was hallucinating. However, the other three adults also experienced unusual events.

Late January, 1972. Ellsworth Cramer awoke abruptly about midnight to see a gray cloud, three to four feet high, jump up from the foot of his bed and coast through the closed, closet door.

February 23. Ellsworth was wakened by the laughter that his wife had heard while changing the baby. He described the musical quality of the laughter as unnerving and said that this incident shook his previously firm skepticism toward the unexplained earlier occurrences.

The major events reported from the downstairs apartment were as follows:

Mid-December, 1971. Clair saw the empty living-room chair rocking persistenly without apparent cause. She saw it again in late December along with her husband, as described below.

Early January, 1972. Clair saw a small rockinghorse belonging to her older son rocking vigorously in the bedroom closet without apparent cause, for about two minutes. The children were in the living room.

February 22. While in bed with her husband at about 10:45 PM, Clair felt "a small body" enter the bed between herself and her mate. When her husband kicked in his sleep, the "small body" seemed to leave and she saw a "wave-like form." She then heard two thuds in the next room and childlike laughter which she described as beautiful but frightening. She woke her husband, Peter, but a search revealed nothing. Peter later reported that he had heard the laughter but had not told his wife lest he increase her fear.

Late December, 1971. Peter Henry, the nuclear engineer, and his wife, Clair, saw an empty rocking chair rocking vigorously, a few centimeters, up and down, with a sustained, steady movement. Peter struck a match to explore for air currents around the chair but found none. Then he placed his hand on the chair to slow it. When he removed his hand, the rocking chair returned to its former pace. Peter described himself as "stunned." He said that this was "the first cold, hard fact" he could not explain.

Early January, 1972. Peter saw the rockinghorse rocking in the front-hall closet with pronounced motion but without apparent cause.

The sum total of claimed observations could be explained normally only on the minimum assumptions of pathological hallucinations by Naomi upstairs and collaborative fraud by the Henry couple living downstairs. This contingency does not readily fit the sequence of events and seemed motivationally improbable in the light of the total social picture—an opinion that the reader will be in a better positon to accept or reject after he has read the original paper.

In mid-February, 1974, Mr. Pierce re-visisted the house to learn what might have happened in the intervening two years. Peter Henry, had since moved to take a better job in another city. Mr. Cramer accepted the inquiry matter-of-factly and said that, following Mr. Pierce's last visit, there were a few minor phenomena over a period of several months and then nothing more. Thus, as is usually the case in accounts of recurrent spontaneous PK, the phenomena were relatively innocuous and they disappeared of their own accord.

THE PEARISBURG POLTERGEIST

More disconcerting, perhaps, was the Pearisburg, Virginia, poltergeist reported by J.G. Pratt (1978b). The presumed center of the activity was a nine-year-old boy, recently taken as a foster child by a 65-year-old woman whose husband had died a year earlier and who was living alone and wanted company and a supplemental income. The boy had become a ward of the state because of the alcoholism of his natural parents.

After a build-up of occasional falling objects over two weeks, a veritable storm of violent events occurred in one 45-minute period on the evening of 19 December 1976. Heavy furniture, as well as a Christmas tree and small objects, moved, turned over, or were tossed about, always seemingly just out of sight. As shown by pictures taken later, the room was thoroughly disordered.

The widow called her nextdoor neighbor, a retired power-company linesman. He came in 15 minutes and was present when a rocking chair turned over in the living room and then a treadle sewing machine toppled in an adjacent bedroom while he, the widow, and the boy were all in the kitchen. The neighbor was sure no one was elsewhere in the house.

The police and Edward, a son living six miles away, were called. The rooms were photographed and the house vacated. When Dr. Pratt reached Pearisburg the following evening, the house was reopened for his inspection and he interviewed all parties concerned.

The third day after the main episode, a second adult son, Donald, and the foster child returned with the widow to the house to gather Christmas things and to do a bit of straightening up. Again, while the boy was in the widow's presence, coming down from the second floor, a cabinet turned over in the first-floor bedroom. They left the house at once.

On Christmas eve, at Donald's home, where the widow and the

boy were staying, a bookcase turned over and a little later, a statuette fell and was smashed. With that, Donald's 13-year-old daughter became hysterical, and the foster child was removed to the police station and later placed in another foster home.

This case is unusual for the brevity and severity of the main onslaught. The police were unable to believe that anyone would want to wreck the house in any conscious normal way or that the widow would have falsified her statements to cover up such action.

The widow responded freely to Dr. Pratt's questioning. It was her belief that the hand of the Lord was at work.

The boy responded to questions quietly and briefly. He said he had not been frightened and that he had seen some of the objects fall. The indications are that he was happy to be with the widow and that he was liked by her and the members of her family. He had been looking forward excitedly to his first experience of a real Christmas.

The retired linesman, who had been called in, admitted that he was frightened by the events he had attended. For two evenings thereafter he had driven several miles to spend the night with his son. He said that some of his fundamental beliefs had been changed by what had happened.

Poltergeist Perspective

Those desiring to pursue the topic of recurrent spontaneous psychokinesis should read surveys by Rush (1977) and Roll (1978). In the Roll survey, covering 116 poltergeist cases since 1600 A.D., there was one person in 80% of the cases who seemed to be the focus of activity. The median age of such persons was 13, and there were roughly as many males as females. About 50% of these focal persons were reported as prone to dissociative states. Another 30% were said to have psychological disorders. These trends were substantially stronger for the 34 cases since 1950—no doubt as a result of more detailed reporting. (*But see* Taboas, 1980.) The median duration of activity in Roll's cases was two months. Visual and auditory hallucinations were not uncommon.

How might spontaneous psychokinesis be fitted into parapsychology? One can speculate that these cases represent uncontrolled pathological breakthroughs of a psychokinetic power existing in all of us, which is normally confined to our own mind-brain relationship and which in laboratory experiments appears in small, directed amounts outside of the body. Poltergeist phenomena are commonly thought to occur under conditions of extreme frustration.

As far as we know, all spontaneous psychokinetic events entail physical power no greater than that expendable by one person in normal muscular activity. Thus, it would be reasonable to suppose that the psychic energy of PK originates in the focal person. Perhaps it will be possible some day to find in the biochemistry of adolescence some clues as to how the central nervous system mediates psi.

12

EXPERIMENTAL PSYCHOKINESIS

INTO THE LABORATORY

To be amenable to scientific investigation, psychokinesis must be intentionally caused at times when it is expected. As described in the discussion of trance mediumship, there were physical mediums in the nineteenth century who claimed to be able to move objects and to perform other miracles in a seance. At that time some well known scientists were inclined to accept these phenomena as real. With the passing years and a dearth of physical mediums, many parapsychologists tacitly assumed that so-called psychokinesis could be produced only by fraud.[1]

There the matter rested until 1934 when J.B. and L.E. Rhine began their experiments with gaming dice. Gamblers often believe they can control unloaded dice and cause wanted faces to come up more often than expected by the laws of chance even under conditions where skill in throwing could be of no use. Are these gamblers always self-deceived? This was the question the Rhines set out to answer.

The Rhines and their co-workers obtained encouraging results from the beginning of their testing, but it was nine years and a half-million die faces later before they published their first paper on psychokinesis (Rhine & Rhine, 1943). The chief reason for this long delay (L.E. Rhine, 1970, p. 26) was a desire to avoid adding fuel to the controversy already raging among some scientists in the 1930s as to the reality of ESP. It was felt that one incredible phenomenon at a time was enough.

PLACEMENT PSYCHOKINESIS

The early laboratory research on psychokinesis centered on die throwing and, more particularly, on attempts to make certain faces or combinations of faces turn up when one or more dice were thrown by hand, cup, or machine.

After the first publication in 1943, the work expanded in several directions, but most notably, about 1950, toward what was called

---

1. Selected aspects of experimental psychokinesis will be discussed in this and the following chapters. The reader may wish to supplement his study by referring to a survey by Rush (1977).

the "placement" of falling objects. The purpose of placement experiments is to cause falling cubes or other small objects to come to rest in particular, prechosen areas after being released down a randomizing chute. Target areas are reversed or alternated within the same test session so as to balance out any constructional bias in the apparatus.

To the uninitiated, this arrangement might seem primitive. To the scientist, its simplicity is appealing. In a scientific experiment, the simpler, the better, when we are trying to fathom first principles. As we shall see in the next chapter, the placement paradigm provides just enough procedural complexity (beyond that of die throwing for faces) to allow some interesting investigations.

The earliest of the placement work was done by W.E. Cox (1951), but the most of it, by far, was by a Swedish experimenter, Haakon Forwald. The following is a brief description of one of Forwald's later experiments (Pratt & Forwald, 1958).

Mr. Forwald was a design engineer for Sweden's largest electrical company, ASEA. He held more than 500 invention patents in many countries of the world on the control of high-voltage transmission, and he traveled extensively as a consultant.

In a manner typical of most of Forwald's experiments, six unmarked beechwood cubes of 16 mm edge length were placed "randomly" by hand into a horizontal V-shaped trough and then released by pushing a button switch at the end of a long electrical cord. A magnetic trip allowed the trough to swing downward about a pivot, so that the cubes would slide out and fall upon a wide, inclined, open gangway covered by coarse cloth. From there, the cubes would roll and tumble out upon a horizontal table top. The vertical descent was about 45 cm. See Figure 12.1

The table top (120 cm in the direction of principal cube motion and 100 cm crosswise) was marked in cartesian coordinates with lines one cm apart. To provide enough friction to encourage rolling rather than sliding of the cubes, a thin, transparent sheet of plastic was stretched over a plate of glass.

When the cubes had come to rest and before they were touched, the X and Y positions of each cube were recorded to the nearest centimeter. Thereafter, the trough was re-set, and the cubes were collected by hand and placed in it, ready for the next release. By comparing opposite corners of a cube with the nearest grid lines, an uncertainty of less than 1 mm was readily obtained.

The standard protocol used by Forwald in almost all of his ex-

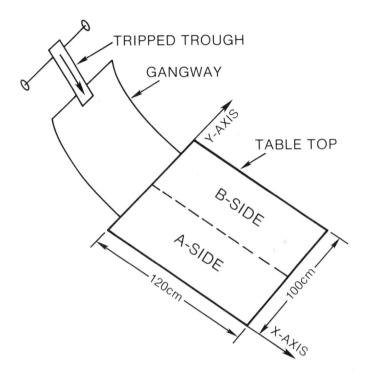

Figure 12.1. Forwald's placement apparatus as used in his Durham, North Carolina, experiment (Pratt & Forwald, 1958). When the trough holding six cubes in a horizontal row was magnetically tripped, it fell to the position shown, allowing the cubes to tumble onto the gangway and down to the table top. Meanwhile, the observers wished for the cubes to roll to the minus or plus Y direction, i.e., to the A or B side.

periments is diagrammed in Figure 12.2. It consisted of a *series* of five experimental *sessions,* each with ten *releases* of six *cubes*—five releases while wishing for the dice to go to "Side A," followed by five for "Side B." Thus, there were 300 cubes to a series. Although the X and Y coordinates of each cube were recorded, only the Y, or transverse, distances were of experimental interest.

Long experience had shown Forwald that his placement effect occurred almost entirely in the first of the five releases for each target side. Therefore, to measure the success of the series in the most sensitive way, a t-test was applied to the difference between the mean positions of the A cubes and of the B cubes in the first release (58 degrees of freedom per series). The remaining four releases could be disregarded; although, as we shall see later, they, too, gave evidence of PK.

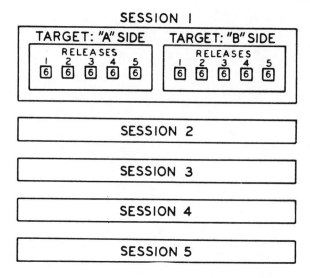

Figure 12.2. Procedure pattern for a standard Forwald placement series (300 cubes, 6 cubes per release). When the target is the *A* side, the subject wishes the cubes to move transversely toward the low values of the *Y* coordinate; for the *B*-side target, vice versa. The purpose of reversing targets is to cancel equipment bias. No attempt is made to influence the primary, *X*-direction motion that is imparted by tumbling from a tilting trough down a sloping gangway.

To perform this particular experiment, Haakon Forwald made an eight-week visit from his home in Sweden to the Parapsychology Laboratory at Duke University in Durham, North Carolina. After building new placement apparatus similar to what he had at home, Forwald spent several weeks working alone and with others to discover under what conditions and in whose presence he could produce the placement effect.

In the course of 11 series, involving various assistants, he found that he could score at about his usual rate when working with Peggie Murphy, the wife of a Duke University graduate student in biology.

In the last twelve days before Forwald's departure for home, two confirmatory series were done in which Mrs. Murphy worked as a co-subject. After each release HF and PM each silently and independently recorded the positions of all cubes and then compared their records for discrepancies before the cubes were touched.

The difference in the mean positions of the first-release *A* cubes and the first-release *B* cubes was 21.5 cm in the first series and 8.8

cm in the second series, these differences being in the desired direction in both cases. The chance probability of the two combined series was 0.0002. A subsequent analysis of variance confirmed the statistical significance of the results (McConnell & Forwald, 1967). In the chapter that follows I shall discuss Forwald's work in greater detail.

SYSTEMS IN EQUILIBRIUM

In a pretheoretical field such as parapsychology the current state of knowledge is difficult for outsiders to ascertain. Within such a field, however, at least among those who are scientifically trained, there is often a consensus as to what is known and what is doubtful. In the area of psychokinesis, for example, it is generally accepted that control of the final resting position and orientation of falling objects is an established phenomenon. What is unknown at present are the range of possible targets and the energetic upper limit of "the power of thought." We want to know, for example: To what extent can physical systems in stable equilibrium be disturbed by psychokinesis?

If one adheres to the conservation of energy principle, the source of psychic energy is a matter for investigation. Is the energy needed for PK drawn from the physiological systems of one or more persons? Would the upper limit of available PK power thus be set by the physiological strength of the contributing individuals? This is a crucial question that cannot yet be answered.

Even for well done experiments there are often serious problems of interpretation. We have seen in Chapter 10 how Schmidt's random number selection by beta rays suggests that nuclear decay can be controlled by PK. But we also noted that control of electron flow at the atomic level in his associated apparatus is an operationally indistinguishable explanation for his results.

What other evidence of atomic PK might be sought? Can local temperatures be raised or lowered as sometimes subjectively perceived in spiritualist seances? Schmeidler (1973) found that a professional psychic, Ingo Swann, could cause apparent temperature changes as measured by an electrical resistance thermometer isolated inside a thermos bottle.

Can chemical processes be triggered directly by thought? Some challenging evidence for the projection of mental images onto photographic plates was obtained even before World War I by a professor of psychology at the Imperial University of Tokyo (Fukurai, 1931). More recently, the work of Eisenbud (1967) with a psychic, Ted Serios, has left most parapsychologists interested but uncertain.

Can biological systems be influenced by PK? The work of Grad (1965; 1967) at McGill University suggests that the "laying on of hands" may have a measureable psychokinetic influence on the growth of plants and the healing of animals. The possible implications of such an effect for medicine excite the imagination.

After strong evidence for the control of dice was published in 1943, a gap of nearly two decades occured before follow-up questions of the kind illustrated above were seriously asked. Such questions were laid aside as unanswerable in the absence of psychic persons claiming to be able to demonstrate gross PK under laboratory conditions. More recently, however, as indicated by the above-cited references, such persons have been found. Perhaps the most dramatic developments have been in the direct movement of visible objects in stable equilibrium.

MOVEMENT OF OBJECTS

In Leningrad in 1968, motion pictures were presented by a neurophysiologist, Dr. G.A. Sergeev, purporting to show two phenomena produced by the nearby waving of empty hands: (1) the sliding of ordinary objects weighing a few grams across a table top under an inverted transparent box, and (2) the swinging of the needle of an enclosed compass resting on a table.

Various parapsychologists of the Soviet Union and eastern Europe have concerned themselves with Nina Kulagina, the housewife who produced these phenomena. Western parapsychologists, tourists, and journalists have visited Leningrad to watch Kulagina in action. Prints of her films have filtered into the U.S.A., where they have been commercially exploited as well as scientifically examined. Reports by Western parapsychologists (Pratt & Keil, 1973) who had watched Kulagina in action were encouraging but not conclusive.

Meanwhile, after seeing the Kulagina film, a biochemical research technician in New York City thought that with some practice she might be able to do the same thing. She had already produced statistically significant results in a dream-telepathy experiment, and in her everyday life she had experienced several striking instances of spontaneous ESP. After some months of trying, she was able to produce small but definite psychokinetic motion. A motion-picture film showing her moving objects under a bell jar was presented by Honorton (1974) of Maimonides Medical Center along with the young lady herself, Miss Felicia Parise, at the annual meeting of the Parapsychological Association in Charlottesville, Virginia, September, 1973.

At the same meeting, Watkins and Watkins (1974) reported some laboratory experiments done with Felicia Parise at the Foundation for Research on the Nature of Man in Durham. In these experiments Miss Parise produced three striking PK effects under well controlled conditions: static 15° displacement of a compass needle, actuation of an electronic metal detector, and blackening of photographic film within opaque envelopes.

At the same meeting, Puthoff and Targ (1974) of the Stanford Research Institute offered a detailed preliminary report of experiments with an Israeli psychic-showman, Uri Gellar, and with an American artist-psychic, Ingo Swann, giving evidence that they could affect complex physical systems in the laboratory.

For several years I had been assigning an increasing, subjective probability to the proposition that the psychokinetic displacement of physical systems in stable equilibrium is possible. At the close of the session on PK in stable systems at the Charlottesville meeting, I was asked to comment impromptu on the current situation. Here are excerpts from my remarks on that occasion (McConnell, 1974b):

> As a physicist I find it difficult to grasp fully what we have just seen and heard about gross psychokinetic phenomena. . . . Instead of trying to evaluate the present situation, I shall give you the perspective in which I see it. . . .
>
> The question that many of us are asking is this: "Are the gross PK effects that we have heard discussed and seen on film here today real or fraudulent? This is the same question that other scientists have been asking for 40 years about ESP. The answer depends, not only upon the evidence in the journals, but also upon the honesty and competence of those who gathered that evidence. These latter factors can be assessed only by getting to know the experimenters intimately.
>
> In the pretheoretical stage of a field of science every newcomer must repeat for himself the basic experiments because there is no generally accepted body of belief—nothing he can take on faith. Soon after I entered parapsychology in 1947, I guided an experiment in wishing with dice which yielded results that were not very dramatic but that I could not reasonably explain by ordinary means (McCon-

nell, Snowdon, & Powell, 1955). Also, I had studied successful experiments done by persons whom I later came to know and trust.

Consequently, for the last 20 years I have been fully convinced of the reality of psychokinesis as shown by falling objects. Although this is a weak kind of PK that might be explained in terms of controlling existing physical energies, it has forced me to remain open-minded toward the more dramatic physical effects that were common in psychical research in past generations and that now in recent years seem to have reappeared. . . .

On the basis of what we have seen here today, I think we must prepare to accept the fact that there is no reasonable basis for denying the ability of some people to change a stable physical system, even when that system is isolated against such change as far as present knowledge in physics can determine.

Since 1973 there have been further reports of the work of Nina Kulagina in Leningrad (Keil & Fahler, 1976; Keil, Herbert, Ullman, & Pratt, 1976), and these, coupled with private communications from parapsychologists whom I have known for many years, compel me to believe with a probability close to certainty the proposition that psychokinesis does occur involving gross energy inputs at a rate of at least 10^{-4} watts (McConnell, 1976c).

METAL BENDING

In the decade of the 1970s the psychic entertainment business flourished. Chief among the stage performers and book writers was Uri Geller, whose possession of genuine psychic ability had been presumptively established by the work at Stanford Research Institute. However, neither SRI nor any other laboratory has reported successful, controlled experiments confirming Geller's claims for "metal bending," the phenomenon of which he was the first recognized proponent.

His flamboyance has been something of an embarrassment to parapsychology. On the one hand, there is a growing belief that gross PK of some kinds does occur. On the other, Geller's reluctance to engage in laboratory research except on his own terms, has forced parapsychologists to shrug their shoulders when asked about this stage magician. The skeptic must bear in mind that his behavior is what one might reasonably expect of a person with his personality and background, regardless of whether he was bending table spoons by mind or muscle.

The question of the reality of PK metal bending may now finally be moving off dead center as a result of the work of J.B. Hasted, a metallurgist at Birkbeck College of the University of London. As a result of Geller's television performances in London in 1973–74, a number of subjects, mostly children, reported the bending of metal objects allegedly by direct mental action. Working with some of these children, Hasted (1976, 1977) and Hasted and Robertson (1979) claim to have produced metal bending in the laboratory with strain gage instrumentation and adequate controls against fraud and experimental error. If these effects can be replicated in other laboratories under comparable auspices, Hasted will have significantly broadened the study of psychokinesis.

13

UNCONSCIOUS CHARACTERISTICS OF PSI

TASK-STRUCTURE EFFECTS

The evidence for the psychokinetic control of falling objects is of two kinds: total scores that are above chance expectation, and characteristic variations in the rate of scoring success within experimental sessions. It is the latter that I shall discuss now.

A high, total score is the hoped-for result of all usual experiments; while a patterned change in scoring is not something ordinarily desired by the subject. The patterns that occur are sometimes called "position effects," but "task-structure effects" might be a better name. They are commonly found in ESP data but have been most dramatically and persistently observed in PK records. They are of evidently psychological origin, and they often seem to follow gestalt principles.

Task-structure effects occur in parapsychological experiments in which a simple task is repeated many times, as in guessing cards or throwing dice. The most common task-structure effect is a decline in the ability of the subject to "hit his target" as the experimental session progresses. This is sometimes followed by a scoring recovery, either after a pause in the data gathering or as the end of the task approaches. In the latter case, the scoring curve is sometimes described as *U*-shaped.

Comparable curves of changing performance have been found in many areas of psychological measurement in which a person is required to make a long series of similar responses. For instance, in studies of recall from memory of a series of words or syllables, a decline in success rate usually occurs as the subject proceeds down the list, and sometimes there is a later rise in success—caused, presumably, by the psychological prominence of the approaching end.

From an evidential point of view, the importance of task-structure effects is that they are psychologically interpretable and yet are largely immune to some of the experimental criticisms that have been commonly offered against psychokinesis. To the extent that such effects are found in existing data when not anticipated, they are not easily explainable by such counter-hypotheses as the loss of unsuccessful data, optional stopping of an experiment, dice bias, recording errors, and fraud in recording the data (Pratt, 1944; 1947a; 1947b; 1947c; 1947d; Rhine and Humphrey, 1944a; 1944b; Rhine, Humphrey, & Pratt, 1945).

SCORING PATTERNS IN PLACEMENT PK

The work of Haakon Forwald was introduced in Chapter 12. His cube-placement data exhibit some of the most remarkable task-structure effects on record. I shall review a group of ten experimental series that he designated as S82 to S91. These were done between March and November of 1960 for the purpose of investigating the dependence of the psychokinetic effect upon the design of the cube-releasing mechanism (McConnell & Forwald, 1968).

The apparatus construction and the data gathering in these experiments were carried out by HF at his home in Sweden. I suggested the arrangement of the apparatus and analyzed the data. In all of these experiments, Forwald used his standard data-gathering pattern, which I have already explained in Figure 12.2.

In these ten special series, in contrast to Forwald's earlier work, each cube was given its own number, which appeared in ink on all faces with a special mark on one of the faces. This allowed the cubes to be placed in the same order and orientation for every release so that the behaviors of the cubes could be individually studied.

I shall list these ten series and then explain them:

S82 and S83: Tipping trough.

S84 and S85: Inclined trough.

S86 and S87: Inverted, longitudinal trough.

S88 and S89: Inverted, transverse trough.

S90 and S91: Tipping trough.

To provide a base line of performance in these ten series, the first two series (S82 and S83) and the last two (S90 and S91) were done with the pivoted-trough equipment that Forwald had been using since he performed his first series eight years earlier. The inclined gangway and horizontal grid were as sketched in Figure 12.1, but the grid measured 112 × 80 cm. This apparatus has now been brought from Sweden by the Smithsonian Institution at Washington, D.C., for its historical collection.

Of the five pairs of series, the middle three employed new ar-

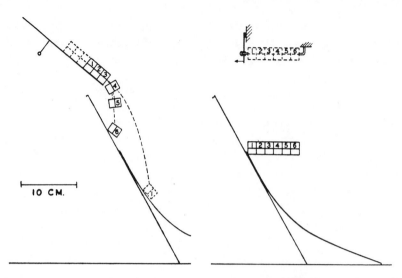

Figure 13.1. Mid-air cube patterns for two of Haakon Forwald's four cube-releasing devices. All distances are to scale. Solid cubes are shown at the instant of first contact after free fall. Broken-line cubes are at an earlier or later time. The placement effect appeared with roughly equal strength for all four releasing arrangements. (Source: McConnell and Forwald, 1968.)

Left: Fixed, inclined trough, as used in Series S84 and S85. Cubes were released by dropping a gate at the lower end of the trough. (Gate is not shown.) For Series S82, S83, S90, and S91, the gate was removed and the trough was allowed to turn about the pivot from a horizontal position to a stop at the position shown (in the manner of Forwald's earlier research).

Right: Fixed, inverted, longitudinal, aligning trough, as used in Series S86 and S87. (Trough not shown.) Cubes were held by end pressure only. For Series S88 and S89 the cube stack was turned 90° about a vertical axis into a transverse position.

rangements for releasing the cubes. In the first new arrangement (S84 and S85) the old, pivoted-trough was used but remained fixed in its tilted position as shown on the left half of Figure 13.1, and the cubes were released by the magnetic tripping of a gravity-operated gate at the lower end of the trough. The motion of the falling cubes was studied by high-speed photography and found to be characteristically different for the fixed and tipping troughs.

In the other four series (S86 to S89) the cubes were suspended in a horizontal stack, held only by pressure applied to the ends. When the pressure was magnetically released, the cubes fell freely in a row until they struck the wide, inclined gangway below. For Series S86 and S87 the axis of the cube stack paralleled the direction of the principal horizontal motion of the cubes, i.e., the X direction as shown in Figure 12.1, so that one end of the cube stack struck the high side of the inclined plane first and the cubes would interfere with one another as they tumbled down to the horizontal plane. This is shown to the right in Figure 13.1. In Series S88 and S89, the cube stack was perpendicular to the X motion, so that all cubes struck the inclined gangway at the same instant and traveled down it, elbowing each other on the way. The target effect was separated from the effects of the several releasing mechanisms by analysis of variance of the transverse or Y displacement of the final resting positions of all cubes.

Despite the dramatically different methods of release, the psychokinetic placement effect was found with roughly equivalent strength among all four arrangements. To exhibit the task-structure effect clearly, the data from all ten series have been combined in Figure 13.2. For each release with the A side as target, the final

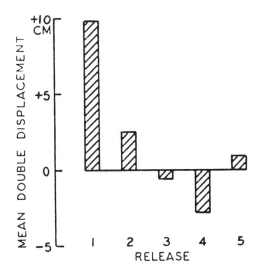

Figure 13.2. Falling-cube placement effect produced by Haakon Forwald by releasing six wood cubes to tumble down an inclined gangway onto a table top while wishing for the cubes to move laterally. The graph represents the pooling of 50 experimental sessions involving four different cube-releasing devices. Within each session, cubes were released five times wishing for motion toward "Side A", followed by five times for "Side B." Height of bar corresponds to the average transverse position of Side-B cubes, minus the average position of Side-A cubes. Each bar results from 600 cube positions. The empirical standard deviation of the bar heights is 0.8 cm, calculated from within-bar variance.

Y position of each numbered cube has, in effect, been subtracted from the final Y position of the same cube in the corresponding release for the B side. These differences have been averaged separately for each of the five releases in Forwald's standard procedure (Figure 12.2). Each bar in Figure 13.2 corresponds to 600 cube positions. The standard errors of the mean, or statistical uncertainties, of the five graph bars did not differ substantially from their average standard error, which was 0.8 cm.

Several features of this "U-curve" deserve mention. The first release has the desired direction of deviation and a magnitude that is nearly 12 times the standard error of mean. This corresponds to a chance probability of about 10^{-30}. The second release has a deviation that is 3.0 times its standard deviation, and is therefore statistically significant. The third and fifth releases are not significantly different from chance expectation. The fourth release is in the wrong direction, with a chance probability of less than 10^{-3}.

This reversal of placement from the desired direction in the fourth release might be thought of as a case of subconscious target avoidance. Naively viewed, the below-chance minimum of the envelope of the bar graph might suggest an adverse attitude (boredom, perhaps) rather than simple fatigue—since the latter would presumably result in a chance deviation. As in all psychological research, one must be cautious in attributing motivations. Similar curves had been obtained for many years by HF. By the time of the present series, they were expected and welcomed.

We can now say that the explanation for this curious effect probably lies in the structure of the mind/brain rather than in the subject's affective response to his task. An exposition of the reasoning behind this momentous statement must wait until the next chapter.

TARGET MISSING

We have just seen that, in repetitive psi experiments, non-chance scoring patterns may occur that reflect the way in which the data were gathered. In particular, we get within-session scoring decline and recovery curves. We call these data-structure effects. Several other extrachance scoring oddities are sometimes found in repeated-trial psi tests. I shall discuss these under the rubric, "target missing."

Assume that you consciously want to guess correctly a deck of cards and that you have some ESP ability, but that, subconsciously, you want to fail. How many different ways can you avoid a target and still tell yourself that you are trying?

You might subconsciously turn off your ESP, and the resulting correspondences between targets and guesses would be mathematically random. What will happen, however, if you cannot turn off your ESP? Suppose you subconsciously know the correct answer in spite of yourself. How might you avoid revealing it in the guesses you give? Almost anything you do under these circumstances will leave some nonrandomness in the data that might be detected by suitable analysis.

The most obvious way to avoid giving right answers is to give wrong answers. However, a subject who is naive about statistics would probably give too many wrong answers, so that his final score might be significantly below chance. A common term for this is "psi missing"—which is confusing because it might seem to mean psi absent. Until a better suggestion comes along, I shall use the expression "target missing by reversal of sign."

There are other ways of trying to hide your ESP. Instead of simply guessing wrong, you might subconsciously respond, not to the intended target, but to the card that is immediately before or after the intended target in time or that is adjacent to it in space. This kind of target missing could be called "proximal displacement" scoring.

The first large-scale investigation showing this effect was by Whately Carington (1940), who noticed that his subjects scored above chance expectation on picture targets scheduled for the days ahead and behind the intended day in his ESP picture-drawing experiments.

If one is subconsciously trying to avoid making correct ESP guesses, there is no need to guess a nearby target. One could just as well systematically substitute one target for another. In card guessing, one might, for example, always call a spade for a heart. This behavior seems to occur frequently. Its first investigation was by Cadoret and Pratt (1950). The most thorough study yet done was by Kelly, Kanthamani, Child, and Young (1975). This effect has usually been labelled "consistent missing," but that expression fails to make clear what is missing or being missed. I suggest, instead, the expression, "target missing by target substitution."

Although I have discussed target missing in terms of purposive target avoidance, it is not now possible to determine in a particular case whether such an effect is caused by a subject's subconscious wish to fail, by unmotivated subconscious confusion, or by some mind/brain mechanism not yet imagined by the parapsychologist. In our search for an explanation we may find a parallel in Freud's investigation of the unconscious.

FREUDIAN CONCEPTS

Freudian theory has structural, dynamic, and developmental aspects. Structurally, according to Freud, the personality embodies three elements: the "id," the "ego," and the "superego." Dynamically, these three entities interact by the flow of so-called "psychic energy" originating in the id. In normal development, according to Freud, the human personality progresses through "oral," "anal," "phallic," "latency," and "genital" stages, until it reaches stability in adulthood (Hall, 1954). When the personality fails to develop normally, the individual seeks a Freudian psychiatrist and is given a kind of treatment known as "psychoanalysis," which differs in certain respects from other forms of psychotherapy.

It is not my intention to endorse or to disparage Freudian theory. It should be noted, however, that, to the extent that the detailed explanatory mechanisms of Freud have empirical reality, they can be described in other words and separated from the Freudian conceptual framework. The eclectic view is that there is nothing unique in Freudian theory that makes it more true or less false than other competing theories.

There is no doubt that Freudian mechanisms are real in the sense that in extreme cases they can be recognized as controlling behavior. In general, however, attempts to analyze individual behavior in terms of these mechanisms are so often wrong that the method of psychoanalysis is unacceptable to most American psychologists.

Our concern in parapsychology with Freudian theory arises because certain "defense mechanisms" postulated by Freud or, at least, analogs of these defense mechanisms are found in connection with the appearance or nonappearance of psi phenomena.

As we shall see, Freudian defense mechanisms are forms of unconscious self-deception that involve antagonisms among conscious and unconscious aspects of human personality. These mechanisms, which appear to some extent in daily living, are evidence for potential multiple personalities in all of us. They support the hypothesis that some altered states of consciousness represent the temporary dominance of aspects of personality that have a continuing existence in us.

Freud speaks of the id, the ego, and the superego. The id is the animal in us. It is pleasure-seeking, instinctual, infantile, impatient, irrational, amoral, ineducable, unconscious, and out of touch with reality. The superego is the god in us. It represents conscience and values. It, too, is irrational, unconscious, and unable to distinguish fantasy from reality. The ego is the essence of man. It is the conscious, rational part of the mind that struggles with the id and the superego.

This tripartite theory of the mind was developed late in Freud's career. Prior to 1920, his structural conceptualizing was in terms of the conscious versus the nonconscious, with the latter divided into the "unconscious" and the "preconscious." For our present purposes we shall ignore the id, the ego, and the superego, and concentrate on the unconscious, but we shall avoid fine distinctions in unawareness. The "unconscious," as I shall use the term, is any part of mentation that is not readily available for introspection. I intend this statement as description rather than definition. Moreover, in the present state of our knowledge, we cannot usefully attempt to identify conscious and unconscious mentation with brain structures. Therefore, we must discuss the workings of the unconscious from a purely behavioral point of view.

There are three Freudian defense mechanisms of possible interest to parapsychology: "repression," "displacement," and "reaction formation."

Repression is the temporary or permanent, purposeful forgetting of ideas that cause anxiety. In parapsychology the frequent inability of the experimental subject to express in waking speech or writing what he knows by extrasensory perception strongly suggests Freudian repression in those cases where the subject nevertheless is able to communicate his knowledge by muscular automatism or to reveal it in dreams or in hypnotic trance.

Displacement in psychoanalytic theory is an arbitrary shifting of affect or interest from one object or objective to another that may be closely or remotely similar. For example, some Freudian analysts explained the attractiveness of smoking partly by its appeal as a substitute for sucking a nipple. (Presumably, this was before nicotine was recognized as a physiologically addictive drug.)

In parapsychology the term "proximal displacement" refers to a systematic response to targets adjacent to the designated target. The shift may be in time or position. The related effect, "target substitution," is the systematic substitution of one target for another in multiple-choice psi experiments. Both proximal displacement and target substitution in parapsychology are analogous and perhaps, in some sense, identical with Freudian displacement.

Reaction formation, in the Freudian lexicon, is a form of reality denial. A person may believe that he loves another unreservedly when, in fact, the exaggerated trappings of love conceal a compulsive hostility. In a similar fashion, conformity may hide rebellion; aggressiveness, timidity; etc. In parapsychology the analogous effect is target missing by reversal of sign so that the test subject scores consistently below chance when he attempts to score above.

These distortions of purpose occurring in psi experiments can be convincing evidence of the reality of psi phenomena if they are sufficiently persistent and unambiguous to rule out chance as an explanation. Both conceptually and experimentally, these knowledge-avoidance effects are a major challenge to the parapsychologist.

Whether Freud's theories will play a large role in the understanding of the mind is uncertain, but he has given us two ideas that are clearly relevant to parapsychology: (1) the brain is functionally multipartite and (2) the nonanalytic operation of the brain may suffer serious logical distortions.[1]

---

1. Freud's (1921) unequivocal acceptance of the reality of telepathy was coupled with an ambivalence that put him in the camp of present-day scientists (McConnell, 1981, p.223).

14

PROGRESSIVE ORGANIZATION AND AMBIVALENCE PRINCIPLES IN PSYCHOKINETIC DATA

INTRASESSION SCORE DECLINE IN DIE-FACE PK

The occurrence of intrasession score declines in experimental parapsychology was noted by G.H. Estabrooks (1927) at the Harvard Psychological Laboratory in a classic card-guessing experiment that anticipated the procedures of J.B. Rhine. The first systematic study of the decline effect in card guessing was done by Ina Jephson (1928).

In the intervening half century, intrasession score declines have become a familiar feature of parapsychological research and have received much speculative attention trying to link them to existing psychological concepts. In this chapter, in a search for unifying principles that might apply to all "task-structure effects," I shall focus upon the score declines found in a die-throwing experiment reported by McConnell, Snowdon, and Powell (1955).[1]

In this experiment a pair of dice were automatically photographed within the totally enclosing die cage pictured in Figure 14.1. Under the control of the experimenter, the cage was motor driven, end-over-end, at a rate of 7.5 half-turns per minute. The inner surface of the cage was studded with rubber bumpers, so that the dice tumbled randomly from one end to the other.

The data given here represent the dice "thrown" by 386 student subjects, who participated singly and once only, after agreeing to wish for one, prechosen, target die-face number to appear as often as possible.

The die faces were also hand-recorded by the experimenter on pages arranged with three adjacent columns of 12 throws each, as shown in Figure 14.2. As indicated in that figure, two pages of machine-thrown dice were preceded, in every case, by one page of dice thrown by the student from a rough-lined cup into a tray.

It is important to note that throughout every experimental ses-

---

1. This experiment is among the more carefully done in the literature of parapsychology. Critics of the field are invited to search for possible weaknesses in it, beginning with a recent review which gives supplementary analyses as well as biographical summaries of my co-experimenters (McConnell, 1982b).

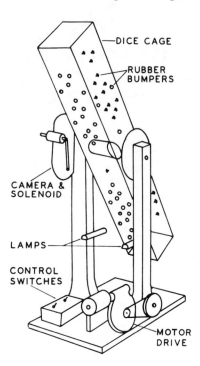

Figure 14.1. The motor-driven die-throwing machine, sketched from a photograph. The die cage, drawn in a turning position, was 90 cm long. A nonresettable counter for serially numbering each half turn is not visible.

sion there was a short rest period of about two minutes duration after every 36 throws of the dice pair (e.g., after the 4.8 minutes required for the three columns of the machine-thrown data half page). In that rest period the number of target faces (hits) in each of the three preceding columns was counted and recorded on the data sheet. Thus, data gathering took about 40 minutes per subject.

The total number of target hits in the 18 columns of the three data pages is shown in Table 14.1. As anticipated from previous die-throwing experiments reported in the literature, a statistically significant decline in scoring rate was found within the half page of the data. This is shown in Figure 14.3, in which the three columns represent the summation of all half pages of all subjects. The bars of the graph show the excess or deficit of target die faces relative to the number expected by chance.

When evaluated by a t-test, the difference between the first and third columns of Figure 14.3 was found to have a chance probabil-

Table 14.1

NUMBER OF SUCCESSES (TARGET DIE FACES) OCCURRING IN EACH COLUMN
POSITION OF THE THREE DATA PAGES (EXPERIMENTERS COMBINED).

Number of subjects = 386. Number of die-face trials per subject for each
position = 24. Nominal p-value = 1/6.

Half page	Page 1 Cup-thrown			Page 2 Machine-thrown			Page 3 Machine-thrown		
Upper	1572	1509	1544	1553	1585	1524	1636	1566	1518
Lower	1512	1520	1512	1572	1475	1509	1592	1566	1477

ity of .005. The data from the machine-thrown dice (whose accuracy had been verified from the photographic film) were found to have a somewhat stronger decline, with a chance probability of .002. As explained in the original report, these numbers have been corrected for any dice bias.

The total decline between the first and third columns of Figure 14.3 is 353 die faces, which I shall calculate from Table 14.1 by the following, slightly roundabout procedure. (The reason for describing the calculation in this particular sequence will be apparent later.) If the three pages of data are combined as though they were one, the deviation from chance in the upper left column of the combined page is 1572 + 1553 + 1636 − 4632 (= + 129), where 4632 is the chance-expected score. Similarly, for the upper right, lower left, and lower right corners, respectively, the deviations are

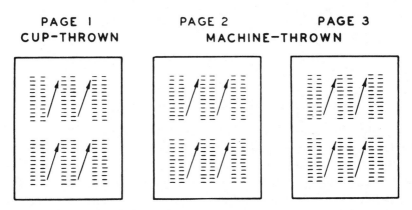

PAGE 1
CUP-THROWN

PAGE 2
MACHINE-THROWN

PAGE 3
MACHINE-THROWN

Figure 14.2. The layout of the three data pages used for each of the 386 test subjects. Each of the six double columns on a page had space for 24 die faces thrown two at a time. A rest period after every half page (72 die faces) controlled the emergence of psychokinesis.

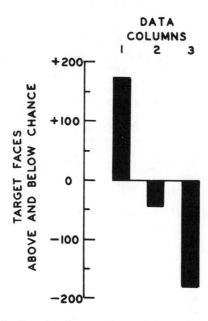

Figure 14.3. The decline in the number of favorable (i.e., target) faces obtained while wishing in an uninterrupted sequence of 36 throws of a pair of dice. As they were thrown, the fallen die faces were recorded in three columns of 12 throws on each half data page. All half pages for all subjects have been combined in this figure. For each column the chance-expected number of favorable faces is 9264 ($p = 1/6$) and the observed standard error is 90. (This approximates the theoretical value of 87.9)

-46, $+44$, -134. Thus, the sum of the deviations for the two lefthand columns on the combined page is $+173$; while the right-hand columns total to -180. The difference, or "half-page decline," is $+353$ die faces.

EVALUATION AND CHALLENGE

If one does not have a working familiarity with statistical method, one cannot readily judge whether a decline of 353 die faces is an ordinary chance fluctuation from zero or something more interesting. In Figure 14.4, I have provided a graphical analysis by which the nonmathematician can judge these results directly.

The half-page decline at the end of the experiment was calculated above to be $+353$ die faces. In Figure 14.4, I have calculated the decline as it existed after every ten subjects throughout the experiment. In this way, one can watch the growth of the decline

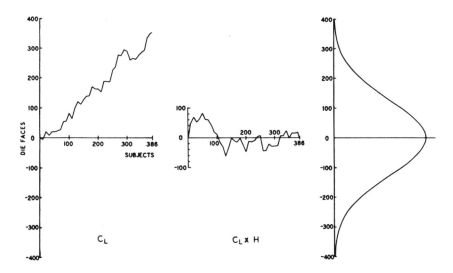

Figure 14.4. Chronological accumulation of the scoring-rate decline (C_L) and the interaction ($C_L \times H$), for 386 subjects as computed after every ten subjects. Since these are single-degree-of-freedom components of variance and since the denominator of the variance ratio has a large number of degrees of freedom, they can be expressed directly in target die faces and their final values can be evaluated by visual inspection against a single, normal curve of error drawn appropriately for the length of the experiment as shown. The final value of C_L (353 die faces) equals the difference between the first and third columns of Figure 14.3 and corresponds to a two-tailed probability of .005. The interaction ($C_L \times H$) has not been found meaningful in the history of parapsychology. Throughout this experiment the $C_L \times H$ curve shows only chance fluctuations around the expected value of zero.

and compare it to its short-term fluctuations. This chronological sequence is shown in the lefthand graph (which is labelled C_L, because this decline is known technically as the "linear component of the column main effect" in the analysis of variance of these data).

At the right hand in Figure 14.4, I have drawn accurately to size the chance-determined "normal curve of error" against which the decline of 353 die faces must be evaluated. For any ordinate value, the abscissa or horizontal distance from the y-axis to the curve is proportional to the probability of getting a scoring deviation from chance expectation equal to that ordinate value. The probability value .005 means that the sum of the areas between the y-axis and the upper and lower tails of this curve beyond the ordinates, plus and minus 353, is one two-hundredth of the total area enclosed by this normal curve. Once the above explanation of the curve is understood, it will be intuitively obvious that reaching a deviation of 353 from zero would be a highly unusual event if chance alone were operating.

How such a curve might typically look in the case of a purely chance experiment is shown in the middle graph, labelled $C_L \times H$. (Technically, this is what is known as the "interaction between the half page and the linear component of the column effect.") It is a mathematical function with no psychokinetic meaning, even though it is calculated from the same data as C_L. The final value of the curve is -3 die faces, arrived at by using the same deviation totals as before $(+129, -46, +44, -134)$. To get the decline, C_L, these numbers were added after multiplying by $+ - + -$. To calculate $C_L \times H$, one multiplies, instead, by $+ - - +$. Throughout the course of the experiment, this interaction curve "walks randomly" back and forth in the vicinity of zero, as one would commonly expect if chance alone were operating. I have discussed this aspect of the experiment more completely elsewhere (McConnell, 1982b).

Thus, while it seems reasonably certain that the decline effect shown in Figure 14.3 is the result of something beyond chance, this conclusion raises a puzzling question about psychokinesis.

On the average, at the beginning of each half page of data gathering, after the subject had had a short rest, he and the experimenter were able to achieve the result they desired: the target die faces came up more often than expected by chance. This period of success lasted perhaps 1.6 minutes (the time of the first column). By the end of the second column, at 3.2 minutes, the average PK effect had disappeared and the score (middle bar) was close to chance. In the final 1.6 minutes, corresponding to the third column in Figure 14.3, the effect actually reversed and the dice behaved in opposition to the desires of subject and experimenter. The negative deviation is two standard deviations long and cannot readily be dismissed as a chance effect. Why the reversal?

This is the same effect as that obtained by Haakon Forwald in Column 4 of Figure 13.2 while wishing falling cubes to move laterally. Evidently, we are on the trail of a fundamental peculiarity whose understanding might lead to the unraveling of the mystery of the elusiveness of psi and perhaps eventually to its useful control.

FREQUENCY OF COLUMN SCORES

In an analysis of variance of the data-block scores of the just previously described experiment (McConnell, 1982b), I noticed that there was a slight but significant discrepancy between the residual variance (3.58, with 1540 degrees of freedom) and the theoretical binomial variance for dice computed from npq (3.33). Calculations showed that this difference could not be accounted for by dice bias and must, therefore, represent uncontrolled psychological variables affecting the emergence of psychokinesis. The word "psychological" is crucial. Because the observed effects, to be described below, appear only in connection with the essentially random sequence of target-face numbers used in the experiment (McConnell, Snowdon, & Powell, 1955), those effects can have no meaning except in terms of the wishing of the subject and the experimenter. They cannot have an instrumental or other adventitious origin.

As it happened, the meaning of this excess residual variance was to be found in the frequency distributions of the column scores on the experimental data pages. It will be recalled that each column contained 24 die faces and that, as shown in Figure 14.2, there were three columns per half page, three pages per subject, and 386 subjects in the experiment. The score for any one column is, of course, the number of target faces in that column, and must lie in the range 0 to 24. The frequency distribution of scores expected for 24 thrown dice is given by the algebraic expansion of $(5/6 + 1/6)^{24}$. The shape of the expected distribution is similar to that already discussed in Figure 10.2b, which showed the expansion of the binomial $(3/4 + 1/4)^{16}$. In both cases the histogram has its maximum at 4 and very few scores above 8.

The most direct method of evaluating the discrepancy between an experimentally observed distribution of scores and a theoretical distribution is to calculate the "poorness-of-fit chi-square" and then read the associated chance probability of so great a discrepancy from a table of chi-squares, using as the number of degrees of freedom one less than the number of score categories.

In the present experiment, all scores above 9 were grouped with the 9s so as to give 10 categories. The theoretical distributions employed were based, not on a die probability of exactly 1/6, but on probabilities appropriate to the hypothesis under test.

For example, when all of the 6948 column scores of the experi-

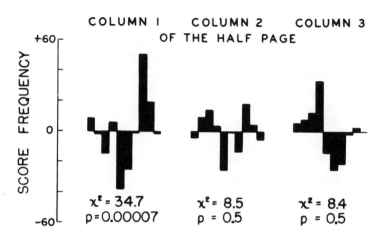

Figure 14.5. The deviations of the frequency of observed data-column scores (0 to 9+) from an expected distribution that was computed to offset any dice bias. In this figure all six half-pages per test subject are combined and each distribution applies to 2316 scores. From a comparison with Figure 14.3, it appears that poorness-of-fit accompanies positive scoring, while goodness-of-fit (small chi-square) associates with negative scoring (i.e., with scoring opposed to the wish of the subject). However, this is only partially true. From Figure 14.6 it will be evident that the poorness-of-fit *in Column 1* of the half page is *negatively* correlated with positive scoring.

ment were fitted against a theoretical frequency distribution that was calculated so as to eliminate from the resulting difference the decline effect shown in Figure 14.3, the resulting chi-square had a chance probability of .001. From this, one concludes that the factors causing the poorness of fit are more complex than a simple column-to-column decline in the probability of die-throw success.

SCORE FREQUENCY VERSUS SCORE DECLINE

As a first step in searching for a relationship between score decline and poorness of fit, McConnell and Clark (1982a) tabulated the column-score frequency distributions associated with the data of the half-page decline shown in Figure 14.3. The result is presented in the three histograms of Figure 14.5, where each of the ten bars, reading from left to right, corresponds to a column score in the range 0 to 9+. The height of the bar represents the excess or deficit of scores of that size relative to a theoretical distribution which was chosen to control against any dice bias without diminishing the decline effect.[2]

By comparison of Figures 14.3 and 14.5, it will be seen that the positive deviation of the score total in Column 1 (Figure 14.3) is accompanied by a highly extrachance distribution of scores ($p = 10^{-4}$), which in turn results mostly from an excess of 7s and 8s (Figure 14.5). In Column 3, the same deviation of score total—but in the direction opposite to the wishing—is generated by a very ordinary distribution of scores ($p = .5$).

Actually, the situation is more complex than might be supposed from Figures 14.3 and 14.5. The pattern of score-total deviations and column-score distributions is further explored in Figure 14.6, column-by-column and page-by-page. Like Figure 14.5, Figure 14.6 shows the differences between observed scores and a theoretical distribution adjusted to remove dice bias but retain the decline effect.

In this connection, it should be noted that the creation of a strong decline effect by a simple shift of die-face probability requires only a barely noticeable poorness of fit relative to the frequency distribution for the probability 1/6. Hence, decline and poorness of fit may be largely independent features in the same data.

In the occurrence of the poorness-of-fit chi-squares of Figure 14.6 the following features can be discerned. As in Figure 14.5, the interesting chi-squares occur in Column 1. The greatest chi-square occurs at the beginning of the experiment, in Column 1 of Page 1. It decreases generally to the right, from column to column, and downward, from page to page. As the chi-square decreases from column to column, the desired psychokinetic effect decreases and then reverses. This is seen most easily by comparing Figures 14.3 and 14.5. On the other hand, as the chi-square decreases from page to page (Figure 14.6, Column 1), psychokinesis "organizes" itself into a stronger positive deviation in Column 1 and a stronger negative deviation in Column 3. The difference in the scoring decline effect between Page 1 and Page 3 is significant at the $p = .05$ level.

In Figure 14.7, the target-face-count and score-frequency data are split by experimenter. The experimenter (M) with the greatest chi-square has the weakest decline effect and a slightly negative total score deviation; while the experimenter (P) with the smallest

---

2. In the remainder of this chapter I have borrowed heavily from McConnell and Clark (1982a).

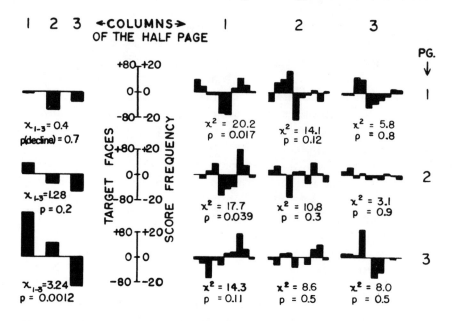

Figure 14.6. *On the right:* Data-column score frequencies as in Figure 14.5, but separated by page (with upper and lower half-pages combined). *On the left:* The corresponding deviations of the target-face count from chance expectation, as in Figure 14.3.

As the poorness-of-fit chi-square decreases for Column 1, the Column-1 total score improves from page to page. Meanwhile, in Column 3, with no evident change in the poorness-of-fit chi-square, the target-hit score grows negatively from page to page. (Chi, which is shown for the scoring declines in the figure, is the difference between the first-column and third-column target face counts divided by the standard error of the difference. For each of the nine total-score deviation bars, the chance-expected number of favorable faces is 3088 based on $p = 1/6$.)

chi-square has a strong decline and a slightly positive total score deviation. (The latter fact may perhaps best be thought of as the result of a longer persistence of positive control before the reversal tendency dominates.) All three experimenters showed a psychokinetic effect, but it was "best organized" for P and most poorly for M. The countervailing trends in chi-square and score total are reminiscent of the column and page variations in Figure 14.6.

Whatever its meaning, there is a pattern in these data that is of causal origin. It doubtless reflects the natural limitations that reduce psychokinesis from godlike omnipotence to an imperfect human striving.

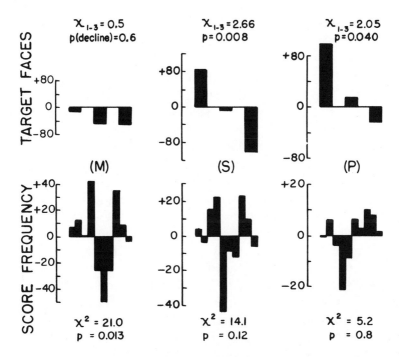

Figure 14.7. Similar to Figures 14.3 and 14.5, but separated by experimenter. The ordinate scales for both target-face count and score frequency have been adjusted for the different number of subjects per experimenter so as to show percentage changes equally. The number of subjects were: M(171), S(128), P(87). A countervailing trend, similar to that shown in Figure 14.6, is evident between poorness-of-fit and the strength of total-score effects.

THE ORGANIZING PRINCIPLE

The purpose of experimentation is to guide further experimentation toward the goal of eventual understanding. When pattern is discovered in data and its meaning is unknown, the experimenter must seek a hypothesis, i.e., guess at an explanation in terms of relationships among generalized, nonobservable quantities.

In the data patterns of this experiment McConnell and Clark (1982a) perceived the operation of two psychological principles as mutually multiplying factors. One of these we called "the organizing principle" and the other, "the principle of ambivalence."

In our theorizing, the organizing principle has to do with clearing the mind and marshalling the attention of the psychokinetic agent. We surmise that the procedures within the testing session were such as to induce increasing order in the psychokinetic action. We suspect that this will occur progressively in any psychokinetic testing session of the kind that we used.

Specifically, it is our hypothesis that the organizing principle manifests itself in a diminishing range of awareness, i.e., in an increasing state of mental dissociation. We prefer to describe this state simply as one of "passive alertness." (See Chapter 6.) It has been discussed in other language by professional psychics as a preparatory state for performance. In parapsychological research it has been induced by the use of hypnotic procedures, progressive relaxation, sensory isolation, or the Ganzfeld (an environment of uniform sensory stimulation by noise and translucent blinders). (For a discussion of these techniques see Chapter 7.)

In the present experiment the operation of the organizing principle was presumably encouraged by the simple, repetitive nature of the psychokinetic task and by the rhythmic turning of the motor-driven die cage; while the intervening rest periods were short and quiet enough to cause no disruption of mood. The absence of observers and the repeated act of calling and recording die-face digits may also have been important.

The evidence for the operation of the organizing principle in the present data is two-fold: (1) the inter-column and inter-page decreasing chi-square of fit of the column scores to the chance-expected binomial distribution, and (2) the page-to-page increasing magnitude of the scoring-decline effect.

A large poorness-of-fit chi-square, when accompanied by a total-score deviation close to chance, may indicate erratic psychokinesis. For example, in the first column of the Page-1 column-score distributions of Figure 14.6, there is an excess of scores 7 and 8, balanced by an excess of 0 and 1 scores (where the score of 4 is chance expectation). Psychokinesis occurred, but was unstable as to sign.

Had these 7 and 8 scores been created, instead, by "constant" psychokinesis (i.e., by a small constant psychokinetic shift in the target-face probability within the first column of Page 1), all scores above 4 would have tended to be in excess, and scores below 4 would have tended to be in deficit. The resulting, hypothetical deviation in total score in that column might have been statistically significant, whereas, in fact, it was close to zero.

The force of this possibility can be seen by a comparison with the total-score deviation and poorness of fit in the first column of Page

3 of Figure 14.6, where a total-score deviation significant at the .01 level was achieved despite a poorness-of-fit chi-square smaller than in Page 1.

In this explanatory scheme, the data of the three experimenters all show psychokinesis but with varying degrees of organization, i.e., among these experimenters, when the poorness-of-score-fit chi-square is smaller, the decline effect is stronger (Figure 14.7).

If, despite its limitations, this interpretation is essentially correct, then the data confirm the empirically well established idea that psi performance can be improved by short-term preparation for experimental testing by inducing a favorable state of dissociation (Chapter 7).

In the present experiment, fitting each testing session into a 50-minute hour allowed, on the average, only about five minutes for experimenter and subject to get acquainted. Perhaps the first two pages of data per subject served as preparation for the more successful third page (Figure 14.6). If so, then a more adequate psychological preparation of the subject and experimenter before the throwing of the first dice might have resulted in a greater overall psychokinetic effect.

Alternatively, these findings suggest the following experimental possibility. Whereas, in most parapsychological experiments the effectiveness of psychological preparation can be inferred only by a comparison of results obtained with different preparational procedures, in the present experiment the progressive effect of preparation can be "watched" in the course of the experimental session. This direct exhibition of the effect of preparation might provide an efficient method for the testing of protocol variations.

THE AMBIVALENCE PRINCIPLE

The brain is coupled to, or exhibits, consciousness—we know not which. People, as conscious entities, engage in willing or wishing. We accept the fact that, when the brain has a conscious wish to do so, it can cause muscular motion of the body. However, as a result of many experiments similar in principle to the present one, it now appears that consciousness in its volitional aspect has access to another power which is capable of reconfiguring matter (e.g., controlling falling dice) without the intervention of the motor pathways of the brain. The exercise of this power has been called psychokinesis. As a practical matter, psychokinesis is so limited in apparent scope that its occurrence is still in dispute among scientists outside the field of parapsychology.

According to the principle of ambivalence proposed by McConnell and Clark (1982a), the unknown causal train from conscious wish to the psychokinetic execution of that wish passes through a dual channel exercising affirmation and negation. These tend to balance each other and thus prevent the desired psychokinetic end result.

Under various circumstances the positive and negative tendencies may be temporarily out of balance so that either the desired result or its logical opposite occurs. (The nature of the "logical opposite" is presumably defined by the perception of the brain and not by absolute logic.)

It would appear that the ambivalence principle, unlike the organizing principle, cannot be controlled by dissociation techniques. It can, however, be manipulated by the structure of the experiment and doubtless in other ways.

In emotional terms, it is as though there is a balance between hope for, and fear of, psychokinetic success. Initially, in any segment of a testing session, after proper preparation, hope tends to dominate and a positive effect is achieved. As the effort of willing continues, the balance shifts from affirmation to negation. In some cases, the decline in average success may pass through the level of chance expectation and a reverse effect results, as in the present experiment. In general, it can be said that, as an empirical fact and for reasons entirely unknown, sustained volition tends to shift psychokinetic control from affirmation to negation even though, at a verbal level, volition seems more or less constant.

The occurrence in the literature of inclined and U-shaped scoring curves, in addition to the more common declines, suggests that the balance of ambivalence is determined psychologically and not simply by physiological factors. This would not be surprising, since motivated behavior nearly always involves selecting between competing desires. On the other hand, at both neurological and behavioral levels, the concept of dynamic balance between excitation and inhibition is frequently encountered in the explanatory literature of psychobiology and it is almost universally assumed that the brain necessarily must regulate opposing processes, whether they be psychological or physiological.

McConnell and Clark (1982a) suspect that, in its entirety, the manner of operation of the ambivalence principle is largely a matter of genetic endowment and that it can be correlated with personality traits, although one is not yet able to say how. Exceptionally psychic persons are presumably those for whom ambivalence is readily shifted in the direction of affirmation. Conversely, it may be supposed that there are "born losers" whose psychic ability tends to defeat their conscious ambitions—in gambling and perhaps in living, generally. The possible sociological importance of further investigation is apparent.

15

HYPNOSIS AS PSYCHOKINESIS

ABSTRACT

The hypnosis research of L.L. Vasiliev and colleagues done in Leningrad between 1921 and 1938 has long been regarded by parapsychologists as evidence for extrasensory perception. The present author reviews part of that research and argues that those experiments in which a subject obeys nonsensorily conveyed suggestions to fall asleep and to awaken must instead be regarded as involving psychokinesis. Vasiliev's work, taken in historical perspective, suggests that the distinguishing feature between hypnosis and "mere suggestion" may be the utilization of psychokinesis by the hypnotic operator. Some possible implications of this finding are mentioned for parapsychology, for psychology, and for society as a whole.[1]

THE WORK OF L.L. VASILIEV

Some research done in the Soviet Union nearly half a century ago appears to have a crucial bearing upon the hypothesis that hypnosis is a parapsychological phenomenon. This research was reported in a book titled, *Experimental Studies of Mental Suggestion,* written by L.L. Vasiliev and published in Russian by the Zhdanov Leningrad State University (Vasiliev, 1962).

The book describes hypnotic research done by Vasiliev and his colleagues between 1921 and 1938. Its publication had to wait more than 20 years, for the duration of World War II and until the death of Stalin. Viewed as a parapsychological investigation, this work appears to be as good as any from the West. It is regrettable that it has been largely ignored.

I shall not try to cover the entire period of Vasiliev's research. Instead, I shall present a segment of the work done in 1935 and 1936 by three men, L.L. Vasiliev, I.F. Tomashevsky, and A.V.

---

1. If correct, the hypothesis I present in this paper is of profound importance. It is therefore not surprising that this paper was rejected for publication by six of the major journals of psychology and parapsychology.

Despite a four-year search, I have found no reason to doubt my thesis that psychokinesis is the essential element of hypnosis. Under the circumstances, believing in the importance of this paper, I have no choice but to publish it privately and without change, for the scrutiny of my peers.

So that no more time will be lost in ascertaining the truth of the matter, I have added in the following chapter the journal-referee criticisms as well as earlier correspondence with Drs. E.R. Hilgard and T.X. Barber. These men are widely regarded as the leading exponents of two opposing schools of hypnotic theory. It is their work that is challenged by my hypothesis.

Dubrovsky. The work was carried out at the Bekhterev Institute for Brain Research in Leningrad, where Vasiliev and Tomashevsky were physiologists and Dubrovsky was a medical hypnotist.

Following the lead of similar work by the French experimenters, Janet, Gibert, and Richet in the 19th Century, Vasiliev and colleagues investigated the possibility that a susceptible person could be put to sleep or awakened by the command of a hypnotic operator given from a distance under conditions that excluded sensory communication.

LEAD-CHAMBER EXPERIMENT

From among a number of Vasiliev experiments concerned with remote hypnosis, I shall first describe a series of 29 trials done under well controlled conditions in which the purpose was to put the test subject to sleep from a distance without regard to when she might later awaken.

The method of monitoring the subject was as follows. A small, soft rubber ball filled with air was connected by a long rubber tube and pipe to a bellows-operated stylus resting on a carbon-tape drum recorder located in another room. The subject reclined in a darkened isolation chamber with the ball tied to the palm of her hand. She was instructed to press the ball rhythmically throughout the experiment, although, in fact, she ceased to do so when she fell asleep. In this way, a permanent record could be made.

This particular experiment was carried out in a suite of rooms at the Bekhterev Institute, and involved one female subject as the receiver and two experimenters, one, the observer, and the other, the sender. In Figure 15.1 is shown the floor plan of the suite. The receiver lay on a bed inside a Faraday cage, labelled 2, in the large round room. To shield against radio waves, this cage had its sides, top, and bottom made of soldered sheet iron, one mm thick, and had an iron door that sealed tightly.

The sender was three rooms away, a distance of 13 meters, inside a lead-sheathed chamber, which is marked 1 in room A. The observer was in the side room marked B, and with him was the recording drum, 3, and an electrical signaling button, 4, whose functions I shall explain in a moment.

A diagram of the lead chamber is given as Figure 15.2. It was 1.8 meters high and one meter square—big enough to hold a chair and a wall shelf. The sender entered through a hole in the top, after which he lowered the lid so that its edges were sealed in a gully

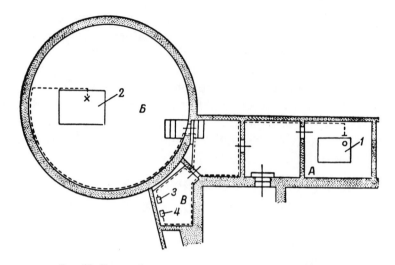

Рис. 22. План лаборатории с новым размещением приборов.

А — комната индуктора (*1* — стинцовая камера); *Б* — комната перципиента (*2* — камера Фарадея);
В — комната для регистрирующих приборов (*3* — кимографическая установка для регистрации
сна и бодрствования перципиента, *4* — кнопка для включения электромагнитного сигнала в стинцовой камере для индуктора).

Figure 15.1. Plan of laboratory in which *1* is a lead-covered chamber holding the sending experimenter in the two-experimenter tests, *2* is a Faraday cage holding the receiving subject, and *B* is the room for the observing experimenter, which contains a drum recorder (*3*) for monitoring the receiving subject and a button (*4*) for signaling the sending experimenter.

filled with mercury. The lead was 3 mm thick, which would effectively shield against a large range of electromagnetic radiation, including ordinary radio waves and soft X-rays.

On the outside of the lead chamber was an electromagnet, *2*, that was operated by the signaling button in the observer's room. Opposite the magnet, but on the inside of the lead chamber, there was an iron armature that could be tripped by the observer so as to turn off a battery-powered signaling lamp. With this arrangement there were no wires passing through the shield that might carry stray radio waves.

The experimental procedure was the following: After a restful conversation in the round room the receiver entered the Faraday cage and was instructed by the observer, who then closed the cage and went to the recording room, closing all doors behind him.

In the recording room he started the drum recorder and a stop watch, pushed the button to signal the beginning of the experiment to the sender, and recorded the time of day.

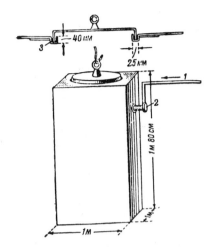

Figure 15.2. Lead-covered chamber, showing method of sealing lid in mercury gully to prevent electromagnetic radiation leakage.

Рис. 23. Внешний вид свинцовой камеры для экранирования индуктора. Вверху схематически изображено устройство для герметизации крышки.
1 — ввод из регистрационной комнаты; *2* — электромагнитная катушка; *3* — ртуть.

Meanwhile, the sender had gone to the lead-chamber room, *A*, taking with him one of three envelopes previously prepared by another experimenter. The sender climbed into the lead chamber, closed the lid, switched on the lamp, and opened the envelope, which contained one of three assignments: (1) Suggest sleep from within the lead chamber. (2) Open the lead-chamber lid and suggest sleep while standing on the chair with head protruding from the lead chamber. (3) Lift the chamber lid and stand on the chair, but do not suggest anything.

The sender opened the hatch or not, as required, and awaited the starting signal. He then continued to follow his instruction until he received a second signal from the observer, telling him that the subject had stopped pressing the rubber ball and was asleep. At that time the sender gave the assignment paper to the observer, who entered its instruction into the log.

Thus, the following three conditions were met:

1. Until the end of each test the observer in room *B* did not have knowledge of the particular assignment and merely acted as observer and recorder.

2. The sender opened the assignment envelope only when he was inside the closed lead chamber.

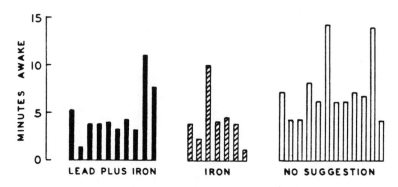

Figure 15.3. Data from two-experimenter tests, showing times to fall asleep under three experimental conditions: with remote suggestion when shielded by lead chamber and iron Faraday cage, with remote suggestion shielded by iron Faraday cage only, and without suggestion. The mean observed times were 4.71 ± .86 min, 4.21 ± 1.06 min, and 7.40 ± .98 min, respectively.

3. The subject was left alone to herself while the experiment took place.

The data of all 29 of the test sessions are shown in graphical form in Figure 15.3 The solid bars represent the time to fall asleep with mental suggestion given from within the lead chamber. The shaded bars are the same, but without lead-chamber shielding. The open bars are the time to fall asleep without suggestion.

With suggestion and with both iron and lead shielding, i.e., from within the lead chamber, the time averaged 4.71 ± .86 minutes. With suggestion and only iron shielding, the average time was 4.21 ± 1.06 minutes. Without suggestion, the time was 7.40 ± .98 minutes. For the cases when suggestion was given, the time difference between iron shielding and iron-plus-lead shielding is not statistically significant. The time difference between the no-suggestion and the pooled suggestion conditions is significant at the $p = 0.02$ level. Thus, suggestion at a distance was successful despite iron shielding; while the addition of lead shielding had no determinable effect.

ROULETTE-WHEEL EXPERIMENT

Before discussing the above results, I want to describe briefly another, longer series, done under somewhat similar conditions, but requiring only one experimenter.

In this experimental variation the receiving subject was placed,

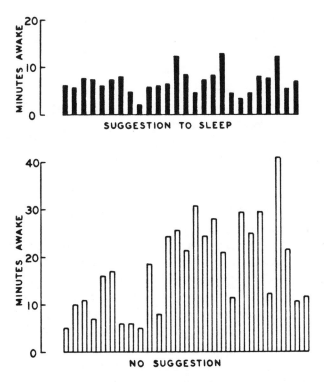

Figure 15.4. Data from the one-experimenter, roulette-wheel tests, showing times to fall asleep with the subject in the Faraday cage and the experimenter in room *B*. The mean observed times, with and without remote suggestion, were 6.8 ± .5 min and 17.7 ± 1.9 min, respectively.

as above, in the Faraday cage. The sender went to the recording room, where he started the drum recorder and at the same time gave a spin to a special roulette wheel containing an equal number of black and white sectors. If a black sector appeared, he made silent suggestions to go to sleep. For a white sector, he carried out the same experiment but without making suggestions.

The results of 26 sessions with suggestion and 27 without, are shown in Figure 15.4 The average time to fall asleep was 6.8 ± .5 minutes with suggestion and 17.7 ± 1.9 minutes without. The difference is statistically significant with a chance probability of less than 10^{-5}.

The subjects in this series were a man and three women, concerning whom Vasiliev says only that approximately the same number of experiments was done with each. In this and all similar experiments reported in Vasiliev's book, the subjects, for the most part, were clinical patients suffering from hysterical neurosis, although in some successful tests they were normal volunteers.

INTERPRETATION

Should we accept these results at face value? One cannot properly make a judgment from a second-hand account, but must go to the original report. There are two English translations of Vasiliev's book, one of which was done by the U.S. Government, presumably at the request of the Central Intelligence Agency.

I have described data from Chapter 7 of this book. Chapter 8, which deals with successful tests of the same kind conducted over distances up to 1700 km, is also of exceptional interest.

How are we to interpret these results? If we accept the hypothesis of a parapsychological interaction between the sender and the receiver, should we call it extrasensory perception (by the receiver) or psychokinesis (by the sender)? Did the sender send information which the receiver then accepted and acted upon of his own volition? Or did the sender directly affect the brain of the receiver? One might say: Was it a "suggestion" or was it an "order"?

From an operational point of view, I believe it must be called psychokinesis. If we speak of free will in these circumstances, we must mean that there was conscious consideration resulting in a choice. Although at the beginning of the test session the receiver may be presumed to have consciousiy put him or herself into a receptive frame of mind, there is no evidence whatsoever that, as the sender began his suggesting, the receiver consciously decided to accept his advice to go to sleep. Indeed, in the many experiments done by Vasiliev, but not reported above, in which the receiver was awakened by suggestion from a distance after having been hypnotically put to sleep, a conscious decision to accept a suggestion would seem to involve a contradiction in terms.

IMPLICATIONS

If, as illustrated in these experiments, it is possible for one person to initiate or terminate behavior in another person by means of psychokinesis, are there implications for ethics, medicine, sociology, or philosophy? Perhaps it is too soon to say.

We do not yet know the range or strength of psychokinetic ability and its distribution in the population. Nor do we know the degree and distribution of susceptibility to it. There is some information, but it is of a general and preliminary nature.

Parapsychologists believe that psychic ability, as shown by its reciprocal phenomena, extrasensory perception and psychokinesis, is widely but unevenly distributed in the population. They have found that the kinds of information that can be transferred by ESP include imagery and emotion, as well as the digitialized bits in card guessing. This suggests by analogy that one might project psychokinetic commands of great complexity. Moreover, as mentioned in Chapter 12, the maximum emergent energy rate in psychokinesis under exceptional circumstances is probably at least 10^{-4} watts (McConnell, 1976c). This is a small but not inconsequential fraction of the energy consumption rate of the human brain.

The situation with regard to susceptibility is clearer. Vasiliev's experiments were carried out in a hypnotic context. Both experimenters and subjects believed that they were engaged in a hypnotic experiment. In Chapter 4 of Vasiliev's book, which deals with suggestion of motor behavior from a distance, there can be no doubt that the subjects' behavior was typically "hypnotic." I see no reasonable basis for denying the inference that the defining element of true hypnosis, as distinct from response to "mere suggestion," is the use of psychokinesis by the operator. If so, our question about susceptibility to psychokinesis is really (at least in part) about susceptibility to hypnosis. Concerning that topic, there is a large scientific literature. I think it probable that, when the available information is more widely assimilated, it will be agreed that both psychokinetic power and psychokinetic susceptibility are universally but non-uniformly distributed in mankind.

I would like to bring to your attention an ethical imperative that would seem to follow from the idea that each of us may be able to influence directly the brain action of those around us.

In the light of what we now know about psychokinesis, would it not be sinful to wish evil upon, or even to feel hatred toward, our fellow humans, because thereby, to some unknown degree, we may be doing harm to them? That is to say, would it not be sinful unless there is a moral obligation for each of us to attempt by this means to reward those who are good and punish those who are evil?

Hypnosis and Psychology

The foregoing ideas need to be considered in historical perspective. Hypnosis has been investigated extensively by psychologists, especially since World War II. "Psychological Hypnosis" is one of the 41 membership divisions of the American Psychological Association. There are four American scientific and technical journals devoted to hypnosis. From all of this activity, roughly two schools of thought have emerged, which I shall identify by their most persuasive proponents, E.R. Hilgard and T.X. Barber.

E.R. Hilgard says, in effect, that hypnosis is what it seems to be: a mysterious psychological state in which the subject is dissociated and partially subservient to the operator. T.X. Barber, on the other hand, subsumes hypnosis under other familiar categories of behavior, thereby demystifying it.

According to Barber: "the concept of *hypnotic trance* and related concepts—*hypnotized, hypnosis,* and *hypnotic state*—are not only unnecessary but also misleading. . . . Subjects carry out so-called 'hypnotic' behaviors when they have positive attitudes, motivations, and expectations toward the test situation which lead to a willingness to think and imagine with the themes suggested [by the operator]" (Barber, Spanos, & Chaves, 1974, p. 5). Barber clearly believes that the brain of a hypnotzied person is not in a special state.

Hilgard considers hypnosis as "an altered state of consciousness" (1968, p. 10) without apparent commitment to the existence of a concomitant hypnotic brain state. In using the word "state," he seems to mean merely that something unusual and important is happening that can be characterized by a behavioral syndrome—it being understood that, as with most syndromes, individual differences are the rule rather than the exception.

I side with Hilgard in his "belief in the distinctiveness of hypnotic phenomena" (ibid., p. 21). It seems reasonable to recognize hypnosis as one among a number of occurring dissociated processes that can usually be differentiated in their totalities if not in their details. (By *dissociation* I mean a condition in which a person loosens or loses his normal sense of identity or of command over his cognitive processes.)

There is one feature of hypnosis recognized by both schools that I suspect is significant for the hypothesis that hypnosis is a psychokinetic effect. It is generally accepted that no physiological variable has been discovered whose values can identify exclusively the hypnotic state. This might be expected if dissociation (achievable by various means) is a physiological condition and psychokinesis is a superimposed process that defines the resulting behavior as "hypnotic."

HYPNOSIS AND PARAPSYCHOLOGY

There is irony in the proposition that hypnosis is the psychokinetic influence of one brain upon another. The Society for Psychical Research was founded in 1882 "to investigate that large group of debatable phenomena designated by such terms as mesmeric [hypnotic], psychical, and Spiritualistic" (*Proceedinge of the SPR, 1, 3*).

Eventually, as psychology took over hypnosis research and as spirit research was recognized as conceptually misbegotten, the Society busied itself almost entirely with "psychical phenomena" and the field metamorphosed into "parapsychology" whose proper concern was with extrasensory perception and psychokinsesis.

Beginning about 1960, hypnosis came back into parapsychology in two ways: as a possible training process for improving psychic ability, and as a dissociated state in which ESP might be more readily elicited. So far as I know, it has never been said in the serious literature that hypnosis might *be* a psychokinetic process.

For nearly 100 years parapsychologists have been familiar with the clinical experiments of the French school of psychiatry showing that hypnotic behavior could be produced (it was said) "by shared associations through mental telepathy" without sensory contact. Vasiliev's laboratory work, which sharpens the challenge, has been available in English since 1963. I find it surprising that no one has suggested that hypnosis is mediated by psychokinesis.

My interest in this matter began casually a few years ago. While preparing a classroom lecture on hypnotism, it occurred to me that hypnosis-as-psychokinesis was an interesting possibility that should be kept in mind. Later, in 1978, for the first time and for another purpose, I thoughtfully examined Vasiliev's book.[2] I was impressed by the quality of his work, and in a relatively quick shift of gestalt I became convinced by the logic of his findings that psychokinesis is almost certainly the essence of hypnosis.

I would guess that most parapsychologists will reject this idea—and well they might. If it is true, the following corollaries, among others, deserve consideration:

Psychokinesis has been the subject of intensive research by psychology for many years under the guise of hypnosis.

We are faced with the possibility that hypnosis is an ubiquitous,

---

2. While preparing *Encounters with Parapsychology*.

psi-mediated "brain washing" process that enters, to a greater or lesser extent, into all interpersonal relationships.

We may be "our brothers' keepers" in a more intimate and compelling sense than anyone of much importance since the Renaissance has really believed.

The cultural ramifications seem endless. Neither parapsychology nor psychology is ready for that kind of responsibility. If the above generalizations are plausible, they provide an adequate explanation of why the possibility of hypnosis as psychokinesis has been repressed by parapsychologists.

16

HYPNOSIS, PEER REVIEWED

IN SEARCH OF CRITICISM

In the preceding chapter I suggested, on the basis of the work of Vasiliev, that the essential element of hypnosis may be the psychokinetic control of the brain of the subject by the hypnotic operator. This hypothesis, if true, is important beyond estimation. It seemed doubtful, however, that so obvious a conception could have been overlooked for so many decades.

After a year of consideration in which I could find no alternative explanation for the Vasiliev research, I decided to seek criticism from other scientists. I prepared the paper which you have just read and sent it in February 1979 to Drs. E.R. Hilgard and T.X. Barber, these being the two well-known protagonists whose opinions I had reviewed in the paper. To both I said simply: "Any comment you might care to offer regarding the enclosed manuscript will be warmly appreciated. You need not return the manuscript."[1]

E.R. HILGARD

Dr. Hilgard's letter of reply in its entirety was as follows:

> I have never found the work of Vasiliev very convincing.
> To accept your interpretation of hypnosis as psychokinesis assumes the acceptance of his results as valid.
> Ideo-motor action seems to me much more plausible than psychokinesis as an explanation of what typically goes on in hypnosis.

"Ideo-motor action" is a label meaning unexplained automatic movement resulting from ideas. Because I could not see how a label could be regarded as an explanation for hypnotic behavior or for Vasiliev's findings, I wrote again, in part, as follows:

> I interpret your letter to mean that you might be inclined to accept my identification of hypnosis with psychokinesis if you could accept Vasiliev's experiments at face value, but, because you reject the Vasiliev work, you find nothing of interest in my proposal. . . .
> Does your reservation about Vasiliev's work stem from what you see as technical inadequacy? (Could you give an example?) Or does

---

1. Quotations herein below from my personal correspondence with Hilgard and Barber are printed with their permission.

your lack of conviction arise from the fact that Vasiliev and/or colleagues may have engaged in fraud in gathering their data?

Dr. Hilgard's second letter follows without deletion:

> My feeling of uneasiness about Vasiliev's work is not based on any suspicion of fraud but rather of scientific innocence. The Russians continue to use the idea of hypnosis as sleep, although if they were careful, they would find that it is not sleep, and shows none of the physiological indications of sleep. Furthermore, there is no physiological sign to tell when the person has entered hypnosis.
>
> Because of these uncertainties about hypnosis at a distance, which require some kind of indication that one person has become hypnotized and another not, the possibility of experimenter bias, which could very well be unconscious, is very great.

When he talks about "the Russians" confusing sleep and hypnosis, Hilgard must be referring to a tendency of the Soviet psychological literature, but he can hardly have meant to include Vasiliev, who, as far as I can determine, nowhere uses the idea of hypnosis as a variant of normal sleep.

When he speaks broadly of "experimenter bias" arising out of "scientific innocence," Hilgard may be referring to his only specific criticism, namely, his doubt that Vasiliev's subjects were actually hypnotized in as much as they were not specifically tested for the state of hypnosis.

Hilgard makes the point that there are no physiological tests for hypnosis, but he does not deal with the fact that there are no psychological tests either. The hypnotic "indications" he is asking for are behavioral performance tests that reflect degree of mental dissociation. Dissociation can, and often does occur without any "hypnotizing procedure" and therefore cannot be said to be the defining element of hypnosis. T.X. Barber, you will recall from Chapters 6 and 15, insists that there *is* no defining element and hence there is no such thing as hypnosis.

Despite his call for an "indication that one person has been hypnotized and another not," Hilgard's true concern may be that Vasiliev's subjects had fallen into physiologically normal sleep (determinable, in principle, by EEG) after being given a purportedly "hypnotic" command to "sleep." If so, I can only respond that shifting into normal sleep is a common occurrence in the so-called hypnotic trance and this provides no escape from the fact that in the Vasiliev experiments the subjects were "put to sleep" by commands given from a distance without sensory communication. It would appear that Hilgard has avoided the challenge he was offered.

T.X. BARBER

In his reply to my inquiry Barber began: "I very much appreciate the opportunity to read 'Hypnosis as Psychokinesis.' The major problems I have with the hypothesis is that I do not see how it can explain the following interrelated findings."

Barber then presented a list of behavioral-performance test results commonly regarded as indicating the hypnotic "state" but which can, and often do, occur in the absence of a hypnotic operator. He next conjectured that, if Vasiliev had tried, he might have successfully demonstrated some of these other hypnotic indicators in addition to sleep induction. Barber closed with the statement: "My conjecture can be tested at any time in an experiment with very good hypnotic subjects. I believe that an empirical test could go far in answering the important question raised by your paper."

This was a fine letter as a statement of Barber's well known position on hypnosis, but it did not seem to bear upon my thesis. The induction of other hypnotic phenomena by means of an extrasensorily transmitted mental order had, in fact, been demonstrated by Vasiliev as reported in chapters of his book that I did not review in my paper, but why this would help answer "the important question raised by [my] letter" is not apparent to me.

I wrote again to Barber, hoping to draw him out on the idea that the principle of explanatory parsimony requires we assume (1) that, whatever its nature, the kind of brain control exerted by Vasiliev can likewise occur in the more usual, face-to-face hypnotic situation, and (2) that this control is mediated by the same psychological mechanism that operates, for example, in the so-called psychokinetic control of gaming dice. Barber did not reply.

Although I did not say so, I believe that the interpretation I have provided of hypnosis as a psychokinetic phenomenon will resolve the Hilgard-Barber controversy. Toward that end, perhaps the most useful information to come out of this correspondence was the fact that neither Hilgard nor Barber objected to my description of their respective viewpoints in my paper.

PSYCHOLOGICAL REVIEW

Having drawn a blank in my search for criticism by private consultation, I next submitted my paper sequentially to six journals for which I considered it appropriate. In all cases the manuscript was rejected, and I am thus left with the criticisms of only a small group of editors and referees. So that the process of peer review will not be entirely thwarted, I shall present and analyze these journal responses.

My journal of first choice was the American Psychological Association's *Psychological Review,* which, according to its flyleaf:

> publishes articles that make theoretical contributions to any area of scientific psychology. Preference is given to papers that advance theory rather than review it and to statements that are specifically theoretical rather than programmatic.

To the editor I wrote:

> For such a simple paper perhaps you will agree that there is no reason to waste the time of referees. The manuscript is short. You will perceive the issues, and I doubt that you will feel a need for advice. . . . Yours for less due process, R.A. McConnell

Editor W.K. Estes replied, in part, as follows:

> The problem is not that there is anything wrong with your paper so far as I can see, but just that it doesn't fit into the journal that the *Psychological Review* has become during the past two or three decades. [I] give serious consideration only to papers that would be regarded as theoretical contributions to psychology as that notion is understood by our population of referees. And it will be no surprise to you that, on that criterion, your paper has just come to the wrong place.
>
> While thinking about your paper and what I could say about it, I leafed back through earlier issues of the *Psychological Review* with the thought that at a much earlier period a paper such as yours would have fit in perfectly well. Certainly, that idea was well borne out in the oldest issue I could find on my shelves [May 1936].

What Dr. Estes seemed to be saying is: "Although the evidence may be sound, the idea is too simple to be regarded as 'theoretical' by today's paychologists." Dr. Estes is a sophisticated scientist who understands the role of theory. Hence, his explanation of his rejection of my paper may have been intended as a tactful condemnation of his colleagues.

PSYCHOLOGICAL BULLETIN

Next I tried the APA's *Psychological Bulletin,* which, according to its flyleaf:

publishes evaluative reviews and interpretations of substantive and methodological issues in the psychological research literature.

To the editor, I wrote as I had to *Psychological Review,* adding that I thought my manuscript would qualify as an "interpretation of a substantive issue." Editor R.J. Herrnstein replied as follows:

> I am sorry to say [that your paper] is not appropriate for the *Bulletin.* Although I found it interesting, it is clearly not the sort of integrative review of a psychological literature that we specialize in.

JOURNAL OF ABNORMAL PSYCHOLOGY

Professor A.M. Buchwald, editor of the APA's *Journal of Abnormal Psychology,* rejected my paper with the following comment:

> The hypothesis that the defining element of hypnosis is the use of psychokinesis by the operator strikes me as unduly speculative. Even if one were to accept the results of the Vasiliev experiments and your interpretation of them, the results would not rule out alternative explanations of hypnosis. If the subjects were actually hypnotized prior to the experiments, the results would, at most, show that hypnotized subjects could be affected psychokinetically. I think adherents of both the Hilgard view and the Barber view would argue that this does not show that hypnotic suggestions, in general, involve psychokinesis.

This criticism might be paraphrased as follows: "Even if it be granted that both hypnosis and psychokinesis occurred in the Vasiliev experiments, why assume that they are the same phenomenon?"

Answer: Why not? Both phenomena are totally unexplained and are believed by some psychologists to be nonexistent. These supposedly different phenomena share the same identifying logical element; namely, that the will of the operator is psychologically imposed upon an external entity. Historically, these phenomena acquired different names when they were elicited in different social settings. In the Vasiliev distant-hypnosis experiments there is no way to make an operational distinction. And, more generally, there is no basis for excluding the occurrence of psychokinesis in any hypnosis experiment, regardless of how one might define "hypnosis." If one tentatively grants that both hypnosis and psychokinesis are real phenomena, methodological parsimony applied to Vasiliev's research requires that they be assumed identical.

AMERICAN PSYCHOLOGIST

The APA's all-purpose *American Psychologist* "publishes articles on current issues in psychology as well as empirical, theoretical, and practical articles on broad aspects of psychology." To its editor I wrote:

> Somewhere among the journals of the APA there must be a place for every psychological paper if it is of sufficient importance. Perhaps you will agree that mine is an empirical-theoretical paper with broad implications for psychology.

In due time the appropriate associate editor reported that he and two referees concurred that "the logic and text of your manuscript are difficult to follow and do not find support in the broad literature of psychokinesis and hypnosis." He sent along the referees' comments.

One referee said only that the paper was too specialized for the *American Psychologist.* The other created an 850-word essay starting with Mesmer's belief in animal spirits and continuing in a style appropriate to a classroom lecture, as follows:

> In my everyday, ordinary state of consciousness I draw on all of my senses—I see, I hear, and yet I select out those perceptions that are consistent with my understanding of the consensually validated world. I may deliberately choose to alter my state of consciousness by restricting input of certain perceptions in order to more actively focus on a more limited range of perception. My awareness may no longer reflect the consensually validated world, but rather it is a reflection of my own personal experience. But I always have a choice as to whether or not I wish to engage in such a switch, and it is I who does the switching.
>
> [A fortiori,] the experimenter in a hypnotic situation has *no* tangible powers to move the subject. Rather, the experimenter functions as a teacher who instructs, gives directions, even orders, but it is the subject (student) who carries out these orders, if he chooses.

The last is an affirmation of the doctrinaire position that no one can be controlled against his will by hypnosis. The referee then went on to ask these questions:

> What was the "nature" of the restful conversation [given to prepare the hypnotic subject]? Was the subject given implicit instructions to sleep during the experiment? What about the implicit suggestions inherent in a sealed-off cage with sensory deprivation as a stimulus to sleep? Was the non-suggestion condition given the same "restful conversation" as the other condition?

Only the last question is relevant to the hypothesis under test, and it is answered in the manuscript by the fact that the experimenter learned the suggestion/non-suggestion condition *after* the subject had been isolated.

Other questions followed, sometimes phrased as "statements of concern":

> I am concerned about the use of parametric statistics with such a small number of subjects. [The raw data are presented in the manuscript and the ratio-of-variances test is obviously adequate for the hypothesis under test, which relates to trials and not to subjects treated.] Was there a control group of subjects? [None was needed. In these fixed-sample experiments each subject served as his own control.] I am concerned that the subjects were primarily clinical patients suffering from hysterical neurosis. Would the same results be obtained with a larger sample and with "normal" subjects? [The question does not bear upon the hypothesis under test.]

JOURNAL OF PARAPSYCHOLOGY

Having learned of no weakness in my paper from psychologists, I sent it next to the *Journal or Parapsychology,* where it was rejected. From 300 words of referee comment, the following explain the rejection:

> [Falling asleep under these experimental conditions] can just as readily be conceptualized as a voluntary trying or an unconsciously initiated trying following a telepathic reception, as by a psychokinetic response. . . . I am open to the idea of psychokinetic influences on other people's brains, but there is no clear evidence for it here, and there is a long-established alternative of "ordinary" interpretations [i.e., ESP plus hypnosis].

I responded to the editor, in part, as follows:

> In this experimental situation, if a distinction is to be made between PK and ESP, it must be operational in principle rather than semantic. Granted there was a psychic causal train from agent to percipient, the possible alternatives as expressed in presently available language would seem to be these: Was the information passed to the brain of the percipient and responded to freely (ESP), or did the information control the brain of the percipient (PK)? By "responded to freely," in this situation I mean that the subject's response was consciously and voluntarily executed. For the Vasiliev experiments there would seem to have been no conscious voluntary execution of the command to fall asleep and there was certainly none when the subject, while asleep, was commanded to waken.

My paper creates what Thomas Kuhn calls a "paradigm conflict," which can be resolved only by a gestalt shift. What that means can be illustrated by the following example, discussed at length by Kuhn (1962): Aristotle saw a stone as falling toward its final point; Galileo saw it falling from its initial position. The difference seems trivial, but it led to the break-out of science from the stagnation of the Middle Ages.

Those scientists who are not accustomed to thinking operationally may nevertheless be able to make the necessary gestalt shift by re-reading Myers's (1886) account of the experiments by Gibert and Janet in which Léonie B was put into a hypnotic trance at unexpected times from a distance and against her will. [Further references to similar early experiments will be found in Alvarado, 1980.]

Your referee believes it is impossible to distinguish PK from ESP in these Vasiliev experiments. I disagree for the reasons given in the manuscript. However, if I were to grant your referee's position for the sake of argument, where would it lead us?

We must remember that PK, ESP, and hypnosis are three observable effects of which we have no scientific understanding. Proponents of hypnosis use the word, "suggestion," which has no more explanatory power than "extrasensory perception." One modern school denies that hypnosis has any unique phenomenological existence whatsoever.

Your referee says that ESP and hypnosis are "ordinary" and "long established" interpretations and are therefore preferable to PK. That is his sole reason for rejecting my paper. What does the word "ordinary" mean, other than "long established"? In this case, what is an "interpretation" other than a name? It would appear that your referee's reason for preferring ESP plus hypnosis is simply that these are both long-established names. That is not science but medieval scholasticism.

My PK proposal has scientific content in that it combines two phenomena hitherto regarded as separate. Everyone has been calling this kind of experiment, ESP plus hypnosis. I suggest that it is one phenomenon, PK. This idea has evidently never before been expressed.

Editor K.R. Rao replied, in part, as follows:

All the papers submitted to us are refereed, and the referees' comments largely determine the final decision. Your paper was read by a member of our staff and by a distinguished parapsychologist whose competence may not be questioned. Both recommended that we not publish your paper. After the referees' comments were in, I myself read the paper carefully and felt that the referees' recommendations were justified. . . .

After receiving your 24 March letter, we decided that, in view of your comments, we should seek the opinion of another referee. His comments just came in, and I am sorry to say that his recommendation is: "This paper should not be published in the *Journal of Parapsychology*. Rather than serving to clarify issues, it confuses them." I'm afraid I have to agree with him. I have enclosed the detailed comments of this referee.

Out of this referee's 900 words, I have selected the one paragraph that I believe expresses his position:

> McConnell's attempt to differentiate psychokinesis from extrasensory response by showing that presumably the subject did not deliberately or by conscious consideration, enter into sleep (or whatever the state was in this case) is misguided and ignores both elements of ordinary psychology and what is known in parapsychology. Internally-generated actions need not always derive either from conscious deliberation or choice. This is especially true with regard to slipping into states of mind, affective states, or judgmental frames of mind. Also, many spontaneous cases of apparent psi, as well as considerable laboratory work in nonintentional ESP, suggest that internally-directed (controlled) ESP may occur rather automatically in response to our needs and may influence our thoughts, feelings, or behavior in ways which we do not cause deliberately. The central structure of argument in this paper is on exceptionally soggy ground.

Except for the first and last sentences, which assert my lack of understanding, I accept this paragraph as obviously true. What the referee is saying is that it is well known that, quite without a hypnotic operator, a subject may reach out by ESP and gather information upon which he may then act without a conscious decision to do so .

Let us translate this idea to the Vasiliev experiments and see if it applies. What the referee would like us to believe is that the hypnotic subject wanted (had a need) to go to sleep to please the experimenter. Therefore, the subject, without conscious awareness, reached out by ESP to learn from the sender when to go to sleep. *Voilà!* We have shown that ESP is just as good an explanation as PK, and since the ESP explanation has always been preferred, it would add nothing but confusion to talk about PK.

I see at least two things methodologically wrong with this verbal legerdemain. It is non-operational and it is unnecessarily complex.

Parapsychologists are free, if they wish, to abandon all conceptualization and to say that we should speak of psi, but never of ESP or PK. This does not appear to be methodologically prudent. There are situations where, under our present conceptualization, ESP cannot be PK (e.g., in clairvoyance) and where PK can never be ESP (in the willed moving of stable systems). The distinction is one of causal directiveness to and from a center of consciousness. Where two people are involved, I am proposing that the distinction between PK and ESP be operationally defined: If *A* consciously orders and *B* unconsciously acts, it is PK. If *B* consciously acts, it is ESP. This conforms to common sense and to the concepts of free will and moral responsibility, which are lurking behind this discussion. If, as a result of this definition, most interpersonal psi involves PK, so much the worse for ESP.

The second methodological flaw in the ESP-plus-hypnosis theory is that it postulates two mysterious processes. If, instead, one conceptualizes the Vasiliev experiments as involving PK plus hypnosis, there remains no justification for assuming they are separate processes (except the vested interests of parapsychologists and hypnotists). Once these processes are assumed identical, all kinds of puzzle pieces begin to fall together. I won't tell what I see. That's fun for you to have. But I object to referees and editors using bad logic to suppress my hypothesis.

To return to this same *Journal of Parapsychology* referee: As his critique progressed, his true state of mind began to reveal itself:

> Granted that persons' behavior, thoughts, feelings might be subject to some PK influence, why link this specifically to "hypnosis"? Surely it could occur in other contexts than those usually identified with hypnosis.

The first of the above two sentences says to me that the referee has granted the possibility of the main leg of my thesis, namely, that there was psychokinetic control by the sender upon the brain of the subject in the Vasiliev experiments.

I agree with the second sentence, although I would rephrase it thus: "Surely a lot of hypnosis occurs unrecognized in everyday life."

A little later, the referee says without explanation: "In my opinion, McConnell seriously misrepresents E.R. Hilgard's view of hypnosis." I can only respond that Hilgard did not complain after reading my paper. I suppose that the discrepancy arises from the fact that hypnosis theory is in such chaos that Hilgard's extensive writings are in a class with Freud's writings and the Bible: Everyone makes his own interpretation to support his own beliefs.

If you suspect by this time that there is a hidden emotional factor in the opposition to the publication of my paper, your suspicion may be strengthened by the following excerpts from the same referee:

> I doubt that anyone would be too troubled by this paper—except anti-psi skeptics—if the author were merely suggesting that the procedures (and resultant internal information processing) associated with hypnosis make a person's thoughts and behavior more subject to PK influence. Unfortunately, he does not stop at this more parsimonious point, but progresses beyond any possible inference from the data . . . .
>
> The thrust of this paper seems to revivify the image of the hypnotist as a powerful Svengali with magical powers over the subject. Modern hypnotists and hypnosis researchers are the first to say that this is not the case. . . .
>
> One cannot see where the author is going with his suggestion, how it could really be useful for research, or how it is related in any cogent fashion to earlier research. I could say much more, but I do not think this poorly thought-out paper warrants it.

JOURNAL OF THE *ASPR*

Ever hopeful, I next tried the *Journal of the American Society for Psychical Research*. The editor's rejection in July 1980 was accompanied by the comments of two referees. From the first, I present one paragraph that constitutes his argument.

> The author thinks his central point about the ambiguity between telepathy and PK novel and important. Novel it is not, and whether or not telepathy can be construed as PK (if it is, then the system affected must be physical—e.g., a brain), there is still the related and *well-recognized* problem of whether telepathy should be construed as active or passive. Telepathy is merely the paranormal interaction between the mental states of two individuals, and so it is up in the air, *in the very concept of telepathy* (such as it is), which individual intiates the causal chain.

This referee is a careless reader. The claimed novelty of my paper does not lie in the commonplace idea that telepathy and PK may be indistinguishable under some circumstances. What I propose is that, in the Vasiliev experiments, PK unambiguously occurred and that it constituted the hypnotic process. The referee asserts that, by definition, telepathy may be construed as either passive or active, i.e., either ESP or PK, indifferently. Because *telepathy,* as a word, is controversial and uncertain in its implications, I avoid it as a descriptive label. This referee has embraced a topic for discussion that does not relate to my paper.

From the comments of the second *JASPR* referee, only the first two paragraphs are essential; the rest being speculative asides.

> I do not recommend publication of this paper in its present form for several reasons. While the author raises some interesting and potentially important issues, the presentation is provocative rather than illuminating and fails to provide any justification whatsoever for its central thesis, that hypnosis is a conditon of physiological dissociation (whatever that means) plus a superimposition of PK guidance and control.
>
> The author's basis for interpreting the Vasiliev distant-hypnosis results as PK rather than ESP seems to me to be based on a fundamental misunderstanding of the nature and role of suggestion and suggestibility as applied to hypnosis: He asks, "Was it a 'suggestion' or an 'order'?" and argues for the latter because the subject did not engage in conscious deliberation prior to responding to the (distant) operator's instructions. Effective suggestion, however, *is an order,* one that is accepted and acted upon *without* conscious deliberation. By definition, suggestibility bypasses conscious decision-making and evaluative processes. Thus, I believe the argument presented in the last paragraph [under "Interpretation"] is mistaken. It is also irrelevant, since, even if we were to grant the viability of the author's suggestion/order distinction, this would still not enable us to resolve phenomenal characterization of the effect as either PK or ESP, since orders must be received before they can be acted upon and this implies perceptual input, albeit nor necessarily on the level of conscious registration.

Before sending his comments to the *Journal of the ASPR,* this referee, who is a friend of mine, telephoned to urge that I withdraw my paper because he found it extraordinarily bad and because of the high esteem he has for me. In retrospect, I interpret his recommendation to mean that he wanted to protect my reputation against the charge of senility—a not implausible charge since I was 66 at the time and had published no experimental papers in parapsychology for 12 years.

After a friendly discussion of the merits of my paper, I told him that he should send in his criticisms to the journal so that I could examine them thoroughly. I said that, unless I could discover the error in my thinking, I intended to publish the paper somewhere.

His written comments followed his oral arguments closely on the whole, but I noticed that while, in writing, he called my paper "provocative," on the telephone he described my discussion of the implications of my hypothesis as "waving a red flag in front of a bull."

This referee imputes to me "a fundamental misunderstanding of the nature and role of suggestion and suggestibility as applied to hypnosis." He then points out that effective hypnotic suggestion is *always* an "order" that is acted upon without conscious deliberation. What he is saying is that hypnosis by an operator always involves "mind control." I preferred to reach this controversial conclusion by generalization from the Vasiliev experiments, where the evidence seemed to be more clearcut than what one finds in the circumspect literature of hypnosis, and where the absence of sensory communication "waves a red flag."

This referee's discussion in the remainder of the paragraph I do not understand. He seems to be saying that, even if one accepts my suggestion/order distinction, one will not know whether to call it PK or ESP since even "orders" have to be perceived. I surmise that this is a semantic entanglement, to be explained as follows

In an ordinary social transaction mediated by sensory means, an "order" must be perceived and then the receipient consciously decides whether he is obliged to follow it. That is not the kind of "order" I meant. My use of the word was metaphorical. This is what I said in my paper, under "Interpretation":

> Did the sender send information which the receiver then accepted and acted upon of his own volition? Or did the sender directly affect the brain of the receiver? One might say: Was it a "suggestion" or was it an "order"?

The response of this referee has something in common with those of his predecessors. They all start with the opinion that hypnosis cannot possibly be psychokinesis and then find difficulty supplying reasons for their position. After consideration by a dozen of the best available psychologists and parapsychologists, two of them members of the National Academy of Sciences, the challenge of my paper remains: In some new and awesome sense, are we our brother's psychological keepers?

Part III

THE SOCIOLOGY
OF PARAPSYCHOLOGY

17

SCIENTIFIC THEORY

SCIENTISTS AND METHOD

I have described examples of the laboratory evidence for extrasensory perception and psychokinesis. If you have not studied the original reports of even these examples, let alone the larger body of evidence from which they were drawn, you may not wish to accept the phenomena as experimentally established. I believe it must be agreed, however, that there is at least a prima facie case for ESP and PK. If so, one may wonder why psychologists, physicists, and biologists have not moved into parapsychology in order to examine its claims.

Indeed, for immediate progress in parapsychology it might be more useful to study this "avoidance behavior" of scientists than it would be to learn more about psi phenomena themselves. In this survey of the field I have been exploring a mystery. In the earlier chapters I have presented psychological and evidential background. Now I shall try to answer the question: Why are scientists not interested in parapsychology?

Like any good mystery, this one is solved with a surprising twist, namely, that scientists, almost without exception, do not understand scientific method. Some of the best—even Nobel Prize winners—have often shown little understanding of the way that science works. Most scientists are experts in one area and have some feeling for the relation of their area to the rest of science, but usually they have only a superficial grasp of the whole of science as a social and intellectual enterprise.

If what scientists do is important, surely it is important to study *how* they do it. Competent scientists follow scientific method in their work. Usually, they learn to do this by laboratory training without verbal understanding—in the same way one learns to ride a bicycle. Scientists, as distinct from philosophers of science, are not formally taught the subtleties of scientific method and are almost entirely unaware that they exist.

As a result, with rare exceptions, scientists are incapable of evaluating a truly novel problem. If you challenge a scientist to step into new territory, he will do so if he is able to keep one foot in the old. But if he is required to jump, so that both feet leave the ground, he is traumatized by fear of the unknown—just as though he were an ordinary human being.

WHAT IS SCIENCE?

Our remaining task in this book is to gain a better understanding of science and scientific method and thus to climb to a higher plane of observation from which to judge the reality of psi phenomena.

What is science? Science, or more precisely, the scientific process, is a combination of observation and mental reflection—of sensory perception and thinking. Scientific activity differs from ordinary observation and thinking in only one way: science is disciplined. Thus, when we study science, we see that it is merely an extension of the business of everyday living.

Science consists of disciplined observation combined with disciplined thought, directed toward understanding the generalities of nature. By disciplined observation I mean observation governed by rules summarizing our past experience in making observations. For example, one rule is that you must plan each step before you do it. Another, is that you must record the results as you obtain them. Likewise, disciplined thinking means thinking according to rules discovered from past successes. Science is a methodical search for reality. Intellectual method governs science and is all that importantly distinguishes it from problem solving in everyday life.

It is commonly said that science is "public." Knowledge that is not public, in the sense I shall describe, is not the concern of science. For example, to the extent that religion does not claim to be publicly verifiable, it cannot be a part of science.

Science assumes that there is a physical world outside the observer with an existence that is independent of his thinking about it. Science limits itself to public observation in that physical world.

For an observation to be public does not mean that anyone can make it at any time or that it can necessarily be made jointly with others. If the observation concerns a rare, natural occurrence, not experimentally reproducible, such as an eclipse of the sun, the observer may have to be in the right place at the right time. If the observation is a subjective phenomenon, such as degree of pain, one cannot directly share it with another observer. Nevertheless, both rare and subjective observations can be made "publicly," under the right circumstances and with sufficient ingenuity.

To be accepted as part of the business of science, observations must be repeatable, not only time and time again for a single observer, but for many observers. This is one way of describing what we mean by "science is public."

SYSTEMS AND STATES

It is true that science seems to depend upon certain special philosophic assumptions. However, when examined, these are found to be merely the assumptions we use in the course of ordinary living and which we learn from historical as well as immediate experience. Science assumes, for example, that nature is repetitive, exhibiting patterns that are the same for all time and throughout all parts of the observable universe.

If nature allows the repetition of events independently in various places, the rules governing the action of these events and any description of the necessary starting conditions must be expressed by mathematical functions that show decreased effectiveness with distance. Otherwise, a repetition in one place might interfere with another happening somewhere else. More specifically, we must assume the existence of scientific "systems" or "domains" within which things will occur more or less independently of other domains.

For example, if I expect to demonstrate Newton's laws of motion, I can do it in this room just as well as in the room next door. The result I obtain will not be affected much by what is going on in the room upstairs. Of course, if my experiment involves the pull of gravity, I must be on the earth and not on the moon if I want my results to agree with those obtained by other experimenters on earth.

More generally, if I want an experiment to be repeatable, I must not only describe the apparatus and the conditions of its use: I must also know what is important and what is not for the success of the experiment. This is called "defining the experimental system," and it is one of the unsolved problems of parapsychology.

The difficulty seems to be that one cannot define the system until one knows the rules of the game, i.e., the relevant "laws of nature." And one cannot discover the laws of nature until one knows how to define the system. That dilemma is an essential aspect of pioneering science.

For the most part, what goes on in laboratories the world over is not pioneering science but "normal" or elaborative science. In normal science one already knows a law of nature, and the job of the experimenter is merely to extend that law and to fill in the gaps in our store of factual information surrounding it. Because most scientists engage only in normal science, they have little understanding of pioneering science. This suggests the question: How does science make progress? I shall discuss that question in the next chapter.

Let us now return to the problem of defining the system. To set up a laboratory experiment intended to measure the universal constant of gravitational attraction using a ball rolling down an inclined trough, one must specify the ball, the trough, the mass of planet earth, and the distance from the center of the earth. That is all.

But what about air friction or the gravity of the moon? We know from past experience that both air friction and the pull of the moon will be small for a ball rolling down a trough in this room. These will be what we call "second-order effects." Of course, if we drop the ball from a tall building, so that its velocity reaches several hundred meters per second, wind friction will become a first-order effect.

Will the presence of the observer make a difference? We can be sure that—psychokinesis aside—he would have no measurable effect on the rolling ball if he kept his distance. But if we did a physics experiment involving subatomic particles, we would have to allow for the influence of the observer, or more precisely, for the influence of his observational probe. In parapsychology, as you may know by now, one of the major obstacles to experimentation is the interaction between the experimenter and what he would like to regard as his isolated experimental system.

In specifying an experimental system, it is not enough to describe, vaguely, how important any one factor may be. One must say exactly what factors ("variables") are important and what are unimportant. One must be explicit because the laws of nature we are seeking must be expressed in terms of the variables we select as important.

Every scientific system can be thought of as in a particular condition at a given time. This is known as the "state of the system." The variables that determine this state are usually called "state variables," although they might well be called "system variables." Thus, in order to write a law of nature, we must describe the physical system or domain within which it will be obeyed, and we must specify the state variables in terms of which it will be expressed.

How does one describe the system? This is done by telling how to go about performing an experiment demonstrating the law of nature. And how does one specify the state variables? By saying exactly how they are to be measured.[1]

What do we do with the variables associated with weak, higher order effects? Ordinarily, they will be omitted from the theory—usually because they belong in some other theory, but sometimes because the theory under development is over-simplified and will need modification later.

PARAPSYCHOLOGY AS SCIENCE

The foregoing ideas underlie Western science and modern technology. How well does parapsychology fit these ideas?

As noted earlier, throughout history, psi phenomena have occurred spontaneously. It is only recently and with limited success that they have been produced experimentally. These phenomena are publicly observable, but not easily so.

In science generally, special apparatus, special training, and special physiological ability may be needed to be a successful observer. A color-blind person cannot, himself, do visual color experiments. In parapsychology it is becoming increasingly evident that experiments cannot be done by everyone, or even by all those who are trained in psychology. It would appear that one must, in some sense, be "intellectually innocent" to be a successful parapsychologist. Otherwise one will suppress the phenomena by one's presence.

I am not sure what "innocent" means, but I suspect it means a certain lack of self-awareness, a constitutional set against introspection. The condition I am specifying is not a lack of ordinary introspection. Some of our best experimental parapsychologists would qualify as poets. My guess is that the kind of self-awareness that destroys psi phenomena is what, for want of a clearer idea, I would call irrepressible analytic self-awareness. In the chapter on "Factors Favoring Psi" I discussed this problem in terms of the awareness-related concept of dissociation.

---

1. The principle that we know only through what we do (observe) is associated most often with the physicist-philosopher, P.W. Bridgman (1927), under the term "operationalism" and is an integral element of the method of "logical empiricism." (See below.)

These speculations could help explain why most, technically competent scientists have little use for psi phenomena. The stereotypical scientist may sometimes experience psi spontaneously and unwillingly, but he cannot catch it in the laboratory and he does not feel a high professional respect for his more loosely organized colleagues who can.

The problem we are up against in parapsychology is that of isolating the experimental system—of keeping the experimenter out of the system or at least a fixed variable within it. When the experimenter thinks too much about his experiment, he may be changing crucial conditions.

THE ROLE OF LOGIC

"Logical empiricism" and "logical positivism" are roughly equivalent expressions used to describe scientific method. So far, I have talked about observation, which is the essence of empiricism or positivism. How about the logical end of these terms?

Whatever it may have meant 100 years ago, logic today means "symbolic logic," as set forth definitively by Whitehead and Russell in their *Principia Mathematica* in 1910. Under their system, all of mathematics became a part of logic. I am not a student of logic and cannot estimate what influence the formalism of symbolic logic is having upon the actual working of science. My present concern is with what symbolic logic has to say about the nature of physical reality.

As Whitehead and Russell made clear, mathematics must be viewed as a system of relationships that contain no empirical truth. For example, the proposition "A is greater than B" is a form without observational meaning until we agree that A and B represent, for example, the heights of John and Mary respectively. Then "A is greater than B" becomes a scientific proposition and may be true or false.

Similarly, all mathematical relationships, no matter how complex, may be consistent or inconsistent with the manipulational definitions of the symbols employed, but they are empty and without scientific meaning until they are connected with reality by identifying each noun symbol with observation.

In this view, mathematical manipulation is merely an exposition of tautologies, a display of inevitable implications. Mathematics cannot create new empirical truths. It can only show those truths that are inherent in the observational data with which it starts.

In more practical terms, you get out of analysis only what you put in. Those of you who have worked with computers are familiar with this idea in the acronym, GIGO, which stands for "garbage in: garbage out." This, I take it, is the basic truth of symbolic logic.

I do not belittle symbol manipulation, of which spoken language is the most common example. Speech is what separates humanity from the lower animals. Mathematics is another, more precise form of symbol manipulation, but it is suitable only for relatively simple situations. Human intelligence can be thought of as the ability to perceive logical relationships, whether implicitly by intuition, or explicitly using symbols. All of scientific progress we owe to symbol manipulation. Let us see how this is so.

PERCEPTION AND MODELS

If we open our eyes in a strange room, we catch a few lines, a bit of color and shading, and we perceive instantly: "That object is a chair." In our intellectual apprehension of the space-time universe we begin with primitive sensory cues that our brains integrate into perceptions of immediate, man-sized reality.

Following the scheme of Henry Margenau (1950), I shall represent our primitive sensations by a plane perpendicular to the page of this book, as shown in Figure 17.1. Close to the plane lie our immediate mental constructs, such as chairs, desks, books, and other people. More abstract things are located farther away from the plane. Notice that we cannot reach directly even the simplest objects. They are separate from the plane of perception.

My perception of a mathematics book laid before me would be quite different in flavor and content from the perception of the same book by a man who could not understand its mathematical content but who had spent his life in the manufacture of paper. Perceptions are personal responses. The total reality of the book can never be known to anyone.

It is important to note that we have no immediate perception of submicroscopic reality, nor of astronomical reality that is hidden from the telescope. The remote parts of reality are known to us only through models, based on inference drawn from other models representing, in turn, nearby familiar objects, such as boxes, balls, and sticks.

Even immediately perceivable objects, such as a railroad bridge,

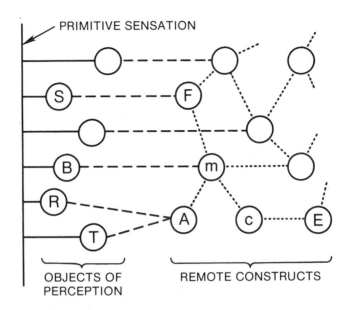

Figure 17.1. Margenau's diagram of physical reality, indicating Newton's Second Law of Motion, $F = mA$, and Einstein's mass-energy equivalence, $E = mc^2$, where F is force, m is mass, A is acceleration, E is electromagnetic energy, c is the velocity of light, S is a spring scale, B is a mass balance, R is a ruler, and T is a timer. Logical connections are dotted. Empirical connections are solid and dashed.

can be scientifically understood only in terms of a model, involving, in the case of a bridge, tension and compression members, interacting with one another, as shown in Figure 17.2. For a bridge, we use a geometric model that provides a direct, spatial analog with reality. For other physical situations we may need mathematical models for which there are less obvious rules of correspondence between the noun elements (constructs) of the model and our intuitive perceptions of immediate reality.

The same is true of scientific efforts to understand psychological phenomena, except that the models may remain ineffably vague and the predictions from those models may be almost wholly intuitive in derivation and hence unprovable by pencil-and-paper symbol manipulation.

What we are aiming to understand in this chapter is the nature of scientific theory. What do we know so far?

A theory will be concerned with a model of some kind, geometrical or mathematical. The model will not be directly perceivable

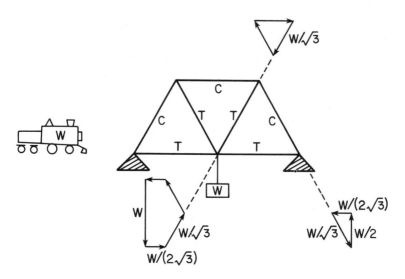

Figure 17.2. Model of a railroad bridge with theoretical force diagrams used to calculate stresses in compression (C) and tension (T) members caused by a load (W). In this simple model there is a one-to-one geometrical correspondence between the bridge members and the model elements.

by our senses, although geometrical models may seem to be. The model must be connected with our perceptions of familiar objects by what are called rules of correspondence. When we represent on paper a geometrical stress model of a railroad bridge, the rule of correspondence is very simple. One line on the drawing is associated with one piece of steel that is to be fabricated and installed. But when we try to identify a psychological construct, such as anger, with the expression on the face of our neighbor, the problem of identification is more difficult and our logical inferences are more likely to be inadequate.

Consider a relatively simple theory of physics, such as Newton's Second Law of Motion: *Force equals mass times acceleration.* We might represent this in Figure 17.1 by three circles distant from the plane of perception and labelled *F, m,* and *A.* We draw dotted lines between the circles to indicate vaguely that multiplying *m* by *A* yields *F.* This is a "theory" because it applies universally to a class of situations and not simply to one set of experimental observations.

But our diagram is not yet complete. It must be connected with the plane of observation by suitable rules of correspondence. *F* (standing for force) we might connect by a line meaning a push or a pull, but it would be better if we insert a spring scale, S, so that our sensory plane connection corresponds to reading a dial.

Mass, M, might be connected to observation by a kick of the foot to determine inertia, but for precision, we use a balance, B, to compare quantitatively the mass of the theory with a standard mass. Acceleration is measured in (meters/second)/second, which we might convert to observation by the ideas of a ruler, R, and a timer, T.

Thus, we have represented Newton's theory of motion. But most theories do not stand alone. This theory will connect with alternate formulations of the laws of mechanics and with other theories involving some of the same circles; so that eventually we have a network of logical operations connecting a large number of mental constructs. By way of an example, I have indicated the constructs in Einstein's mass-energy equation: $E = mc^2$.

Now we can see the meaning of the term "logical empiricism" or "logical positivism." The logical part is in the connections among the constructs distant from the plane. The empirical part consists of the plane of primitive sensation and the nearby objects of perception, which are our measuring tools.

Philosophers who call themselves "logical positivists" are sure that this is all there is to science. However, I suspect they have not paid enough attention to the connections between nearby perception and distant constructs (dashed lines). These are man's creation, not nature's. They are arbitrary. As we shall see in the next chapter, they change as science progresses and are never final.

With this much background we are now in a positon to describe some general characteristics of theory and to distinguish between good theory and bad.

METAPHYSICAL REQUIREMENTS

For a theory to be useful it must possess certain metaphysical attributes. They are called "metaphysical" because their value can be shown from experience but not directly by logic or experiment. Margenau (1950) lists six such attributes. Upon examination these are found to be loosely descriptive rather than discrete or exhaustive. Other philosophers of science have slightly different ways of describing the requirements of a good theory.

According to Margenau, the constructs or noun terms of a theory must first of all possess logical fertility. This means that they must permit logical manipulation. The concept of *mass* is fertile in physics but the idea of *love* in psychology may not be sufficiently definite or indentifiable to be dealt with by symbolic logic.

The second requirement for constructs is that they have multiple connections. Unless there are at least two connections to a construct, there is no possible pathway through it from one observation to another and hence the construct is of no scientific value. In general, the more ways a construct connects to other constructs, that is, the more ways it can be used in theories, the more real or valid it is considered to be.

The third requirement for constructs is permanence. Constructs are defined by their connections reaching toward the plane of observation. These are called "epistemic connections," as opposed to formal or logical connections with other constructs. However we choose to define a given construct, we must stick to it. We cannot call something a house in one theory and a tree in another. We cannot talk about radio waves as an explanation of telepathy unless we are willing to agree that ESP must show all the known characteristics of electromagnetic radiation. We can sometimes add new attributes to a construct but we cannot arbitrarily discard the old.

A good theory possesses a fourth characteristic known as extensibility. It must lead to new discoveries and to a widening range of application. Newton's law of universal gravitation was extensible because it was found to apply to molecules observable on earth as well as to planets in the sky. A weakness of behaviorism in psychology is its inability to encompass neurophysiology and subjective cognition. B.F. Skinner, a leader of neo-behaviorism, asks that the human organism be regarded as a "black box" that has neither internal structure nor awareness.

A fifth requirement for constructs, according to Margenau, is that of causality. To exhibit causality, a valid theory must allow prediction. In the simplest case we start with a set of data at the plane of observation and pass to more distant constructs where, by means of the theory, we compute a new set of data that will be found by measurement when we return to the plane of observation. If we adequately specify one state of a system, that is to say, one set of observational data, the theory must tell us with certainty the state that will follow. In quantum physics, where the two states are specifiable only in terms of probabilities of observation, nevertheless the connection between the states is mathematically precise.

A sixth desideratum for a theory is that it be simple and esthetically pleasing. Among competing theories otherwise in good standing, scientists will generally prefer one that is simple or elegant. This is a subjective judgement that is supposedly of more emotional than intellectual importance. Some prefer the word "parsimonious" to "simple."

How can these ideas be used to develop a theory? My guess is that, for the working scientist, the metaphysical requirements on theory are of exclusionary value. They may suggest when a new theory is weak but not when it is worthwhile.

If anyone has a theory intended to explain the phenomena of parapsychology, and if that theory fails to meet the requirements just described, then the burden of proving the value of the theory will rest upon the theory builder, and he should not be surprised if others are too busy to listen.

What is the purpose of a theory? How do the six characterisics already mentioned contribute to its value? Very briefly, a good theory does two things: (1) It provides a shorthand statement of the known experimental facts, and (2) it guides us to new experiments and new discoveries.

We do not have any good general theories in parapsychology, and I think it may be a long time before we have assembled enough clues to make one. Meanwhile, we must be content to gather data using our intuition and to build what are called "little theories" that have a restricted scope of application and, hopefully, some predictive value within that scope.

18

PROGRESS IN SCIENCE

Thomas Kuhn, Historian and Heretic

In the present chapter, I shall ask you to examine the nature of progress in science, beginning with the following long-established ideas. As you read these statements, are there any with which you would disagree? Think about each one for a moment as you go down the list.

1. Science is the accumulation of truth concerning nature.

2. As science progresses, our total understanding converges toward reality.

3. The unchanging laws of nature are waiting to be discovered (by some combination of luck, diligence, and insight).

4. The purpose of scientific research is to make new discoveries.

5. The past accomplishments of science are described in its textbooks (by which each new generation of scientists takes up its task from its predecessor).

In some important aspect, each of these five statements is untrue. Or at least, there is a historian of science at Massachusetts Institute of Technology who says they are untrue. His name is Thomas Kuhn. In 1962 he published a book called *The Structure of Scientific Revolutions* in which he said many things about the nature of progress in science that were contrary to everyday belief and even contrary to the beliefs of his fellow historians. He has been widely ridiculed by philosophers of science (Lakatos & Musgrave, 1970; Shapere, 1971), but among working scientists he has attracted a large following.

How large is that following? I thought it would be interesting to find out; so I consulted *Science Citation Index*. The result is shown in Figure 18.1, in which the number of citations is plotted for each year since publication. For a book on philosophy to be cited so frequently in the journals of quantitative science is surely unprecedented.

After two decades of growing recognition, Kuhn's rate of journal citation should soon drop, or at least level off, as his ideas become ever more commonplace—just as we no longer cite Pavlov when

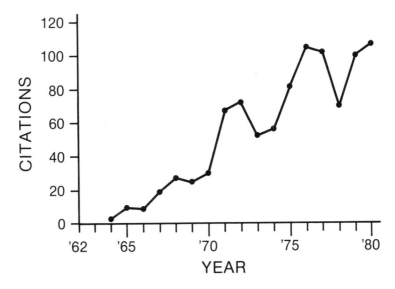

Figure 18.1. Citations per year of Thomas Kuhn's *The Structure of Scientific Revolutions* in the English-language journals of quantitative science since the book's first publication in 1962. The second edition appeared in 1970. Source: *Science Citation Index.* (In 1980, the number of additional citations in *Social Sciences Citation Index* was about three times the number in *SCI.*)

we refer to conditioned reflex, or Einstein when we speak of mass–energy equivalence. Among those who are professionally concerned with progress in science—and among educated people generally—Kuhn's concept of "paradigm" and his distinction between "normal" and "revolutionary" science have become almost as ordinary as biological evolution.

Professor Kuhn's seminal work was first published by the University of Chicago Press as Part 2 of Volume 2 of the *International Encyclopedia of Unified Science.* This encyclopedia was conceived and edited for the furtherance of logical positivism as an erudite theory of knowledge. Strangely enough, Kuhn's ideas have tended to undermine positivism and may, in time, prove to have been a major factor in the disappearance of that school of philosophy (but not of the primitive, noncontroversial methodology of the preceding chapter). Reason and observation remain the holy stones of science, but the priesthood has disappeared from the shrine built for their worship.

I present Kuhn's ideas with diffidence because I am neither a philosopher nor a historian. Kuhn talks at length about scientific theories. Does science produce knowledge, or does it produce theories? Or is a well-established theory a part of knowledge? The answer to the last question is obviously *yes*. A theory is a framework for conceptualizing reality.

Knowledge, in the common use of the word, is an understanding of things as they are. Science is generalized knowledge: knowledge of principles rather than particulars. To the extent that the universe follows immutable patterns, scientific knowledge should be immutable. Scientific knowledge, above any other kind, should be valid forever, once it has been gained. But is it forever? Is it ever gained?

In my chapter on the nature of scientific theory I discussed the idea that knowledge of the world outside ourselves is never direct except, loosely speaking, in the case of man-sized objects within our immediate sensory reach, and that our knowledge of the very small, of the very large, of psychological relationships, and of all generalities, is only by inference built upon abstraction. We are alone, each by himself, in an unreachable universe. Our senses lie to us, telling us that the table we touch is known to us, when all that we know is the perception we have built in our brain out of memory and a few piecemeal sensory clues. Our training in self-deception goes further, making us believe that the atoms themselves can be understood by us, within that table and within the fiery stars.

Viewed in this perspective, our scientific theories, whether or not we call them "knowledge," can scarcely be regarded as immutable. They are representations of an outer reality that we cannot reach. It is a puzzling and awesome tribute to the human intellect that we have made any contact with the world beyond our sense perceptions. If we are to extend further our reach toward the whole of nature and especially toward our fellow men, it might be well to muster all the sophistication of which we are capable. It is in this spirit that I wish to introduce you to Thomas Kuhn's ideas of how science progresses—if not toward an ultimate truth, at least from one theory to a next and better one.

MODELS AND TABOOS

To understand Thomas Kuhn's book, we must grasp two basic propositions: (1) scientific theories deal with models, and (2) scientists are opposed to any important change in those models.

I have already discussed the fact that science is concerned only with models and that, since no model fits completely and many models fit partly, we can never know when a new aspect of reality may be discovered and a better or different model will be needed. (Chapters 1, 5, 17)

The word "model" conveys the idea of an unchanging object in three-dimensional space. You already know that a model in science may be a process rather than a thing and may not use geometry at all. Kuhn employed the word "paradigm" as roughly equivalent to a theory and its model, and I shall use his term in this chapter.

The second basic proposition, namely, that scientists oppose change, is accepted by Kuhn as a given fact with no discussion of its psychological origins. To understand this fact we must go back to a simpler time in history.

It was only a few hundred years ago when anyone who dared to question religious belief might be publicly roasted to a slow and grisly death. Why was this?

The church authorities at that time said that such action was necessary, both as God's punishment for the heretic and to protect the priceless souls of all who might otherwise be led astray by the heretic's teaching.

Today, we know that heretics were destroyed because they threatened the peace of mind of both rulers and ruled. Similarly, throughout all of history, even in the most civilized countries, those who violated the taboos of society were put to death. So died Socrates the Athenian, Jesus the Jew, and Giordano Bruno the Italian.

We may ask why such drastic methods of thought control were necessary in the past, although in our culture, at the present time, immediate death is not the usual form of punishment for ideological heresy. Only through the answer to this question can we understand Kuhn's theory of scientific progress, and only through Kuhn can we understand parapsychology as a revolutionary threat to present-day science.

BELIEF SYSTEMS

"Survival is the first law of nature." Children learn this in the first years of school. The aphorism is stated and accepted but never examined. Its usual interpretations have to do with death by violence or by starvation but never with death by destruction of sacred beliefs.

Each of us finds the will to face life by orienting ourselves toward the world in a way that is comforting or rewarding or that at least minimizes the sum total of our anxiety toward the known and the unknown. Whether we think about it or not, each of us has a "philosophy of life" that we have acquired, mostly by happenstance, from our parents, our teachers, from the printed word and television, and from all other encounters with our environment.

The core of our philosophy, the basic frame of reference in which we perceive ourselves and all specific happenings, is our "world view." We can accept minor modifications in our way of seeing life. That is what happens in the usual educational process. But when our world view as a whole is threatened, we are frightened because we fear the loss of our will to live. We sense death waiting for us around the next ideological corner.

In former times, when the world view of a culture was embodied almost solely in its religious dogma, the heretic who frightened us with his new view of life was put to death. Beginning in the seventeenth century, as the scientific understanding of cause and effect made the trappings of religion increasingly absurd, the people were forced to develop new world views involving many aspects of life other than those specifically religious.

No longer was there a central authority that could insist, even locally, upon a monolithic belief system. Today, cultural authority as to what is true and should be believed is dispersed among many groups: among religious sects, labor organizations, political structures, the service professions, the learned professions, and, of course, within the general public which holds our legacy of common belief. With the fragmentation of ideological authority, death to the heretic cannot—at least in free countries in time of peace—be summarily ordered by any one of the power centers.

This does not mean that people no longer have a world view or that it will be any less vigorously defended against change. What has happened, as belief systems became more variegated, is that people have developed new defenses against new ideas.

This is not the place for a detailed examination of this topic. For present purposes we need to recognize two facts.

1. Any attack upon another person's belief system is an attack upon his will to survive and he can be expected to resist it accordingly.

2. The established beliefs of science play a small part in the belief system of the layman but a large part in the world view of the scientist. The leaders, as well as the followers of science, have built into their lives the orthodox scientific beliefs of our time and will resist by every means any new idea if they perceive it as a threat to their conception of "the meaning of life." They have developed an emotional attachment to the theories they learned at their professor's knee. They cling to the old models of reality as an infant to its mother. This has been increasingly true of scientists since the seventeenth century as religious values have lost ground.

I do not wish to suggest, however, that scientists are peculiar in this respect. With the decline of religious influence, our cultural sense of purpose has fragmented, so that many groups place their private values above those of the rest of society and above any appeal to reason. As the confusion and panic grows, there are nihilists who reject all existing world views and seek only the destruction of civilization and a return to some unimagined, primitive way of life.

If this is the true explanation of scientific conservatism, should we deplore and seek to eradicate it, or should we admire and foster it? The right answer is not easy to choose, as the following argument shows.

Conservatism in science is essential, just as in every other group activity of society. The world has too many troublemakers who are forever coming up with new ideas before the old ones have been explored. As things are now arranged, these dilettanti are ignored. It is all but impossible to get a hearing for a new idea before the time has come when its consideration is unavoidable. Perhaps this is as it should be.

If by the wave of a magic wand we scientists could be released from our neurotic fear of basic novelty, we would all be nosing around like caged rats, endlessly curious but accomplishing nothing. There are many dull jobs to be done in science, and even the more creative work requires peace of mind and a slow pace. It is necessary that things be arranged so that the gathering of knowledge can be a quiet, routine occupation, with ordinary rewards and limited perspectives.

On the other hand, it would be perverse to insist that the present arrangement is the best possible. As Max Planck, the discoverer of the quantum of light, described the situation in his autobiography:

"a new scientific truth does not triumph by convincing its opponents and making them see the light, but rather because its opponents eventually die, and a new generation grows up that is familiar with it." There ought to be some way to circumvent wise old leaders who, even in their more liberal moments, can never accept a new idea as fully worthy of investigation.

THE RHYTHM OF SCIENCE

With this much of an introduction, we are ready to begin the consideration of Thomas Kuhn's book, *The Structure of Scientific Revolutions*.[1] The central theses of Kuhn's historiography of science is that science is not a cumulative, growing enterprise but that it rebuilds itself anew in a series of revolutions. The well-established observational facts are not changed as a result of revolution, but in a conceptual sense much of the old structure is destroyed and replaced with something different. Stated in this way, Kuhn's basic idea seems inescapable.

Kuhn divides the process of science into two alternating stages, which he calls "normal science" and "extraordinary science." Normal science is the familiar type of research based upon accepted explanatory models or paradigms. To serve in this way, a paradigm must have two characteristics: it must be sufficiently unprecedented and successful to attract an enduring group of adherents and sufficiently open-ended or incomplete to leave work for those adherents. Extraordinary science is what takes place in the transition from one paradigm to another. It has been more descriptively called "revolutionary" or "crisis" science.

In somewhat greater detail, the history of a field of science may, in a typical case, be traced through the following seven steps:

1. A preparadigm period of confusion.
2. The beginning of mature science with the emergence of a prevailing paradigm from among primitive theories.
3. A period of "normal science" in which the paradigm is explored and elaborated.
4. Crisis in which unexplainable anomalies are increasingly apparent.
5. Emergence of a new paradigm.

---

1. In discussing this work I shall follow a condensation that appeared in the *Journal of the American Society for Psychical Research* (McConnell, 1968).

6. Revolutionary struggle between the old and the new.
7. Victory for one side and return to normal science.

PREPARADIGMATIC SCIENCE

For mathematics and astronomy the preparadigmatic phase was completed in pre-history. For other fields the conceptual achievements of familiar great names marked at least roughly the beginning of normal science as follows: motion—Aristotle; statics—Archimedes; physical optics—Newton; chemistry—Boyle and Boerhaave; electricity—Benjamin Franklin; evolution—Charles Darwin. Only the behavioral sciences of man are still in the preparadigmatic stage.

Data gathering in the preparadigmatic period is likely to be random, casual, superficial, and observational rather than experimental. Experimenters will draw upon what is ready-to-hand or from related crafts. Chemistry, for example, began out of the art of metallurgy and the blind searching of the alchemists, who knew what they wanted but had no correct knowledge of how to get it.

Lacking a theory to tell where to dig, no one in such a period can afford to dig deeply. The result is a morass of data, combining the simple with the complex, and the true with the false, while leaving many gaps. Competing schools develop. The more creative members of these schools are truly scientists; yet the literature that results seems almost a caricature of what we think of as "scientific."

Kuhn says very little about preparadigmatic science. This seems to be an area where more historical research would be worthwhile. He says nothing at all about the status of psychology and, of course, does not mention parapsychology. (In psychology it could be argued that Freud and Pavlov have provided two competing paradigms. Or it could be said that psychology today has many paradigms—and, hence, none in the Kuhnian sense.)

NORMAL SCIENCE

The first conquering paradigm ends the felt necessity for each worker to rebuild his field from its foundations; encourages more precise, esoteric, systematic, and expensive research; allows selectivity and specialization within the field; and guides fact collection and theory articulation.

---

2. Some of the difficulties that arise in this situation are illustrated in Appendix E: "Governmental Assistance to a Pretheoretical Science."

A paradigm is incomplete. Like an accepted judicial decision in the common law, it is an object for further development. It must be more powerful than its competitors in solving some problems or in making certain predictions. But its strength may lie partly in its esthetic appeal or mostly in its promise of future successes.

Normal science is the actualization of that promise. The foci of effort in normal science are three: (1) the determination of intrinsically significant facts, (2) the verification of theory by comparison with observation, and (3) theory elaboration. Thus, what Kuhn calls "normal science" might instead be termed "elaborational science."

The paradigm tells the working scientist what problems are worthwhile, what are impossible, and what are to be dealt with by applying the pejorative epithet, "metaphysical."

The word "metaphysical" is convenient to have at hand. Metaphysics according to the dictionary means: "that division of philosophy which includes ontology, or the science of being, and cosmology, or the science of fundamental causes and processes; or, in a looser sense, all of the more abstruse philosophic disciplines; and, in a narrower sense, ontology alone."

That is what a philosopher means by "metaphysics." When a scientist calls an idea or a subject "metaphysical," he usually means: "Perhaps I shall accept it, but I shall not study it."

Let me give an example. Both Aristotle and Descartes had detailed explanations for the force of gravity. After Newton wrote his inverse-square law of gravitation, $F = mm'/r^2$, inquiry into the cause of the force, F, between the two masses, m and m', became "metaphysical." The adherents to Newton's theory said: "Don't ask why. Just accept it as a given truth." Those who opposed Newtonianism argued that its reliance upon innate forces would return science to the Dark Ages.

The Newtonian point of view easily won the day, but it is interesting to note that, still later, using a new paradigm, that of general relativity, Einstein did away with gravity as an innate tendency and made it a geometrical property of space.

At any time in history, the prevailing paradigm tells what problems may have solutions and what are metaphysical. In the words of Kuhn (1962, p. 37): " . . . a paradigm is a criterion for choosing problems that, while the paradigm is taken for granted, can be assumed to have solutions. To a great extent these are the only problems that the [scientific] community will admit as scientific or encourage its members to undertake. Other problems, including many that had previously been standard, are rejected as meta-physical, as the concern of another discipline, or sometimes as just too problematic to be worth the time."

In addition to paradigms, normal science has "rules." These are explicit or implicit abstractions from paradigms and are deployed as guides to research. Rules may be classified into four groups: (1) Accepted scientific laws and statements (such as, matter is inde-structible). (2) Accepted instruments and techniques (for a long time physiologists opposed use of the techniques of physics). (3) Quasi-metaphysical commitments (e.g., the laws of mechanics must specify corpuscular motion and interaction). (4) Higher level commitments (e.g., the assumptions that phenomena are repeat-able and that the world can be ordered with increasing precision).

Where do rules come from? Often from the paradigms in many fields. Collectively they represent the professional world view of scientists and give coherence to science as a whole.

Rules are much harder to recognize than paradigms, and are likely to be tacit rather than explicit. The education of young sci-entists concerning the rules of the profession is by model or ex-ample and only rarely by formal discussion.

The difficulty that scientists have with the findings of parapsy-chology is not so much that they do not fit into existing paradigms but that they seem to violate the rules that scientists unconsciously live by. I shall discuss this in my final chapter.

CRISIS

Since a theory deals with only some selected aspect of nature, it is not surprising that eventually every theory will be found to be an over-simplification and will be unable to encompass all of the obser-vations that seem to be within its province. In the process of trying to verify the predictions of a theory or to extend its range of applica-tion, experimenters, sooner or later, will find its limitations.

Paradigm research is a marvelously successful process, not only for the fulfillment of the aims of normal science but for its own ultimate subversion—the latter because it leads to specialization so that esoteric experiments will be done, and done with a precision that will reveal anomaly.

Discoveries of anomalies, contrary to textbook opinion, are rarely sudden and are usually the work of more than one man. This is because they involve both experimental fact and conceptual assimilation (Kuhn, 1962, 53 ff.).

In our list of the three objectives of normal science there is no mention of a search specifically for facts that cannot be fitted into current theory. Such a search is rarely undertaken. Only minor novelties are welcomed. Any major anomaly will be regarded as a research failure, i.e., as the result of carelessness, incompetence, or fraud on the part of the experimenter (Kuhn, 1962, pp. 59, 77 ff.).

Scientists prefer to ignore unexpected discoveries as long as possible. They will wait until the anomaly clearly questions the heart of the prevailing paradigm, or until the anomaly has practical importance, or simply until a long time has passed.

In the case of psi phenomena, which violate the underlying assumptions but not the explicit dicta of prevailing paradigms, and which are not demonstrable at will and have no evident practical value, scientists have been pretending for nearly 100 years that no scientific problem exists.

Eventually it happens that the evidence for an anomaly permeates the consciousness of enough scientists so that a state of intellectual crisis comes into being. Vigorous escape activity results in a loosening of the rules of science and a conceptual blurring of the existing paradigm through proliferation of its versions. Extraordinary research is undertaken that attempts to isolate the breakdown in the paradigm, to magnify the anomaly, and to give it structure. Scientists turn toward normally neglected philosophy, examining the rules and doing "thought experiments."

REVOLUTION AND BEYOND

Sooner or later a new paradigm, or at least a hint of it, emerges, and the revolution begins. A scientific revolution is a time of intellectual disorder within the field where it occurs. Because the contending proponents develop different world views, they cannot communicate with one another on a reasoning basis. Often they cannot even agree as to what the problem is and, therefore, what would constitute a solution.

Paradigm change has been compared to a political revolution. There is first a spreading sense of the inadequacy of existing institutions. Estrangement leads to eccentric behavior. There is a growing commitment to a new paradigm, followed by polarization of opinion and battle without quarter. Revolutions, whether political or scientific, change institutions in ways that institutions prohibit. During the changeover, society is not fully governed. Logic and experiment are never enough to settle the issue; force may be needed (Kuhn, 1962, p. 92).

After every scientific revolution the textbooks are rewritten to teach the new paradigm. The net effect is a revision of history like that described in George Orwell's *1984*. The old ideas are discarded as false. Why dignify in print what science has made it possible to discard? The heroes of science are remembered; their works are forgotten or revised. Thus is science falsely made to appear conceptually cumulative and the latest paradigm made to appear a better approximation to ultimate truth.

Science is a rare enterprise among civilizations. Its practitioners constitute a self-perpetuating elite, living within a culture but not responsible to it for validation. One of the questions that Kuhn's book raises but does not answer is why the civilization of Western Europe, and no other, gave rise to a dominating science. This suggests a further question: Will science as a growing enterprise continue to exist in the age of anarchy that lies ahead?

THE ROLE OF GENIUS

Despite the importance of his insights, Kuhn's picture of progress in science is seriously deficient. It reveals nothing about the creative process or about the people who make discoveries. Concerning the creative process, nothing is yet known; although we may suspect that extrasensory perception is somehow involved. Concerning the creative individual, history books can tell a great deal.

By way of illuminating the gap in Kuhn's scheme of science, and to convey some conception of the nature of genius, I have abstracted a biography of the astronomer, Sir William Herschel (1738–1822), from *Pioneers of Science* by Sir Oliver Lodge (1893). Lodge (1851–1940) was a Fellow of the Royal Society and a physicist of some reknown. He was also one of the early presidents of the Society for Psychical Research.

Sir William Herschel was born at Hanover in 1738, the son of an oboe player in a military regiment. The father was a good musician, and a cultivated man. The mother was a woman of strong character and profound ignorance. Herself unable to write, she set her face against learning. . . .

It was a large family, and William was the fourth child. We need only remember the names of his younger brother Alexander, and of his much younger sister Caroline. . . .

At the age of seventeen, William became oboist to the Hanoverian Guards, shortly before the regiment was ordered to England. Two years later he removed himself from the regiment. . . . At the age of nineteen, he was thus launched in England with some French, Latin, and English, picked up by himself; and some skill in playing the hautboy, the violin, and the organ, as taught by his father. . . .

He lived as musical instructor to one or two militia bands in Yorkshire, and for three years we hear no more than this of him. . . . He next obtained the post of organist at Halifax; and some four or five years later he was invited to become organist at the Octagon Chapel in Bath, and soon led the musical life of that then very fashionable place. . . .

While at Bath he wrote many musical pieces—glees, anthems, chants, pieces for the harp, and an orchestral symphony. He taught a large number of pupils, and lived a hard and successful life. After fourteen hours or so spent in teaching and playing, he would retire at night to instruct his mind with a study of mathematics, optics, Italian, or Greek, in all of which he managed to make some progress. He also about this time happened upon some book on astronomy.

In 1765 his father died. . . . William then proposed that his brother, Alexander, should come over from Hanover and join him at Bath, which was done. Next they wanted to rescue their sister, Caroline, from her humdrum existence, but this was a more difficult matter. Caroline's journal gives an account of her life at this time:

> *My mother would not consent to my being taught French, . . . so all my father could do for me was to indulge me (and please himself) sometimes with a short lesson on the violin, when my mother was either in good humour or out of the way. . . . She had cause for wishing me not to know more than was necessary for being useful in the family; for it was her certain belief that my brother William would have returned to his country, and my eldest brother not have looked so high, if they had had a little less learning.*

However, seven years after the death of their father, William went over to Germany and returned to England in triumph, bringing Caroline with him: she being then twenty-two.

So now began a busy life in Bath. For Caroline the work must have been tremendous. For, besides having to learn singing, she had to learn English. She had, moreover, to keep accounts and do the marketing. . . .

William, who was deep in optics and astronomy, used to sleep with the books under his pillow, read them during meals, and scarcely ever thought of anything else. He was determined to see for himself all the astronomical wonders; and there being a small Gregorian reflector in one of the shops, he hired it. But he was not satisfied with this, . . . to the sister's dismay, who says:

> *And then, to my sorrow, I saw almost every room turned into a work-shop. A cabinet-maker making a tube and stands of all descriptions in a handsomely furnished drawing-room; Alex putting up a huge turning-machine (which he had brought in the autumn from Bristol, where he used to spend the summer) in a bed-room, for turning patterns, grinding glasses, and turning eyepieces, &c. At the same time music durst not lie entirely dormant during the summer, and my brother had frequent rehearsals at home.*

Finally, in 1774, at the age of thirty-six, he had made himself a 5½-foot [focal-length] telescope, and began to view the heavens. He soon began another telescope, and then another. He must have made some dozen different telescopes, always trying to get them bigger and bigger; at last he got a 7–foot and then a 10–foot instrument, and began a systematic survey of the heavens; he also began to communicate his results to the Royal Society. . . .

I read another extract from the diary of his sister, who waited on him and obeyed him like a spaniel:

> *My time was taken up with copying music and practising, besides attendance on my brother when polishing, since by way of keeping him alive I was constantly obliged to feed him by putting the victuals by bits into his mouth. This was once the case when, in order to finish a 7-foot mirror, he had not taken his hands from it for sixteen hours together. In general he was never unemployed at meals, but was always at those times contriving or making drawings of whatever came in his mind. Generally I was obliged to read to him whilst he was at the turning-lathe, or polishing mirrors—Don Quixote, Arabian Nights' Entertainments, the novels of Sterne, Fielding, &c.; serving tea and supper without interrupting the work with which he was engaged, . . . and sometimes lending a hand. I became, in time, as useful a member of the workshop as a boy might be to his master in the first year of his apprenticeship. . . . But as I was to take a part the next year in the oratorios, I had, for a whole twelvemonth, two lessons per week from Miss Fleming, the celebrated dancing-mistress.*

The music, and the astronomy, and the making of telescopes, all went on together, each at high pressure; the Herschels knew no rest. Grinding mirrors by day, concerts and oratorios in the evening, star-gazing at night. It is strange his health could stand it.

The star-gazing, moreover, was no dilettante work; it was based on a serious system—a well thought out plan of observation. It was nothing less than this—to pass the whole heavens steadily and in order through the telescope, noting and describing and recording every object that should be visible, whether previously known or unknown. The operation is called sweeping. . . .

Four distinct times in his life did Herschel thus pass the whole visible heavens under review; and each survey occupied him several years. He discovered double stars, variable stars, nebulae, and comets; and Mr. William Herschel, of Bath, the amateur astronomer, was gradually emerging from his obscurity, and becoming a known man.

Tuesday, the 13th of March, 1781, is a date memorable in the annals of astronomy. "On this night," he wrote to the Royal Society, "in examining the small stars near η Geminorum, I perceived one visibly larger than the rest. . . . I suspected it to be a comet.". . . It was no comet, it was a new planet; more than 100 times as big as the earth, and nearly twice as far away as Saturn. It was presently christened "Uranus.". . .

Since the most ancient times of which men had any knowledge, the planets Mercury, Venus, Mars, Jupiter, Saturn, had been known, and there had been no addition to their number. Galileo and others had discovered satellites indeed, but a new primary planet was an entire and utterly unsuspected novelty.

One of the most immediate consequences of the event was the discovery of Herschel himself. The Royal Society made him a Fellow the same year. The University of Oxford dubbed him a doctor; and King George III sent for him to bring his telescope and show it at Court. . . .

The King ultimately appointed him astronomer or rather telescope-maker to himself, and so Caroline and the whole household were sent for, and established in a small house at Datchet. . . . From being a star-gazing musician, Herschel thus became a practical astronomer.

The King offered £2,000 for a gigantic telescope to be made for Herschel's own use. Nothing better did he want in life. The whole army of carpenters and craftsmen resident in Datchet were pressed into the service. Furnaces for the speculum metal were built, stands erected, and the 40-foot telescope fairly begun. It cost £4,000 before it was finished, but the King paid the whole. . . .

In 1783, Herschel married an estimable lady who sympathized with his pursuits. They moved now into a more commodious house at Slough. Their one son, afterwards the famous Sir John Herschel, was born some nine years later.

But the marriage was rather a blow to his devoted sister: henceforth she lived in lodgings, and went over at night-time to help him observe. For it must be remarked that this family literally turned night into day. Whatever sleep they got was in the day-time. Every fine night without exception was spent in observing: and the quite incredible fierceness of the pursuit is illustrated, as strongly as it can be, by the following sentence out of Caroline's diary, at the time of the move from Datchet to Slough: "The last night at Datchet was spent in sweeping till day-

light, and by the next evening the telescope stood ready for observation at Slough."

Caroline was now often allowed to sweep with a small telescope on her own account. In this way she picked up a good many nebulae in the course of her life, and eight comets, four of which were quite new, and one of which, known since as Encke's comet, has become very famous.

The work they got through between them is something astonishing. He made with his own hands 430 parabolic mirrors for reflecting telescopes, besides a great number of complete instruments. He was forty-two when he began contributing to the Royal Society; yet before he died he had sent them sixty-nine long and elaborate treatises. One of these memoirs was a catalogue of 1000 nebulae. Fifteen years after, he sent in another 1000; and some years later another 500. He also discovered 806 double stars, which he proved were really connected, from the fact that they revolved around each other. . . .

It was the beginning of a science of the stars. Hitherto all the energies of astronomers had gone out towards the solar system. It was the planets that had been observed. Tycho had observed and tabulated their positions. Kepler had found out some laws of their motion. Galileo had discovered their peculiarities and attendants. Newton and Laplace had perceived every detail of their laws. . . .

Herschel discovered the life and activity of the whole visible universe. No longer was our little solar system to be the one object of regard, no longer were its phenomena to be alone interesting to man. With Herschel every star was a solar system. And more than that: he found suns revolving around suns, at distances such as the mind reels at, still obeying the same law of gravitation as pulls an apple from a tree.

This excerpt from Sir Oliver Lodge tells us something we could not learn from the theories of scholars such as Kuhn, namely, that the gaining of radically new knowledge requires individual determination and romantic freedom.

Parapsychology cannot be evaluated without some feeling for scientific pioneering. Unfortunately, we shall not get competent evaluation from the normal-science experts who are in charge of national scientific affairs, most of whom have never had a courageous scientific thought in their careers.

19

FRAUD IN PARAPSYCHOLOGY

THE CASE OF S.G. SOAL

Like other fields of science, parapsychology has had its fraudulent experimenters. I shall describe two of these, and the reader may properly wonder how many more there are who have not been uncovered.

Some day, when psi phenomena are universally accepted, the case of S.G. Soal may well be regarded as the most interesting of its kind. Perhaps by then our knowledge and control of psychopathology will ensure that fraud involving the manipulation of data over an extended time can no longer occur in controversial fields of science.

Samuel G. Soal (1890–1975) was born in Yorkshire, England. At age 20 he graduated from East London College with first-class honors in mathematics. He took his M.A. in 1914 and served his country in World War I from 1915 until he was wounded at the Battle of the Somme in 1917. Later, he rose to the position of Senior Lecturer in Mathematics at Queen Mary College.

From 1922 to 1961 he was active as a member of the Society for Psychical Research and in 1950 was chosen as its president. In 1945 he was awarded the D.Sc. degree by the University of London for his research in parapsychology.

Soal's early parapsychological work was in sittings with trance mediums. In one series of such sittings he obtained strikingly evidential messages from a communicator whom he later found to be still alive—thus raising interesting questions of interpretation (Soal, 1925). Soal dissociated readily and produced automatic writing, some of which was published in the *Proceedings of the SPR* under a pseudonym (Soal, 1929).

Later, Soal turned his attention to experimental parapsychology. In an effort to duplicate J.B. Rhine's experiments, he recorded 128,350 card guesses while testing 160 selected subjects over the years 1934–1939. His results were always near chance expectation, and on various occasions he publicly derided the success of American card guessing.

In November, 1939, under the persistent urging of an English experimenter, Whately Carington, Soal re-examined his data, looking for coincidences between his subjects' guesses and the target cards before and after the intended card—an effect analogous to one that Carington (1940) had discovered in picture-drawing experiments.

To his surprise, Soal found that two of his subjects had scored at an above-chance rate on the target cards immediately before and after the proper card. He then extended his search until he had covered eight cards forward and eight backward. The resulting scoring for the entire set of patterns was clearly extrachance, with p-values of 10^{-3} and 10^{-4} for the appropriately calculated chi-squares for these two subjects.

These findings were reported in detail by Soal (1940), who thereafter carried out experiments with the same subjects over a period of two years under a variety of seemingly fraud-proof conditions (Soal and Goldney, 1943). This work was expanded and published in book form by Oxford and Yale University Presses. (Soal and Bateman, 1954).

Soal continued his research in parapsychology until his retirement, but none of his later work was as convincing as that just described, and much of it was unsuccessful.

Strong suspicion was later cast upon Soal's work by two members of the SPR (Scott and Haskell, 1974). The resulting discussions by well known parapsychologists are essential reading for a sociological understanding of parapsychology (Barrington, 1974; Beloff, 1974; Goldney, 1974; Mundle, 1974; Pratt, 1974; Stevenson, 1974; Thouless, 1974).

By a computerized examination of large segments of Soal's data from one of his two successful subjects, another member of the SPR, Markwick (1978), was able to demonstrate to the satisfaction of all parties concerned that these data had been fraudulently manipulated to produce apparent ESP. (Goldney, 1978; Pratt, 1978a; Randall, 1978; Scott, 1978; Thouless, 1978).

Broadly stated, Soal's ability to carry on successful deception over a period of several years stemmed from the fact that he assumed fully the role of senior experimenter. For example, when target lists were prepared in advance, it was usually done by Soal alone. In preparing target sheets of random numbers for some test sessions, it appears probable that he inserted extra 1's, which he later was able to convert to other digits to match the subject's guesses. So far as has been determined, he executed his feats of legerdemain unassisted save by a prodigious memory.

At first glance it seems strange that a scientist should devote himself wholeheartedly to a life of professional fraud. Markwick (1978) offered two vague explanatory hypotheses under the headings, "dissociated manipulation" (p. 272) and "data massage" (p. 274). From her discussion it would seem that, in the first instance, she was thinking of a nonreprehensible falsification by a secondary personality in Soal's body, while in the second she had in mind reprehensible falsification "by Soal himself."

THE W.J. LEVY CASE

Before discussing the Soal case, I shall present the Levy case for comparison. W.J. Levy came to the Institute for Parapsychology at Durham, North Carolina, in 1969 as a summer trainee before entering the Medical College of Georgia. In collaboration with others more technically qualified, he developed an automated procedure for testing small mammals in shock avoidance. Building upon the psi research of Rémy Chauvin, at the Sorbonne in Paris (Duval & Montredon, 1968), he devised a routine in which the animal, by using ESP, might avoid a mild electrical shock randomly applied to one half or the other of the floor of a small rectangular cage. In the absence of sensory clues, the animal, pausing by chance in either half of the cage, would receive shocks 50% of the time. However, by extrasensory anticipation of the shock location, the animal might avoid discomfort by jumping at the proper time to the other half of the cage.

In this arrangement, after a certain number of trials, the animal exited to a holding cage in a Ferris wheel, which then advanced to admit the next animal. The entire operation, including the recording and analysis of the data, was carried out under the control of a digital computer. Over a period of several summers, under Levy's guidance, the technique was developed to the point where gerbils showed dependable successful avoidance rates of the order of 55%, where 50% was chance expectation.

Because of his diligence, managerial skill, and apparent ability to produce dependable psi phenomena, Levy joined the permanent staff as director of the Institute after receiving his medical degree in June, 1973.

In June of 1974, Levy's uncalled-for attention to the apparatus recording his experiment aroused the suspicion of his co-workers, who, by the use of independent monitoring apparatus, were able to show that he was creating "successful" trials by shorting loose wires. His resignation as an employee of the laboratory was promptly accepted, and the details of the affair were appropriately reported in the journals of the field (Rhine, 1974; 1975; Davis, 1975).

Two factors help explain how such an important discovery as that claimed by Levy could be allowed to go unchallenged for several years.

Like all laboratories in this field, the Institute for Parapsychology operated on a financial shoestring. It had long served as a national training center for students, but, of necessity, there was only minimal supervision by professionally trained scientists. Levy, although not trained in scientific research, seemed to fill the laboratory's need for productive leadership, and by the force of his personality, tended to dominate the activities in which he engaged.

From the outset, Levy's success was recognized as a turning point for parapsychology if, indeed, it was authentic. No attempt was made by others to replicate his work because the necessary investments in equipment and technique were beyond the capabilities of the half-dozen parapsychologists, worldwide, who otherwise might have dropped what they were doing and turned to this animal research. Levy had the ball, and it was easier to let him run with it.[1]

COMPARISON OF THE SOAL AND LEVY CASES

The Soal and Levy cases have both similarities and differences. The nonchance scoring pattern that Soal discovered (1940) almost certainly represented a real ESP effect.[2] Likewise, it is probable that Levy was dealing with an unexplained nonchance effect at the beginning of his research, although some may think it more rea-

---

1. Perhaps as a result of the Levy affair, very little research is currently underway investigating the possibility of psi in animals. For a review of the literature, see Davis (1979).

2. It is interesting in this connection that Soal's "target displacement" effect was independently confirmed by John R. Smythies (1974), a neuropsychiatrist with an international reputation as an editor of neuroscience reference works. While he was at the University of Edinburgh in 1951, Dr. Smythies observed the displacement effect with one out of four hospitalized patients, with selection-corrected chance odds of one in 10,000. He did not bother to publish his findings at the time because they seemed inconsequential compared to Soal's—a feeling that became inappropriate 23 years later when Soal's work came under attack.

sonable to ascribe his initial success to experimenter PK on the animal brain rather than to animal ESP.

It may be suppositionally inferred in both the Soal and Levy cases that, as the monotonous experimental routine destroyed the enthusiasm of the experimenter, psi vanished. Experimental failure led to fraud. It is at this point that an explanation is needed.

As individuals, Soal and Levy seem to have had little in common. Soal, in the words of Markwick (1978, p. 273) was "a strange personality: obsessive, absorbed, secretive, and subject to bouts of dissociation." No one, to the best of my knowledge, has publicly characterized W.J. Levy's personality. In my brief acquaintance I found him to be intellectually aggressive, technically oriented, brash, and lacking in warmth. I have heard no suggestion that he suffered, or was skilled at, mental dissociation.

MORAL RESPONSIBILITY IN A MULTIPLE PERSON

Markwick's alternative hypotheses attempt to assess Soal's behavior in moral terms by separating guilt or innocence from the evil consequents of action—attaching them, instead, to the intent of the do-er. According to prevailing social doctrine, a person may commit a crime with his body but not necessarily with his mind. In the criminally insane, some essential element of the brain is presumed to be disconnected or malfunctioning. Thus, an insane person is not to be blamed, and yet, for the same action, a sane person suffers opprobrium.

For this biological myth to be socially useful, the citizenry must believe that a dichotomy exists between mental responsibility and nonresponsibility, and there must be professionally expert witnesses who can testify in court as to whether the wrong-doer was, or was not, an evil person at the time of his crime.

Much nonsense has been written about this problem. One school of New Left psychiatry goes so far as to deny that mental illness exists. This supposition, however, has been definitively answered (Murphy, 1976).

The truth is quite the opposite: None of us is entirely sane. All of us think and behave psychopathologically some of the time, and many of us do it most of the time—although only a few seek professional help for mental illness.

There are, of course, kinds and degrees of insanity. In the present cases, the crucial question would seem to be: Were Soal and

Levy constantly and uniformly aware of their dishonesty, or were there times when their thinking included no memory of their continuing betrayal of the principles to which they were committed by their social relationships to their colleagues? If in some sense they had forgotten the past (in so far as it should guide the present so as to attain a future consonant with the past) then to some degree they were acting psychopathologically.

Stated in this way, the problem is seen to be universal. All of us are evil at times in our lives, and at those times we seem to be rather successful in suppressing memories of the obligations we are violating. Presumably, the same mental mechanisms that allow forgetting of principles can allow the repression of the violation of those principles. One might expect this kind of moral disability especially in those minds with the greatest power of concentration.

Our first impulse is to deny that this kind of forgetting should be called psychopathological. It seems remote from the mental illnesses that fill our psychiatric institutions. Perhaps our whole conception of psychopathology is mistaken?

In the past few years the psychiatric profession has been paying increasing attention to an illness known as "multiple personality," which was first intensively explored eight decades ago. To decide whether Soal or Levy were victims of multiple personality, we need to know more about this illness. In Chapters 3 and 4, I introduced the topic historically and theoretically. At this point I shall expand our conception of it.

The Prevalence and Implications of Multiple Personality

Clinically diagnosed multiple personality requires the existence of two or more consciousnesses occupying the same brain either simultaneously or sequentially. These consciousnesses are defined by their accessible memories, which, although never identical, will usually overlap. The existence of more than one personality is acknowledged when control of motor activity is known to pass from one personality to the other in a matter of seconds without warning. Often this transfer takes place under appropriately rewarding circumstances. As in the case of schizophrenia, the behavior of the patient is often motivationally transparent to a knowledgable observer.

Certain beliefs have grown up concerning multiple personality that I suspect are incorrect. It is supposed that the multiple-personality patient will be recognizably hysterically neurotic, that the pathological changes in personality will be sufficiently dramatic to be evident to a skilled observer, and that the changes will be sudden.

These are, indeed, characteristics of cases in which there is a clinical referral. In general, however, there is no unique "condition" of multiple personality—merely a continuum ranging from very sick to quite well. As discussed in Chapter 4, we all suppress certain memories, either temporarily or permanently. We all have mood changes, to one degree or another, and they need not be sudden. These changes differ in degree but perhaps not in principle from the changes in pesonality that were observed as mental illness by Morton Prince (1905), Walter Prince (1915, 1916), and Cornelia Wilbur (Schreiber, 1973). The repression of memories of isolated events is part of the psychopathology of everyday life recognized by Freud (1901). When one or more constellations of memories are *intermittantly* suppressed, we have what is commonly meant by multiple personality.

With our present level of psychological knowledge we can only guess at the extent of psychopathology in mankind. My hunch is that any sensitive observer who is familiar with the literature of multiple personality will recognize the symptom of recurring suppression of memories of important but unpleasant events in some of his fellow workers, despite the fact that multiple personality is characteristically concealed by the patient from himself and from the world.

Although one might expect a census based on the casual recognition of suppressed (single or grouped) memories to overestimate the incidence of multiple personality (by including permanent suppression), I suspect that it would instead grossly underestimate the more pathological, intermittant problem. It is my guess that, given the appropriate circumstances, at least 80% of the population can be inducted into moods in which they are capable of morally despicable acts from which they would shrink in horror in their better moments.

They (we) change to other personalities that have adequate "ego strength" (sense of self-command and self-sufficiency) but that are supported by constellations of memories in which whole categories of affective and narrational history are, to a greater or lesser degree, eliminated. Sometimes the change is triggered by association with other emotionally aroused people, and mob action results.

More often, the shift between personalities is a private, gradual matter, knowable to others only by weak inference.

I base these speculations in part upon personal observation and in part upon public history. Prominant in my mind, as mentioned earlier, is the frenzied glee shown by the people of Berlin after Hitler's early victories. Similar demoniacal joy in evil is found many times in history, but in World War II it was recorded for the first time on motion-picture film so that its true madness could be intuitively obvious to others later.

The foregoing expanded view of multiple personality differs from the generally accepted view in three principal ways: (1) The usual sensorimotor disabilities of hysterical neurosis need not be present. (2) The memories temporarily lost may be affective rather than detectably narrational, i.e., may be nonverbal memories. (3) The transition from one personality to another need not be discontinuous but can occur (or be induced) gradually. Although it might seem to the clinical observer that the pathology of continuous-transition cases of multiple personality is less severe, there is reason to suppose that the possible changes in personality can be as great as in discontinuous cases.

I suspect that individual potentiality for personality change can be estimated from the occurrence of other, more benign forms of mental dissociation. I suspect, too, that none of us has a "true" or "total" personality, and that, for many of us, there is not even a "primary personality." It is always a matter of degree. All of us are many persons in one.

Stated in this way, the idea of graduated, multiple personality may seem like a nonthreatening "point of view" rather than a revolutionary proposition. Nevertheless, this conception of multiple personality raises interesting sociological questions, of which I shall mention two:

1. If culpability for wrongdoing is always a matter of degree, perhaps we should revise our penalogical procedures. Would it not make more sense to execute the badly dissociated murderer and to try to salvage the criminal who was more aware of his wrongdoing and therefore more "guilty"?

2. When the continuing existence of civilization depends upon the sanity of men chosen to guard the nuclear bombs, how safe are we from accidental oblivion through the agency of multiple personality?

Soal, Levy, and the Reality of Psi

Given our present ignorance in psychology, little can be said diagnostically about Soal and Levy. Judging from the limited evidence, Soal was probably a multiple personality in the classical sense. Levy, most probably, was not. To what extent Levy continuously retained—or, indeed, ever possessed—memories of devotion to scientific truth and of community with others, we do not know. Multiple personality is only one of many psychopathologies.[3]

Elsewhere (McConnell, 1977a), I have discussed how the problem of fraud should be logically dealt with in assessing the case for and against psi phenomena. The possibility of dishonesty must be allowed in evaluating every experimenter's contribution to the total evidential picture.

Earlier (McConnell, 1975b), I discussed the motivations of scientists compared to other professions and described the intellectual, methodological, and social constraints upon fraud that are found in science.[4] Because fraud and other possible, unrecorded procedural misadventures can never be excluded with any high degree of certainty from second-hand evidence (i.e., from scientific-journal reports), the evidential value of any one experiment, or all of the experiments from a single investigator, is very limited (regardless of the chance probability that may be associated with the null hypotheses under consideration in his experiments).

Since no one piece of evidence can be strong, the case for the reality of psi phenomena must rest upon the quantity and diversity of that evidence. To attempt to prove psi by one "perfect experiment" is an impossible enterprise.

---

3. Anita Gregory (1980) offers a subtle and persuasive explanation for scientific fraud that makes no mention of multiple personality (i.e., of transient memory defect) but is based, instead, on alienation, pride, intense commitment to a scientific idea, and, by implication, on errors of logic in relating self to society.

4. These constraints are effective only in a healthy society. Perhaps the ultimate in collusive nonscience as evidence of cultural decadence will be found in an exposé by Pendery, Maltzman, and West (1982).

20

WITH FRIENDS LIKE THESE . . .

PARAPSYCHOLOGIST AS MARTYR

Critics of parapsychology may be surprised to learn that opposition to its advancement sometimes arises within the field itself. I shall give two examples, illustrating, respectively, what I have called right-wing and left-wing appeasement.

In 1972, *Science,* the interdisciplinary journal of the American Association for the Advancement of Science, rejected a paper by Honorton, Ramsey, and Cabbibo (1975), describing an investigation of the influence of experimenter friendliness upon the ability of volunteers to produce ESP with an automated, random-number guessing machine. Because I had been asked by *Science* to serve as a referee, the matter of the rejection eventually came to my attention and I assisted the senior author in uncovering the reasons for the journal's unfavorable action. We found that the criticisms of the three referees who recommended rejection were almost entirely improper.

Eventually, the paper was published within the field of parapsychology in exactly the form in which it had been rejected by *Science,* together with the correspondence with the editor of *Science* and the nonconfidential criticisms by the rejecting referees as forwarded to the authors by *Science.* This was an unusual eventuality—perhaps a "first" in the history of science—almost certainly so for the journal, *Science.*

Because my present comments deal solely with the later difficulties in publishing this paper in a parapsychological journal, the reader is referred to the paper and correspondence, as published, to make his own evaluation of *Science's* rejection. Since the matter is necessarily somewhat technical, for the convenience of the reader I have included as Appendix F hereto, an explanatory summary of the errors made by the *Science* referees.

Originally, I thought that any journal in the field of parapsychology would be delighted to publish a fully documented exposé of prejudice shown against this scientific discipline by the world's most important journal of science. To my puzzlement and dismay, after the paper by Honorton, et al., had been submitted to the *Journal of the American Society for Psychical Re-*

search, I learned that the editor and some members of that Society's Publication Committee and Board of Trustees were strongly opposed to publication. The authors were told that the experimental paper itself was excellent and would gladly be accepted with minor modifications to conform to the *Journal's* style, but that the *Science* correspondence and referee's comments would not be welcome even though the flyleaf of the *Journal of the ASPR* proclaims that "Responsibility for the contents of any article appearing in the *Journal* rests entirely with the contributor and not with the ASPR," and not withstanding that this journal normally carries the widest imaginable range of materials that can be fitted in under the heading "scientific." This anomalous behavior by parapsychologists controlling their own journal seemed even more interesting than the earlier rejection by *Science,* and I pursued it accordingly.

Correspondence with the editor and with a member of the Publication Committee yielded a congeries of reasons for rejection that added up to a judgment that it would be inexpedient and perhaps unethical to attack *Science* openly in this manner. Forthwith, acting without the foreknowledge of the authors of the rejected paper, I wrote to half a dozen leading American parapsychologists (including the editor of the *Journal of the ASPR*) who were young enough, I hoped, to be interested in aggressive opposition to prejudice by *Science* against their field.

I sent copies of the *Science* and *JASPR* rejection correspondence and a statement of the issue raised by the *JASPR* rejection as I saw it. I asked that the matter be discussed openly by correspondence within this select group of parapsychologists—not to coerce publication in *JASPR,* but with a view to clarifying our own thinking concerning the proper stance of parapsychology vis-a-vis society with immediate reference to what might be called "right-wing appeasement" in public relations. ("Left-wing appeasement," i.e., pandering to popular interest in parapsychology, I suggested as a topic for later consideration.) What I got in return from this younger group of parapsychologists can be most simply described as a null response. It was evident that unwillingness to offend the scientific establishment could not be explained simply as due to the timidity of old age.

Meanwhile, without my knowledge, the senior author of the rejected paper had struck a deal with the editor of *JASPR* by which the question of publication would be reconsidered by three referees to be jointly chosen by the editor and senior author. In due time, two of these recommended publication, and the paper was finally accepted.

Because I had been determined to have this paper and appended material published somewhere, my correspondence file dealing with its rejection is several centimeters thick and comes from scattered parts of the English-speaking world. Included is a letter solicited by a member of the *JASPR* Publication Committee who opposed publication, in which the Chief Executive Officer of the American Association for the Advancement of Science explained that he could see nothing unethical in publishing the editorial and referee comments from *Science*. It is interesting that a senior parapsychologist with long experience in the publishing world and with a finely honed sense of justice had to seek an authoritative answer to so elementary a question of professional ethics.

The following paragraph from the editor of a well known psychiatric journal, whose advice had been sought informally by a member of the Board of Trustees who opposed publication, may add a piece to the puzzle.

> I cannot speak to the legal aspects of the problem you pose in your letter of August 1. From my own affective standpoint, I would be annoyed as hell if the anonymous opinions of my reviewers were spread upon the pages of another journal to which the rejected author had gone. I would regard it as a breach of faith, a transgression of custom, and an act which I would not regard as proper, right, desirable, or preferred. I use all of these words because, taken together, they may add up to "ethical." But, maybe, I would just be suffering from an assault against my irrationally defended sense of territoriality or privacy.

Another member of the Board of Trustees who opposed publication (a psychiatrist) explained his position, in part, by this sage observation: "Truth has a way of rising to the surface at its own rate, and premature efforts to throw it in the face of the infidels sometimes delays the process."

The systematic scientific investigation of ESP began with the founding of the SPR in 1882, and the literature shows that the reality of the phenomenon was convincingly demonstrated not long thereafter. What are we to make of the fact that, one-hundred years later, the leaders of the field are not in a hurry to give up the martyr's role?

LEFT-WING APPEASEMENT

Another major problem of the field as seen from the outside is that many parapsychologists lack a keen sense of scientific propriety. They are willing to consort publicly in writing with laymen who pretend to be scientists but whose orientation is antithetical to science. Perhaps because their own training has been deficient, some parapsychologists do not understand that the world is managed by hierarchies of specialists and that for various reasons— some justified, some not—these elites jealously guard against intrusion by technically incompetent outsiders.

For years, my private urging to fellow parapsychologists to be selective in choosing their professional company had fallen on deaf ears. Recently, I was reluctantly led into action by the publication of a popular anthology, co-edited by a well known parapsychologist. After discussion with the editor of one of the two leading U.S.A. parapsychological journals, I prepared a review, which is reproduced below in shortened form with some added explanatory comment in brackets. (Single copies of the original review as offered for publication and then privately printed in 1978, will be sent to any reader of this book upon request.)

ON THE DISTINCTION BETWEEN SCIENCE AND NONSCIENCE IN A PRETHEORETICAL FIELD

R. A. McCONNELL

This book review was prepared for the *Journal of the American Society for Psychical Research* with the enthusiastic encouragement of the editor. It was subsequently rejected for publication as unsuitable in content. I am distributing it privately because I believe that parapsychologists and their critics should be aware of the methodological crisis that it reflects within the field.

—RAM

Reviewer's Perspective

Until the leaders of psychology and physics can accept the idea that the evidence for psi phenomena deserves serious attention, there will be little financial support for parapsychological research and little scientific progress in the field. Hence, it is important to know why those leaders reject psi phenomena.

One reason is that those who presume to speak for parapsychology often show that they do not understand the difference between *science* and *nonscience*. The distinction can be told in one word: self-discipline. In a well established field that distinction is maintained by means of an authority structure. In a pretheoretical field, such as parapsychology, all is chaos. Everyone is free to represent himself to the public as a distinguished and thoughtful leader.

The very existence of a field of science depends upon maintaining a line of demarcation between the professional investigator and the undisciplined enthusiast, between scientific searching and popular fantasizing. The truth of this statement is perhaps nowhere more evident than in a book for the layman in which the separating line has been obliterated. As such a book, *Future Science* [Anchor Books, 1977] is well worth examining.

There are no observable phenomena in the universe that are unscientific *per se*. Although the topics covered in this book are such that it would be difficult to say anything scientifically useful about them, my attention will be directed, not to the topics, but to their treatment.

In reviewing this book, I cannot speak for my diverse fellow parapsychologists, but I shall reflect accurately, I am sure, the methodological viewpoint of orthodox science.

Peripheral Information

How should a book be judged? By its content, of course—but by its content in relation to its intended audience, and also by its purpose or pretentions, and by the position and reputation of its authors/editors.

The present book is evidently intended for intelligent but scientifically illiterate adults, i.e., for average college-educated Americans. As will be shown later by excerpts, the editors offer this book, not as entertainment, but as a serious attempt to foresee the future.

[I have deleted at this point a one-page, factual, neutrally-toned summary of the professional backgrounds of the editors and authors.]

Future Science is divided into six major sections. Because my primary concern is with the creative contribution to the entire work by the editors, one of whom is a Member of the Parapsychological Association, I shall not attend directly to each of the chapters by the individual contributing authors, but, for the most part, shall look through the eyes of the editors. I shall exhibit their opinions expressed in their own commentary scattered throughout the book. To avoid inadvertently misrepreseenting them, I shall quote rather than paraphrase.

Scope and Purpose of the Book

The following quotations from the editors' *Introduction* and from their comment preceding Section I: *Setting the Perspective,* show their serious, scholarly purpose and the scope of the work, which includes and extends beyond parapsychology.

> The expanding perimeter of human knowledge has brought pioneering scientists in many frontier areas face to face with events that cannot be easily explained in terms of present scientific concepts of reality. . . . the all-too-frequent reaction by other scientists has been to disregard these unusual occurrences or to discount the reports as "pseudoscience". . . .
> This regrettable attitude is a debasement of true science. It conceives of science as a body of knowledge rather than as a method of knowing. In doing so, it becomes dogmatic, doctrinaire, and has been properly labelled "scientism." A firm rejection of this attitude was made by physicist P.W. Bridgman, when he said in *The Logic of Modern Physics:* "It is difficult to conceive anything more scientifically bigoted than to postulate that all possible experience conforms to the same type as that with which we are already familiar, and therefore to demand that explanation use only elements familiar to everyday experience." (pp. 13–14)

> Our overview starts from the year 1882, when the Society for Psychical Research was founded in England. . . .
> The Duke experiments led to the definition of parapsychology most often used: the branch of science that deals with psi interactions, i.e., behavioral or personal exchanges with the environment which are extrasensorimotor—not dependent on the senses and muscles. "Psychical research" is a synonym for parapsychology. . . .
> In recent decades, some investigators have come to feel that even the traditional domain of parapsychology needs to be expanded in the scientific search for understanding of unusual phenomena. . . .
> Many other investigators of the paranormal now recognize the need for convergence of psychology and physics. . . .
> There have been many terms proposed for the burgeoning field that studies the physics of paranormal processes. Among them are paraphysics, parascience, psycho-energetics, psychophysics, and psychotronics. These terms are not synonymous, although they have a great degree of overlap. All of them, however, can be distinguished from both parapsychology and psychic research by the wider spec-

trum of purportedly paranormal phenomena allowed within the scope of investigation. . . . (pp. 22–24)

[So far, this is a fine statement of intent, to which no scientist could raise serious objection.]

The Forces and Geometry of the Occult

Selections from the editors' comment preceding later sections of the book have been chosen to show the content of the book and the editors' evaluation thereof. Section II: *The Occult Forces of Life,* for example, present "articles describing various traditions, ancient and contemporary, that claim to have identified an unusual form of energy as the key to understanding paranormal phenomena." (p. 55)

Section III: *The Geometry of the Paranormal* "presents another concept: the multidimensional, dynamic structure of space." (p. 122) ". . .Our intention in this section is to examine a number of intimately related ancient ideas that purport to explain a wide variety of paranormal phenomena." (p. 127) In the words of the editors:

> Levity is held to be not merely negative gravity or the absence of gravity but rather a *primary force* characteristic of counterspace, resulting from the etheric formative forces arising in the nonphysical world. Gravity thrusts outward from the earth, pulling matter downward; levity streams inward to the earth from the cosmos, supplying the means, for example, of getting Newton's apple up in the tree in the first place. (Is this not one of biology's great mysteries: how did the apple get *up* there?) (p. 127)
>
> The last article . . . looks at specific research into geometric forms relating to the concept that space is dynamic, energetic, and has higher-dimensional geometric properties that can transform themselves into three-dimensional space. This is an area where many puzzling phenomena are met. Perhaps the best known goes under the name "pyramid power." It has gained wide attention, even appearing on the cover of *Science Digest* (February 1975) as a feature article. [How one can sharpen razor blades, enhance plant growth, etc., etc., by storing the test object under a cardboard pyramid is described on pp. 194–197 of *Future Science.*]
>
> A pyramid, however, is only one-half of a crystal shape. We have already seen that von Reichenbach's crystals (indeed, all crystals) apparently are natural transformers or generators of nonphysical energy. Is the crystal structure a key to controlling energy through form? Is this also the reason that wizards traditionally wear conical hats? Is this the rationalizing concept behind the "sacred geometry" of true magic and arcane religions? (p. 128)

One example of a large-scale phenomenon is the geographical feature called ley lines. These perfectly straight lines, only a few feet wide, stretch across a landscape for miles—in some cases, hundreds of miles—and form a network or grid upon the surface of the Earth. First noticed and named by Alfred Watkins in England at the turn of the century, it was soon found that these lines of great antiquity were associated with ancient sacred sites such as pagan temples, burial mounds, and terrestrial zodiacs, or the churches and cathedrals later built above them. . . . Indian serpent mounds are said to be a principal feature of ley lines. . . . the so-called "dragon lines" of China may be the same thing as ley lines.

The paranormal aspect of ley lines, however, is the assertion that they can be dowsed, according to an article in *The American Dowser* (August 1974). In this way, it is claimed that they have been found to have a corresponding underground energy flow of great speed—a flow that at certain intersections and terminal points appears to be at right angles to the surface of the earth. Along these lines underground water domes and mineral deposits are said to have been found and, on the surface of the ground, ancient stones which local traditions maintain are "charged with power." (pp. 128–129)

This gridwork is said to coincide with a wide range of natural and paranormal phenomena, including the following: the "Bermuda Triangle" and its purported corresponding eleven areas of strange disappearances ("windows" into hyperspace?) equally spaced around the globe above and below the equator; the planet's tectonic plates; the overlapping of the center of all world magnetic anomalies at the nodes and edges of the crystal-like lattice; the occurrence of all global centers of maximal and minimal atmospheric pressure at the nodes of the grid; paths of hurricanes, prevailing winds, and global currents follow the ribs of the grid; the large deposits of mineral ores which lie along faults or folds in the Earth's crust, which in turn often follow the grid's ribs; and the frequent location of birthplaces of ancient cultures at the intersections of the grid. . . .

Nor is this energy structure limited to the earth and its atmosphere. The lattice, the Soviet investigators say, exists throughout the cosmos and accounts for the creation of planets, stars, and galaxies. This material, at first glance, appears to be highly speculative, but the evidence cited in Bird's article could be rechecked by other investigators.

From crystals to galaxies is a great leap, but, if clear and reasonable linkages can ultimately be shown, or if both crystals and galaxies can be demonstrated as particular cases of an underlying principle, then our probe into cosmic mysteries may have uncovered a unifying concept—the dynamic structure of higher-dimensional space—for bridging science and religion. "Pick a flower and trouble a star," say the mystics. Is science about to demonstrate this? The articles presented here give indications of it. But they also demonstrate the massive amount of work that needs to be done if esoteric philosophy is to be examined through modern scientific procedures. (pp. 130–131)

Occult Physics and Technology

Section IV: *From Physics to Metaphysics* is introduced with the thought: "A Maxwell or an Einstein who will give us a unified theory of paranormal phenomena is greatly needed. Even if history shows that such a person was not among the authors presented here, we feel that their contributions will eventually be recognized by the person as instrumental to his or her conceptual break-through." (p. 207) This section contains a paper by ———, which will be epitomized separately herein below.

As the editors describe it, Section V: *The New Technology* deals with "dowsing devices, the Hieronymus machine, the or-gone accumulator (which is a functional element in the cloud-buster), the Motoyama device, [and] radionics. We could add the Priore device, the Lakhovsky multiwave oscillator, the Moray free-energy device, and Drown radiovision to the list, along with many others." (p. 339)

> Not surprisingly, there are also indications that the ancients had a grasp of technology far more sophisticated than is generally believed. Hints of this abound in all directions: the 1513 Piri Reis map, based on ancient sources, charting the Antarctic shoreline apparently prior to the last Ice Age; a mechanical computer found in Greece and dated 65 B.C.; electric batteries used in Babylon four millenia ago. . . .
>
> [Is it possible that] much today appearing mythical and fantastic is really the degenerated remnant . . . and distorted memory of once-real ultrasophisticated technology? Might amulets, talismans, and scepters, for example, really be now-misunderstood psychic devices or psychotronic generators used for purposes such as healing, de-fense against other psychic energies, etc?
>
> The UFO [unidentified flying object] phenomenon is a focal point for these mysterious hints about strange energies, advanced technol-ogy, and historical mysteries. . . . (p. 342)
>
> The ramifications of the new technology are enormous. Consider the theological implications of indisputable evidence of survival beyond the grave. Consider the effects on drought and famine if international weather engineering through the cloudbuster were be-gun. Consider the energy crisis facing Western civilization in terms of a crystal energy device which could tap the planet's gravita-tional field and turn it into electricity or in terms of the Moray radiant energy device which apparently taps an unnamed cosmic energy to provide (as T. Henry Moray, the inventor, claimed to have done in the 1930s) 100,000 watts of electrical power from a 60-lb package.
>
> In the face of looming catastrophe and global disaster of many

sorts, is it not time to ignore dogmatic voices of resistance which say
that these things are pseudoscience, and mount a coordinated research program? Unconventional though these devices may be, they
may offer enormous hope to a faltering world up against the limits of
its physical and metaphysical constraints. Thus, we present a variety
of devices for consideration here, recognizing their speculative nature and slender claims for authenticity. Yet if only one apparatus of
this group is found to be practical, the benefits to humanity could
make the research worthwhile. (p. 344)

[I have omitted here a friendly, three-page, uncritical presentation of excerpts from a professor of materials science at a large
California university who describes his private theory of magneto-
electric waves traveling through negative space/time at 10^{10} times
the speed of light and in which he applies this theory to curing
lower-back pain using a wobbly dowser's wand, consisting of a
weight glued to the end of a 26-inch rod of one-quarter-inch spring
steel. My noncommittal, summarizing comment was that these excerpts "should suffice to allow a judgment as to the scientific value
of this paper."

In the entire review, my only unfavorable comment, other than
that offered in my initial "Reviewer's Perspective" which is presented above, was confined to my final section, which follows.
Nevertheless this review was rejected by the editor of the *Journal
of the ASPR*.

In fairness, I must add that the editor was dedicated and competent and that I usually agreed with her professional judgments. She
must be given major credit for all that her journal accomplished in
her 25 years of service. I believe that her judgments invariably
reflected the sentiments of her advisers.]

Evaluation

There are two questions that I would leave with my readers:
What is the significance of this book, and what attitude should
members of the Parapsychological Association take toward a fellow member who co-edits such a book? The latter is a question
that each person must answer for himself. It is my purpose merely
to state the question as clearly as possible.

Perhaps it would help to ask: What attitude would the members
of the American Astronomical Society take toward a fellow member who had published evidently worthwhile telescopic observations but who edited a book for the general public that endorsed

astrology as a future science? I believe the dilemma is essentially the same in the two cases.

The parapsychologist who wants to take a stand on this matter may wish to begin by rating himself as to orthodoxy. After scanning *Future Science,* if he draws back in horror, then on this matter he thinks as a professional scientist.

Individual parapsychologists cannot have it both ways. Either one accepts the methodological viewpoint of science or one should cease to desire and to expect favorable recognition by the scientific profession.

The broader question of this book's significance is one that I asked more generally five years ago: What dangers to parapsychology are inherent in the demands of the populace for emotional satisfaction? (McConnell, 1973) It may be time for a re-assessment.

For ecological reasons the long-range prospect for the support of science by society as presently constituted can only worsen (McConnell, 1982c). In the last half-decade the breaking down of Western culture, including its standards of institutional excellence, has continued as expected (Somervell, 1946). (The latter fact can best be understood by linear thinkers by means of examples such as the current "grade inflation" found in the universities despite the falling Scholastic Aptitude Test scores of entering freshmen.)

The question of paramount importance is whether study of the nature of man can provide us with a new value system before the final abandonment of the old takes all of science, including parapsychology, into oblivion. Each of us can try to estimate the quickening pace of disintegration by keeping track of culturally degrading events as they occur, or are accepted, for the first time. The publication of *Future Science,* given all the circumstances, is such an event on my list.

21

OF PEOPLE AND PREJUDICE

TESTIMONY FOR AND AGAINST PSI PHENOMENA

Under the title, *The Enchanted Boundary,* Walter Franklin Prince (1930), then Research Officer of the Boston Society for Psychic Research, published what may have been the first compilation of disbelievers in psychic phenomena. Through that book and its companion work, *Noted Witnesses for Psychic Occurrences* (1928), Prince has left his contribution to the sociology of parapsychology.

Among the many whom Prince listed as publicly testifying to the impossibility of psi phenomena, only a few are remembered today: physicists Michael Faraday, John Tyndall, and Lord Kelvin; biologist Thomas Huxley; psychologists, G. Stanley Hall, Hugo Münsterberg, and Joseph Jastrow; historian T.B. Macaulay.

Those generally remembered persons from Prince's book of "witnesses" who reported first-hand, ostensibly psychic occurrences, came from many different occupations: suffragist Susan B. Anthony, Prime Minister Arthur Balfour, dramatist David Belasco, poet Robert Browning, plant breeder Luther Burbank, mathematician Jerome Cardan, Samuel Clemens ("Mark Twain"), Senator Chauncey Depew, Charles Dickens, hypnotist James Esdaile, General Giuseppe Garibaldi, Goethe, statesman John Drummond Hay, Justice Oliver Wendell Holmes, publisher Henry Holt, Victor Hugo, Jeanne d'Arc, Ben Jonson, hypnotist Auguste Liebeault, botanist Carolus Linnaeus, inventor Hudson Maxim, naturalist John Muir, General James Oglethorpe, General George Pickett, statesman Josiah Quincy, pianist Artur Rubenstein, John Ruskin, composer Camille Saint-Saëns, composer Robert Schumann, Sir Walter Scott, Percy Bysshe Shelley, Socrates (as related in Plato's *Apology*), writer Harriet Beecher Stowe, and theologian Emanuel Swedenborg.

Such a list proves nothing about the reality of psi phenomena, but it does suggest that ostensibly psychic occurrences are widespread and not confined to the ignorant.

My contribution to the sociology of parapsychology will be both more modest and more personal than that of Walter Prince. I hope to shed light on the nature of prejudice in science as revealed by the behavior of opponents to parapsychology whom I have encountered.

Most of my examples are trivial behaviors spanning a day or more. It is through the study of minor, extended, and clearly delineated interactions between people that we can best gain an understanding of attitudes.

I am concerned in this and the next chapter with the larger aspects of prejudice: its manifestations, incidence, and scope. Elsewhere (McConnell, 1977a), I have dealt with the psychological machinery by which scientists deceive themselves regarding parapsychology and, more generally, with the reality-integrating mechanisms by which the thinking segment of the population achieves belief consistency and avoids the discomfort of "cognitive dissonance."

SYMBOL AND REALITY

We are distinguished from other animals by the fact that we deal with two worlds: the real world and its symbolic representation. We assume that there is a congruence between these worlds.

We live our thinking lives in the world of language. As literate beings we carry on our social transactions almost exclusively in symbols. Nonverbal interpersonal communication is emotionally important but intellectually empty.

How well does language represent reality? For the purpose of logical manipulation resulting in predictable observation, how well are our nouns tied to nature? Except in engineering and in the physical and biological sciences, there is only the most tenuous relation between reality and our mental constructs. Because our beliefs are articulated in language, we are free in most areas to believe what we wish—constrained only by our limited, first-hand contact with nature.

That the individual believes what he wishes, is usually conceded with regard to the populace. However, it is equally true of the leaders in all fields of human endeavor except where there is tight feedback to reality. Elsewhere, evaluative decisions are reached intuitively—after which, reasons are sought to justify those decisions to self and others.

Decent, sensible people will, of course, reject this idea that all beliefs about nonphysical reality are twisted to whatever shape will make us comfortable. Nevertheless, the evidence is everywhere about us. How else, for example, are we to explain that in preparation for World War II the German people, including scientists, scholars, and artists, without perceptible resistance, over a period of years, step by step, accepted the destiny offered to them by Hitler in what would appear to have been the strangest intellectual debacle in history?

Even our wisest leaders hold to what I call the "elitist fallacy," namely, the idea that intellectual leaders are to be trusted in matters of intellect, at least within their areas of acknowledged competence. Cambridge Professor C.D. Broad, for example, (1887–1971) was a model of honesty and kindness, and one of the great philosophers of the twentieth century. Writing in another context (1938, p. 141) he said:

> Neither [Henry] Sidgwick nor [Frederic] Myers could foresee that in another 50 years compulsory education would have produced throughout the civilized world a populace of literate imbeciles, ready to believe or to disbelieve anything with equal passion and unreason, and that science would have provided, in the cheap press and wireless, an immensely powerful engine for generating irrational beliefs and disbeliefs at will.

The present point of this quotation is not what it says—which is obviously true—but its implication that there is a class of *ubermenschen* who reject irrational beliefs and disbeliefs. Broad himself was nearly such a person, and in Sidgwick and Myers he was describing two paragons of rationality. However, in my experience, this attribute is much rarer than he seems to have believed.

BELIEF AS A TREASURE

It was not until I circularized the Federation of American Scientists in 1976, after nearly 30 years association with parapsychology, that I learned the extent to which scientists lack interest in the possibility of ESP. I sent a printed letter in a university envelope to 8,500 members saying that I had received an F.A.S. bulletin which began, "As you know, within the space of half an hour the entire industrialized world can be destroyed" and which ended by urging passage of a law to deny the President of the United States the first use of nuclear weapons.

In my letter I commented that, although political action is important, our best long-range hope lies "in the discovery and nurture of new ideas in science—presumably in biology and psychology, where it is reasonable to suppose that we are still near the beginning of an exponential rise in knowledge." I suggested for consideration the specific subfields of genetic engineering and parapsychology. Concerning the latter I said, "I regard it as a reasonable belief that phenomena so intimately concerned with man's mental nature must be important and that their investigation should be given a high priority." On the basis of my reputation as a scientist in other fields, I offered to send without obligation single copies of evidential and sociological bibliographies of parapsychology.

The response rate was two percent from this highly sensitized, nuclear-war-fearing group. This experience illustrates the proposition that lack of interest is a nearly universal defense against any challenge to existing beliefs.

In a scientist, a commitment to seek reality is exceedingly rare except with regard to narrowly selected subject areas within his intentional focus, and then only if the subject is one that coerces truth. A physicist, for example, will normally be forced to exercise devotion to truth within his specialty. By contrast, an economist need have little concern for empirical reality.

Personal commitments are usually not to reality but to belief within a world view. The mature physicist is committed to a conception of physical causality that he shares with his peers. There is nothing discernibly idiosyncratic about it. The mature economist of our time is committed to the Keynesian principle of self-multiplying wealth. Were it otherwise, he could not have earned his doctorate or found employment.[1]

Some unlimited commitment to belief is necessary for bare survi-

---

1. Even in the natural sciences it can take a long time for reality to coerce belief. Examples of persisting absurdities: (1) The building of lighter-than-air dirigibles in the 1920s, although elementary stress analysis showed their vulnerability to the sheer forces visible in the whipping of trees on a windy day. (2) The refusal for more than a generation to respond to the research of Raymond Pearl (1938) of Johns Hopkins University, which showed that heavy tobacco smoking associates with a doubled death rate in the age range 30–50 years. (3) The deployment of fission-power reactors only to discover that the "nuclear priesthood" specified by the Director of Oak Ridge National Laboratory as necessary for the management of massive amounts of radioactive materials (Weinberg, 1972) cannot be created from salaried conscripts. (4) The present denial of the inheritance of intelligence, although scientists all agree that biological function depends upon structure and that structure is determined genetically. (For some who might wish to pursue this last, currently important topic, I have included Appendix G: "Listening Guide to the Controversy about the Relation of Intelligence to Inherited Biological Structure.")

val. Happiness requires a broad spectrum of such commitment. Once a person has crossed the enchanted boundary between adolescence and adulthood (See Chapter 23), the constellation of beliefs making up his world view becomes a commitment that can be altered in only the rarest of cases. Suspension of belief risks psychological collapse.

The foregoing paragraphs are intended to illuminate two definitions: A *prejudice* is a belief to which one gives unlimited commitment. A *philosophy of life* is a collection of prejudices. These concepts are central to an understanding of the status of parapsychology among professional scientists.[2]

GETTING BACK TO PHYSICS

One cannot advocate the study of parapsychology without encountering scientists strongly opposed to the field. And yet, in 35 years the number who have angrily responded to my promotional activities has been surprisingly small. Rarely did I discern animosity directed toward me as an individual. Rather, it must be supposed that the adverse responses reflected anxiety aroused by the purported character of psi phenomena. I shall give examples.

An eminent nuclear physicist kindly served in the mid-1940s as a committee member for my doctoral dissertation on "video storage by secondary electron emission from simple mosaics." Later, I sent him parapsychological reprints from time to time. A generation passed before I learned how strongly he felt about parapsychology. In a speech before the American Philosophical Society he said:

> Flying saucers and astrology are not the only pseudosciences which have a considerable following among us. There used to be spiritualism. There continues to be extrasensory perception, psychokinesis, and a host of others. . . . Where corruption of children's minds is at stake, I do not believe in freedom of the press or freedom of speech. In my view, publishers who publish or teachers who teach any of the

---

2. Upon first consideration, the fraudulant creation, and the irrational rejection, of evidence favoring psi phenomena are seen as two sides of the coin of deception. The charlatan experimenter deceives others; the prejudiced skeptic deceives himself. As a rule, however, fraud and prejudice both involve both kinds of deception. A difference in this respect is only a matter of degree.

Fraud in science indicates a partial breakdown of the perpetrator's portrayal of reality. The need for prejudice implies patchwork among incongruous elements of the holder's belief system. The analysis of the stability of belief systems is beyond the scope of this book. Suffice to say, in the field of science, fraud and prejudice are both irrelevant to the ostensible aim of the enterprise; for they cannot change the nature of the universe.

pseudosciences as established truth should, on being found guilty, be publicly horsewhipped and forever banned from further activity in these usually honorable professions (Condon, 1969).

In 1953, after the *American Journal of Physics* rejected an experimental paper on psychokinesis (McConnell, Snowdon, & Powell, 1955) for a list of reasons that seemed to me to be patently evasive, I sent the editorial correspondence for comment to an eminent physicist with whom I had had a mutually respectful relationship during World War II and who later was to become a U.S. Presidential advisor. He replied:

> If reputable journals refuse to publish your stuff, I would, if I were you, reach the conclusion that it is not worth publishing. [The editor] gave precisely the correct answer to your long and meaningless letter. I would strongly advise you to get back to physics.

TRUTH BY AFFIRMATION

In 1972–73, as one step in a ten-year program to explore the thinking of the intellectual leaders of America on complex, emotion laden subjects, I sent a pair of papers to a selected group of several hundred scientists. These papers, about two unrelated controversial topics, were mailed together in the hope of eliciting comparable responses to each topic.

The first paper was an unpublished socio-legal analysis titled "Affirmative Action in the Universities," in which I began as follows:

> [By the creation of administrative law] the Executive Branch of our government, through its affirmative action procedures, is attempting to carry out a social reform by the use of economic sanctions without the authorization of Congress. In the process, it has abandoned some fundamental freedoms long accorded to worker and management. More important perhaps, the movement here afoot is revolutionizing our social structure irreversibly, for better or worse. It may be a threat to the economic productivity of our industry and to the intellectual excellence of our universities. A question can properly be raised as to why the assumptions underlying this movement have not been publicly explored.

I then examined a range of ideas which, at that time, had not been fully treated in the literature. Examples: Reverse discrimination. Mutually inconsistent policies of cultural paternalism within the Federal Government (e.g., as between Negro and Indian). Biological factors possibly affecting numerical representation of races and the sexes in employment categories and in Ph.D. pro-

grams. Ambiguities deliberately written into the Federal regula-
tions for the tactical advantage of the Department of Labor in
enforcing Affirmative Action.

The tenor of my paper is suggested by the following excerpts:

> The nature of [racial and sexual, economic] injustice is not always
> what is popularly supposed. It is not necessarily a denial of opportu-
> nity or reward "simply" because the victim is a member of a dispar-
> aged group. For biological or other reasons the group, as a group,
> may deserve disparagement in terms of its suitability for a particular
> kind of employment. The injustice lies in investing the individual
> with the average, supposed characteristics of the group rather than
> determining his specific nature.
>
> In this view, unjust discrimination on the basis of race or sex is
> inherent in the thinking process: It results from our ability to gener-
> alize and to deal in simplified concepts. It occurs, not only because
> we are intellectually lazy, but because, for survival, we have learned
> to be intellectually economical. We tolerate a certain error in our
> cognition of our environment because we are finite in our mental
> capacities and are being pressed hard to satisfy our needs as we
> perceive them. . . .
>
> Although discrimination based upon individual merit is an inescap-
> able fact for mankind as a part of nature, discrimination based upon
> group membership is demeaning for the person and, in the long
> view, is destructive of social order.

The second paper (McConnell, 1973) was a scholarly appeal for
a distinction between scientific parapsychology and popular occult-
ism. In my introduction I said:

> The present-day loss of conventional beliefs and the rise of philo-
> sophic anarchy parallel the early Christian era. . . . We are living in
> a crescendo of popular superstition whose only relation to parapsy-
> chology is through the substrate of weak, sporadic, natural pheno-
> mena to which both [the parapsychologist and the common man]
> attempt to relate. The distinction between the interest of the com-
> mon man and that of the scientist in psychic phenomena—a distinc-
> tion based upon discipline, technique, and goals—is lost upon the
> layman and is in danger of denial by scientists, who are repelled and
> frightened by the present populist mockery of reason as a guide to
> life. (p. 227)

The body of the paper gave documented instances of scientific
ignorance among the well educated. Examples: The advocacy by
politically powerful educational leaders of the use of astrology for
the classification of students. The offering of money-making
courses in occult nonsense by American colleges and universities.
A private, ten-million dollar hypno-occultism business pretending

to teach ESP. An "Academy of Parapsychology and Medicine" in which medical doctors accept the use of fake electronic devices to assist in clinical diagnosis.

The responses to these papers were extraordinarily diverse. By a world authority on the multivariate analysis of personality I was told:

> I am greatly impressed by the way in which this [Affirmative Action] document gets to the essentials of the situation, analyzes the inconsistencies in our present position, and works toward a sane solution.

From a Nobel Prizewinner in physiology I received the following letter (here given in its entirety):

> I do not know what revolts me more, the bigotry of your "Affirmative Action" manuscript or the idiocy of your "Parapsychology and the Occult." I shall appreciate your *not* corresponding with me any more in the future.

It was evident from this and other letters that, for some scientists, if feelings about a topic have religious depth, even rational discussion will raise anxiety to an intolerable level.

EXTRASENSORY ANTI-HUMANISM

After the first modern encyclopedic appraisal of experimental ESP appeared in 1940 (Pratt, Rhine, Smith, Stuart, & Greenwood), attacks upon the field of parapsychology in the journals of science became exceedingly rare. In 1978, one such attack did appear, however, in the highly regarded psychological journal, *Perceptual and Motor Skills* (*46,* 1063–1079).

My attention was drawn to this paper because it contained eight statements misrepresenting my published writings. In a rejoinder (McConnell, 1978) I simply juxtaposed each such statement with the relevant material from my writings as cited by the authors.

The matter deserves mention here because the authors called upon behavioral scientists "to make a public disavowal of belief in ESP" (p. 1063).

> We have addressed ourselves to the ESP problem . . . because beliefs of this kind are in the long run anti-humanistic. . . . New discoveries are welcome in any research program. ESP, however, does not represent some brave new frontier of human knowledge; it is nothing more than a thinly disguised form of essentialism, a reversion to a pre-scientific religio-mystical tradition. It relates quite

clearly to the primitive practice of assigning causation to mysterious, impalpable, evanescent inner forces whenever the natural web of causation is not immediately apparent. . . . The deleterious effects of ESP beliefs may be obscure and delayed, but they are real and inevitable. The direction of human affairs based upon misconceptions must, in the long run, produce maladaptive and anti-social effects. (pp. 1076–1077)

At the University of Pittsburgh

In 1947, I became an assistant professor of physics at the University of Pittsburgh with the understanding that my main research would be in parapsychology. After five years, when I had only a little to show by way of publication in conventional physics, my colleagues decided not to renew my contract. The chairman of the department wrote to me concerning my research in parapsychology:

> By and large, we agree that this field is of great concern to physicists and that physicists should be able to contribute to it. No skepticism as to the reality of the reported extrasensory effects was voiced. By and large, we don't think that our department is a good place to sponsor this research on an indefinite basis. We are not well enough established to risk the criticisms (justified or not) that might be brought against us by physicists elsewhere. We prefer to build our reputation in the more conventional fields of nuclear physics and the solid state. The best interests of the department as we see them come before the individual desires of some of us to see work of this kind continued here. We fear that recognition of the department for work of this nature will be long in coming. In the past, controversial theories have sometimes had to await the death of a generation of scientists before they were universally accepted.

In this passage I see no evidence of scientific prejudice. It merely expresses the scientific values that prevail in our time.

I have always been grateful to the author of the above statement. Partly because of his candor, I was able to find outside financial assistance and inside administrative support that allowed me to move to the Biophysics Department, where I was permitted to pursue parapsychology nearly full time among more tolerant colleagues.

My encounters with prejudice against parapsychology among my campus colleagues have been surprisingly few. On one occasion, some years after I had left the Physics Department, a highly regarded member of that department with whom I have always had friendly relations, let it be known to the administration that it was disgraceful that research in parapsychology should be allowed to go on at the University of Pittsburgh. Fortunately for me, those officers who had to respond to this opinion did not agree.

Still later, after word of the affair had reached me, I happened to overtake this faculty member walking on the street. In the course of our conversation I learned that he had not read any of my papers. In response to my question as to the possible importance of psychokinesis, he said, "If such an effect were established, it would be, for physics, the greatest discovery of this century—or any other." He also made it plain that he believed ESP and PK are impossible phenomena.

More recently, I encountered active concern by a departmental colleague lest there be any association between parapsychology and his own research. In 1976, I had welcomed the combining of three biological departments within the University because I hoped this would bring me into close contact with biologists working on brain physiology and behavior. Regrettably, before any common scientific interests could be explored, an organizational problem arose.

As a part of the total administrative shuffle, it seemed reasonable to me that my "Survey of Parapsychology" should be listed with the neurobiology courses rather than with biophysics where it had previously been. At the self-organizing meeting of the neurobiologists I described my course as my only current, teaching contribution to the department and offered to submit its content for review by my colleagues at their pleasure. There the matter rested without discussion.

When I later inquired of the acting leader of the neurobiologists why the minutes of that meeting did not list my course among the proposed undergraduate offerings, I was told that parapsychology was not a part of neurobiology as he defined the term and that he did not wish my course or my name listed with the neurobiology group offerings because to do so might weaken the hard-nosed image he was trying to create.

It is, of course, debatable whether this attitude should be classified as prejudice or as prudence—given our current level of understanding of brain function.

The Author's Belief

In my opinion, based upon the totality of the experimental and spontaneous evidence as I have examined it for a third of a century against the panorama of human experience, the case for psi phenomena has been proved many times over.[3]

This is a social as well as a scientific judgment, which each person must affirm or deny for himself. In doing so, each will be putting his reputation at risk.

I have never met a scientist known for his wisdom who was willing to make a public statement that the case for psi had *not* been proved. This may be only because (parapsychologists aside) I have never met a scientist who otherwise compelled profound respect and who claimed to have examined the evidence for psi carefully enough to make a judgment.

There was a time in my life when I could not conceive that scientific leaders would not examine the evidence for psi if it were brought to their attention. This was followed by a period when I knew as a fact that today's scientific leaders would not examine the evidence for psi but I could not understand why. Now, with age, has come understanding and a degree of acceptance of the blindness of the learned.

Some critics may suggest that my belief in the reality of psi as given above, falls in the category of prejudice. There is a test, however, by which anyone who believes or disbelieves in psi can determine the nature of his commitment. Throughout my professional career I have sought to bring the evidence for psi to the attention of other scientists of the highest competence. By every means within my power I have sought (but with little success) to create and encourage public dispute among scientists concerning this subject. It has been my position that my own opinion should not enter into another scientist's judgment; the evidence must speak for itself. In contrast, the effect of the actions of most of the scientists described above (and of the editors to be described in the next chapter) has been to discourage the dissemination of scientific information to those who might be competent to judge it.

In this regard we might draw guidance from K.M. Goldney who, beginning in 1940, was an active member of the Council of the Society for Psychical Research. Her most important experimental contribution to parapsychology was as administrative assistant to S.G. Soal in his card-guessing work in wartime London in the years 1941–1943. When her claim to a place in history (Soal &

---

3. I am frequently asked whether I am "psychic"—it being supposed that this might have influenced my belief in psi. The only modestly evidential cases of spontaneous ESP for which I can vouch firsthand are described in Appendix H.

Goldney, 1943) was threatened by evidence suggesting fraudulent data manipulation by Soal, she wrote (Goldney, 1974, p. 81): "Of course, an adverse verdict, if established, will destroy individual hopes, even beliefs. So be it, if necessary. 'The world is wide' and the object of all our studies is to find and establish the truth."

Four years later, at age 83, Mrs. Goldney generously praised Betty Markwick's computerized analysis proving Soal's fraud and then repeated the statement quoted above, saying: "These sentences summarized what I felt when I wrote them and what I feel now." (Goldney, 1978, p. 278)

22

GUARDIANS OF ORTHODOXY

THE RIGHTEOUS LAYMEN

Outside the main stream of science there is only sporadic opposition to parapsychology. In 1976, a group calling itself "The Committee for the Scientific Investigation of Claims of the Paranormal" was founded by the editor of *The Humanist,* the voice of the American Humanist Association.

For several years the leaders of this group carried on an educational program in the news media and *The Humanist,* linking parapsychology gratuitously with astrology, witchcraft, unidentified flying objects, and professional seers. Their writings in *The Humanist* were summarized by Rockwell, Rockwell, and Rockwell (1978) largely by means of quotations. The following fragments give the flavor:

> The recognized top academic ESP experts (ESPerts for short) are a *most* peculiar breed of "scientist." . . .

> The failures [of parapsychology] are the result of scientific research being carried out by closet occultists with Ph.D.s. Cult Phuds, to give them a more convenient name, permit metaphysics to interfere with physics. . . .

> The entire field of parapsychology has, from its very beginnings, been crowded with characters as trustworthy as the Emperor's tailors.

Eventually, under the same leadership, the "Committee" started a new journal, severed its affiliation with *The Humanist,* and proudly displayed a list of 75 Fellows and Consultants.

From the beginning, however, there was internal dissension over the question of *objectivity* versus *advocacy.* Should the Committee let the scientific chips fall where they might, or should it sweep them into patterns of truth? The control of the Committee rested with a small, self-perpetuating council dominated by the former editor of *The Humanist.* The decision drifted toward advocacy—no doubt for sound economic reasons. This led to the departure of Marcello Truzzi, a sociologist from Eastern Michigan University, and, later, to a crisis in which Dennis Rawlins, a respected astronomer and one of the founders of the Committee, published a detailed account of his expulsion after he had insisted upon fair play for some astrological data in which he himself disbelieved (Rawlins, 1981).[1] The matter was discussed at length in Truzzi's new journal (1982).

From various sources, including personal correspondence with the Fellows and Consultants of the Committee in connection with a survey by McConnell and Clark (1982b), I infer that these sponsors can be classified as follows:

—Professional writers looking for material for stories.

—Psychologists who dislike the revolutionary implications of parapsychology for their profession.

—Professional philosophers.

—Astronomers who see astrology as a caricature of their profession.

—Magicians who fear that parapsychology's real magic will render them all charlatans.

—A mixed group of scientists and engineers concerned about anti-Darwinism in our educational system.

Despite the broad base of its sponsorship, the Committee for the Scientific Investigation of Claims of the Paranormal remains today a promotional operation managed by laymen. My concern in the remainder of this chapter will be rather with those guardians of orthodoxy who have been appointed by the scientific profession.

THE JOURNAL, *SCIENCE*

Science, published weekly by the American Association for the Advancement of Science, is generally regarded as our nation's most important scientific journal. It is subscribed to by alert scientists in all fields as well as by laymen who wish to keep abreast of all aspects of science. The acceptance of a scientific paper for publication in *Science* is a mark of prestige.

Between 1950 and 1981, I found only four papers on parapsychology in *Science*—all by nonparapsychologists. The first (1954, *120,* 148–149) reported negative experimental findings by two psychologists. Another (1955, *122,* 359–367) was a review by a chemist in which the author concluded, without proof, that all otherwise

---

1. Scholars who are unable to find this nonarchival journal may obtain single copies of the Rawlins paper "sTARBABY" from me for one dollar, postpaid, while my supply lasts—RAM.

inexplicable positive findings in the literature of parapsychology must be fraudulent.

The third paper (1965, *150*, 367), by two opthalmologists, purported to show a correlation between electroencephalographic signals and ESP performance. The work was methodologically so weak it would have been rejected out-of-hand by the scientific journals of parapsychology. The subsequent, well-deserved scorn of correspondents (1965, *150*, 1240–1243) did nothing to improve the image of the field.

The fourth paper, written by a statistician/magician under the scholarly title, "Statistical Problems in ESP Research" (1978, *201*, 131–136) was a trivial reconsideration of some 1940 statistical questions in card guessing plus anecdotal material on the possibility of cheating when subjects are tested under loose experimental conditions. Unbelievable though it may seem, in this paper the experimental work of two parapsychologists was formally referenced and then disparaged without criticism or discussion (Kanthamani & Kelly, 1974a;1974b; Kelly & Kanthamani, 1972). One of these experimenters sent a reply to *Science,* which was rejected and subsequently published elsewhere (Kelly, 1979).

Many parapsychologists were incensed at the selection for publication of a paper of this caliber as representative of the field. *Science* printed two critical letters and promised a second group later (1978, *202*, 1145–1146), which, however, did not appear. Among the suppressed letters was one submitted by the Parapsychological Association.

Over the years, a number of technically excellent experimental papers have been submitted to *Science* and rejected. I have referred to one of these in Chapter 20, in the section, "Parapsychologist as Martyr," and have examined its rejection in detail in Appendix F.

My personal experience with *Science* is best summarized by the following rejecting referee's comment, which I received to a non-experimental paper eventually published elsewhere (McConnell, 1977a):

> I find this is a hard paper to judge. I have no familiarity with the literature dealing with ESP. At the same time I have an initial sense that ESP is fraudulent: I am one of those very people about whom McConnell is writing his paper, and who, he very much doubts, will ever open their minds to what he and others are trying to say. After reading his very readable paper I remain unmoved. I am not now

more interested in learning about ESP; I am not less inclined to believe that ESP is fraudulent. Yet, at the same time, I do not wish to say, straight out, do not publish this paper.

McConnell is trying to show what stands in the way of people's receptivity to research dealing with ESP. He is not, in this paper, essaying a general defense of the genuineness of ESP phenomena; nor giving an account of ESP research. Rather he is offering a contribution, if you will, to the sociology of knowledge (to use Karl Mannheim's famous phrase). He sorts the various assertions opponents make, and comes up with sixteen main types. I believe that, mutatis mutandis, these sixteen types would be often present in the minds of people opposed to some scientific hypothesis, or to some disputed doctrine in the non-sciences. That is to say, McConnell's method has relevance beyond his own purpose. Herein is the great interest of the paper. But I am still not confident that his method is sophisticated enough, even for his own purpose.

What is not clear in this referee's comment is how a belief that "ESP is fraudulent," reached despite "no familiarity with the literature dealing with ESP," constitutes an acceptable basis for opposing publication of the paper.

THE AMERICAN JOURNAL OF PHYSICS

In 1952, as noted in the preceding chapter, I submitted an experimental paper on psychokinesis (McConnell, Snowdon, & Powell, 1955) to the *American Journal of Physics,* a journal devoted to the instructional and cultural aspects of physics. Attempts to encourage the editor to base his rejection upon rationally defensible grounds yielded nothing more satisfying than this memorable paragraph:

> It occurs to me that it is just possible that physicists have such a point of view of the external world that no matter how the results of an experiment like yours are presented, it will be impossible for them to carry conviction. I am not sure for my own part that the effect you are describing is really knowable.

Twenty three years later, with a different editor, I tried again to place a paper in the *American Journal of Physics.* This time it was a lecture I had given to an undergraduate seminar in our Physics Department.

In my paper, which was later published elsewhere (McConnell, 1976c), I defined the field of parapsychology in terms of information and energy transfer and discussed how the purported phenomena clash with current concepts in physics. For human interest, there was a dash of autobiography and a pinch of history involving

celebrated physicists. I gave no data or theory, but offered to mail
a bibliography to any reader.

In his letter of rejection the editor said:

> We are continually bombarded with papers concerning new theo-
> ries about physics. . . . Until such theories are accepted by the phys-
> ics research community, it is not appropriate for our journal to con-
> sider the educational consequences of theories.

When I replied: "What parapsychology presents for our consideration is not theory but purported experimental facts," the editor
responded:

> Your paper falls into none of the categories of papers we usually
> receive. It is, I now see, a testimonial. Testimonials were a regular
> part of church life in the time of my parents.

THE AMERICAN PSYCHOLOGICAL ASSOCIATION

We have already seen in the chapter titled "Hypnosis, Peer Reviewed," that the journals of the American Psychological Association are reluctant to entertain fundamentally new psychological
ideas. The following experience suggests to me that there is a
deeper problem within the psychological profession itself.

In 1969, the *American Psychologist* published a lecture I had
given to an introductory psychology class in which I listed as a
useful reference an earlier paper from the *Journal of Experimental
Psychology* (McConnell, Snowdon, & Powell, 1955). Subsequently, the *American Psychologist* (*25*, 279) carried a letter from
a prominent American psychologist protesting that I had failed to
list also his criticism (*JEP, 51,* 290–292) of the 1955 paper, adding
that "An omission of this sort detracts from McConnell's credibility as a scientist."

Evidently, this critic had forgotten that, in consultation with two
mathematical statisticians, I had prepared a reply to his criticism,
which I had submitted to him and which, after extended discussion
and minor changes, he had recommended for publication in the
Journal of Experimental Psychology—for which he was then a consulting editor. Despite his recommendation, the editor refused to
publish my rejoinder, which eventually appeared in the *Journal of
Parapsychology* (McConnell, 1958). This critic must have forgotten
also that he had sent to me—at my request and over his own
signature—a supply of reprints of his *JEP* criticism so that I might
fulfill my offer to send copies to any *Journal of Parapsychology*
readers who had not seen it. In any case, in his *American Psy-*

chologist letter, although he complained of my failure to refer to his *JEP* criticism, he failed to cite my *JP* rejoinder thereto.

In listing a paper of my own, I had no obligation to cite a technical criticism of it that I believed had already been adequately answered. However, if this skeptic wanted me to play by his peculiar rule, he should have followed that rule himself and referenced my published rejoinder when he cited his own criticism. Instead, he engaged in unwarranted personal disparagement.

I wrote privately to my critic, explaining all of the above in a friendly manner, and closing with: "It seems to me that the image of psychology as a science as well as your good reputation and mine would be enhanced if this matter could be publicly closed on a note of magnaminity from you rather than on one of recrimination from me. What do you think?"

To my surprise, my critic replied that, after several weeks of careful consideration, he had decided to take no further action, giving as his reason that my *American Psychologist* article on "a highly controversial topic [had previously been presented to] an undergraduate audience and provided references that were completely one-sided."

This was not only irrrelevant but untrue. In the body of my lecture, as delivered and as published, I explicitly reminded my student audience that I had given them an advance reading assignment from *Science* (Price, 1955) and I called their attention to a book (Hansel, 1966) recommended by E.R. Hilgard and R.C. Atkinson as a scholarly review of the evidence against ESP. These two, fully cited publications were not only the best available full-scale criticisms of parapsychology but, in turn, their lists of other references damning the field could scarcely have been improved upon. Thus, despite the contrary claim of my critic, I had not provided only one-sided references.

For unknown reasons my critic, still in the prime of life, seemed to have lost contact with reality in this matter. I was left to wonder: what further action on my part would be worthwhile for parapsychology?

Whatever trivial damage may have been done to the image of the field by my critic's defamatory statement could not be undone directly by me. In general, what is required to rectify a libel is not a denial by the injured person but a retraction by the publisher. This would be all the more true in the present case where the critic was a nationally respected authority and the injured party was an unknown outsider defending an unpopular position. I was not about to play David to Goliath in the letters column of a journal.

With this decided, I submitted the matter, first to the editor and then to the Board of Directors of the American Psychological Association, which publishes the *American Psychologist*. My letter to the Board closed with these paragraphs:

> It would appear that an essential ingredient of the situation is the fact that the research concerns "extrasensory perception" and "psychokinesis," phenomena which for nearly 90 years, or the life span of psychology as a science, have been rejected by many psychologists as unworthy of study and in some cases have been attacked with hostility and illogic having deep-seated emotional origins.
>
> May I suggest that the issue which you are asked to consider is not without historic significance, both as regards the subject matter of the research and as regards the willingness of "establishment science" in this time of social crisis [1970] to abide by its proclaimed standards of civility and reason.

The Board considered the matter formally and, like its journal editor, declined responsibility. By letter from the Executive Officer of the APA, I was told that the Board had stated that, if I believed the issue to be of sufficient gravity, I should request examination of it by the Association's Committee on Scientific and Professional Ethics and Conduct.

Under the circumstances, this suggestion by the Board that I go to the APA Committee on Ethics was not responsive to my request that the Board take remedial action for its publication of a misrepresentation of my scientific behavior, nor did it offer an alternate path by which my grievance might be redressed. Whatever the intention of the Board, the effect of its recommendation was to make it appear falsely to anyone unaware of the Ethics Committee's purpose and rules of procedure that the Board's refusal to override its editor was a judicious response to an appellant whose request might better have been directed elsewhere.

Subsequently, by direct communication with the Executive Officer of the APA and with the Secretary of its Committee on Ethics, I verified that:

1. The Board of Directors had not asked its Ethics Committee to consider this matter.

2. The Ethics Committee is an instrument of the APA and its function is not to redress grievances but to protect the psychological profession and the public.

3. If at my instigation an evaluation adverse to my critic were reached by the Committee on this matter, under its operating rules I would not be told of that fact by the APA.

4. The APA, through its Ethics Committee or otherwise, has no power to force an APA member in such a situation to make a public retraction or apology. The APA's only formal option would be to offer the editor's apology for printing an unwarranted defamation. This it had already declined to do.

What the Directors should have done, of course, was to contact my critic informally and bring a little "old boy" pressure to bear. At least, this is what I would have expected of responsible professional leaders. Instead, the Board offered a curiously inappropriate recommendation; for the Board and its supporting professional staff could not fail to know that the purpose and modus operandi of its Ethics Committee rendered their recommendation deceitful.

By my petition to the Board of the APA I had learned something about the thinking of leaders of the psychological profession. How would the bulk of responsible psychologists view the matter?

I assembled all of the documents, including my *American Psychologist* paper (1969) and a summary of the case. The resulting bound file, weighing five ounces, I mailed, first class, with individually signed covering letters to an essentially random sample of 750 Fellows of the American Psychological Association. This sample was drawn from U.S.A. and Canadian psychologists under the age of 70 and included all 295 Fellows of APA Division 9, known as the "Society for the Psychological Study of Social Issues." To this group of Fellows I added a subsample of 75, from the (presumably younger) *Members* and *Associates* of the SPSSI. (This Society is generally thought of as the liberal conscience of the APA, and had been taking public positions on a variety of social issues.)

My covering letter stated: "I am writing to you personally to ask that, after consideration of the evidence, you take whatever steps you deem appropriate to encourage the APA to resolve this publication controversy in conformity with your own ideals."

Because of the targets and nature of my complaint, as well as the format of my mailing, it is reasonable to assume that nearly all of the subjects in my sample read the furnished documents to the point of satisfying themselves, and hence that the response I received accurately reflected the perceived meaning of the matter.

Aside from a few letters that were enigmatic and several others from friendly acquaintances, the remaining replies (26 in number) showed feeling transactions rather than intellectual appraisal. Respondents' feelings were revealed in various ways, e.g., by expressions of sympathy, by hostility toward me, by advice to set the record straight with a letter in the *American Psychologist,* by dismissal of the matter as unimportant, by peacemaking overtures ("Both sides are right"), or by "Why did you send *me* the dossier?"

With so small a response (3%), the respondees were highly self-selected, and no generalization to the population from the nature of the received replies is warranted.

What I had hoped for, but did not get, was perhaps a 20% reply rate. It seemed to me that the minimally proper response from a busy psychologist who was pleased to receive the mailing would have been a two-sentence note, saying: "Thank you for an interesting and apparently well documented psychological case study. I regret I am unable to . . ." From the lack of response, I infer that most psychologists have little concern about professional ethics and the need for honest and generous personal relationships in science.

23

THE CLOSING MIND OF ADOLESCENCE

FORWORD

This was a guest lecture given in October, 1977, in an "antiparapsychological" course for freshmen and sophomores in the Psychology Department at the University of Pittsburgh. For an earlier lecture in the same course, see McConnell, 1976b.

Subsequently, this lecture was rejected for publication by the *Journal of Parapsychology* and the *Journal of the American Society for Psychical Research* as unsuitable for adult readers.

I disagree with this opinion. I am presenting the lecture here because it suggests an educational role for parapsychology and because it may shed light on poltergeist phenomena, which usually involve adolescents. I foresee the study of the nature of man as a preferred form of psychotherapy for the storms of adolescence as well as the basis for a general educational reform.

THE RIDDLE OF CONSCIOUSNESS

What is consciousness? How does human thinking differ from that of a dog or a chimpanzee? The usual answer is that we assist our thinking by means of language.[1] While true in a technical sense, this explanation obscures the essence of our humanity.

Unlike a chimpanzee, we can wonder explicitly about consciousness. We can ask: What are the cosmic implications of our self-awareness? Does consciousness have an extra-material source, or does it arise as a natural property of certain configurations of matter? Will our sense of being and identity someday cease to exist? How does my consciousness relate to that of the persons around me? Are there perhaps other centers of consciousness that do not exist in visible bodies? There are many such questions, but they are all encompassed by: "What am I?"

This may be the most important question one can ask. The writings of wise men suggest that no one knows the answer. At most, we have a few hints—just enough to make it seem certain that there is much more to be learned if we knew how to get at it.

TWO EASY ANSWERS TO A DIFFICULT QUESTION

What do young people do as they become aware of this seemingly unanswerable question? They try to answer it, of course, but after a while they usually become frightened or discouraged.

---

1. Discussed in Chapters 4, 5, and 17.

Sometime around the age of 20 almost everyone feels compelled to settle the matter, at once and for all time, so that he or she will no longer be anxious. The process of responding successfully to the question "What am I?" is known colloquially as "growing up." After that, we are emotionally ready to take our place in the world.

It is difficult to live with uncertainty about one's destiny. If taken seriously, that kind of worry might lead to alcoholism or suicide. Professors do not like to talk about it, but at any large university in nearly every year at least one student ends his life because he has not found a satisfying answer to the question: "What am I?" Most students, to be sure, do not take such drastic action. Instead they find an answer that may not be true but that is good enough for them.

What answers do they find? So far as I can determine, most college students are satisfied by one of two kinds of answers. Some discover that organized religion fills their need for a meaning in life. The rest, for the most part, settle for what seems to me to be a very strange answer. They develop a special thinking skill that allows them to put this question out of mind and to amuse themselves with other questions that are easier to answer, questions that will bring fame and fortune—or, if not fame, then at least economic security as a well fitting cog in the machinery of civilization. This might be viewed as self-discipline for survival. More accurately, it might be called "substitutional thinking." It can be effective in relieving anxiety, and, for many, it is the key to success in life.

Usually the decision to adopt a comfortable set of beliefs or nonbeliefs and to close one's mind for the rest of one's life is taken by the time of the sophomore year in college. Occasionally, one finds a senior who is still open-minded and uncommitted, but the feeling of his teachers is that such a student has already missed his chance and will never be successful because he will not concentrate his attention on the job he must do to earn his livelihood.

WHEN INDOCTRINATION FAILS

The process of maturation explains the slogan of the 1960s: "Don't trust anyone over 30." But I think that slogan missed by ten years. In my experience, with rare exceptions, no one much over 20 is capable of entertaining a new idea that would disturb his or her system of life values.

By that age, with the help of society, we have thoroughly indoc-
trinated ourselves. Once in a while, however, the machinery for
the socialization of the young breaks down, as it did during the
Vietnam War. Large numbers of young men discovered that the
answers or non-answers they had acquired about the meaning of
life could not make them comfortable about going off to battle. As
a result, we had mass rebellion and the beginning of a social revolution. The rebellion was aborted by ending the war.

There are many individual cases where the brainwashing system
that we call "education" fails to give satisfaction. Among them are
the young people who join Reverend Moon's "Unification Church"
and beg for money on street corners while deceiving the public (for
the sake of God) about how the money will be used. Occasionally,
the desperate parents of Moon converts will hire a kidnapper to
capture their child long enough to "re-program" him or her back to
a culturally approved way of thinking. What happens in these cases
might be thought of as a battle of opposing brainwashers.

WHY BELIEFS ARE SACRED

There is a social taboo against talking about the brainwashing of
our youth. Except obliquely, we will not admit that it occurs. We
are told never to question another person's sacred beliefs. But we
are not told why, except that it is impolite to do so. The true
reason is that there is a custom of mutual concealment among
adults: "If you don't question my self-deception, I won't question
yours." The danger each of us fears is the anxiety that would
accompany the creation of a belief conflict or a belief vacuum.

This fear finds expression in the following rule of education in
subject areas that have emotional content: Never ask the student
an unanswerable question or you will make him uncomfortable and
lose his attention.

If one wants to inculcate a new idea, it is good pedagogy to offer it
as a modern substitute for an old, previously accepted idea. If you
are a teacher in what the students call our "Department of Revolution" and your purpose is to promote Marxism—which is a godless
religion, incompatible with older religions such as Judaism and
Christianity—you wrap your ideas in a package labelled "scientific"
and present it to the student at a time when he may be having doubts
about the religious beliefs he acquired from his parents.

In this way, in suitable cases, one can readily substitute Marxism for Christianity. Contrariwise, a good pedagogue would never create anxiety by saying to the student: "I am sorry to confess my ignorance. I know that the Marxist theory of man is in error. I know that the Judeo-Christian concept of man is incomplete. I don't know the true nature of our purpose in life, but I would like to help you look for it." To say that, would be so dissatisfying or disturbing that the student would cease to listen—or so the Educator thinks.

Why Hasn't Science Been Tried?

I am going to risk making you uncomfortable. I refuse to ignore the question: "What am I?" I, too, have not found the answer. But I believe I know a way to search for it, and I invite you to join with me in the search.

What I recommend is the method of science. One may ask: "If it is possible that science can answer this question, why hasn't it been tried?" It has not for a very simple and absurd reason.

For about 100 years psychologists have pre-empted the scientific study of the psyche of man. Until recently, however, like a dog in the manger, they have refused to chew on it. It has been only about 20 years since one was first allowed to use the words "mind" or "mental" in the respected journals of science. Before then, one could talk about stimulus and response, operationalism, conditioning, and physiology, but it was forbidden, upon pain of editorial rejection of one's manuscript, to talk about mind, intuition, inspiration, free will, and all other things that have to do jointly with consciousness and brain. Only recently, that taboo has been successfully broken, and now people of many kinds are moving into the experimental study of mystical states of consciousness, biofeedback, dreams, self-determination—you name it.

However, it is still not entirely respectable to investigate the most important mental phenomena of all, extrasensory perception and psychokinesis. Those who want to do that are more likely to find acceptance in a small-college psychology department than in a large university.

A Modest Educational Proposal

Human self-awareness has been increasing since the beginning of history. In the last 200 years it has begun to spread to all levels of society. In the evolutionary scheme of things, yours may be the first generation of *Homo sapiens* in which great numbers of humans accumulated, through leisure, sufficient self-awareness to be free to ask the question: "What am I?" Toward answering that question, may I offer a modest educational proposal?

"Growing up" extends roughly from age 14 to 20 years. For high school and the first two years of college, perhaps the curriculum should be re-arranged to focus on the nature of man.

Don't we do that now? No, you are being taught, for the most part, by adult teachers with closed minds—unaware, of course, of their own condition. Some are teaching you techniques necessary to earn a living and to think efficiently. Others are trying to help you close your mind, i.e., adopt the culturally prevalent value system. It is a rare teacher who will tell you that we are ignorant of our origin, purpose, and destiny. What you are taught about the basic nature of man is at best superficial and is often wrong.

In my proposal there will be a new hierarchy of studies, known perhaps as "the liberating arts." At the top will be the dual study of consciousness: its understanding through science, and its practice in the humanities.

Instead of reaching maturity by choosing an arbitrary meaning for life, you will be taught to remain forever young by searching for the answer to the question: "What am I?" In pursuing this question, some of you may possibly wish to become parapsychologists and to seek scientific understanding of the relation between mind and brain.

24

RECAPITULATION

THE QUEST FOR IMMORTALITY

In this book I have presented a variety of topics and some unfamiliar ideas. Before attempting a synthesis to show the status and meaning of parapsychology, I shall refresh your memory of what was said in the first 23 chapters.

In the last half of the nineteenth century extrasensory perception was generally recognized by scientists to be incompatible with their beliefs about nature and, therefore, of necessity, to be either non-occurring or "supernatural." Spiritualists turned this scientific opinion to religious advantage by using ESP to prove to the credulous that mediums can communicate with the dead. They argued: "If ESP is scientifically impossible and nevertheless occurs, it must happen by spirit agency."

Spiritualists were interested, not in science, but in the denial of death. Evidence purporting to prove postmortem survival consisted of (a) claims by the living to be either direct representatives or reincarnations of the dead, supported by (b) the production of psi phenomena presumed to be possible only through the agency of the dead. With the acceptance of psi phenomena in the laboratory as a natural manifestation of the living, the case for postmortem survival of individual personality has come generally to be regarded as the product of bad logic and a desire for immortality. Parapsychology may eventually help resolve this desire by revealing the meaning and necessity of death in relation to consciousness.

DIVIDED CONSCIOUSNESS

For the production of ESP it was found that so-called spirit mediums usually enter a trance of one kind or another. Laboratory experiments have since confirmed that psi phenomena are more likely to occur to people when they try to abandon their feeling of individual identity. As they loosen their sensory grasp of reality, they are sometimes able to reach out and make direct, nonsensory contact with their environment. Those conditions in which partial loss of sense of reality take place are known as "dissociated states."

Dissociation phenomena were long neglected by psychology—in part, because of the antithesis between dissociation and the condition of analytical self-awareness in which the rational activities of science ordinarily take place. Recently, psychologists have begun to explore dissociation under the rubric "altered states of consciousness." But psychology still largely ignores multiple personalities, which exhibit perhaps the most challenging of all such states. This neglect is puzzling because a large body of evidence on this subject was gathered at the beginning of the twentieth century by Morton Prince (1905, 1929) studying Sally Beauchamp and by Walter Franklin Prince (1915, 1916) studying Doris Fischer. Their most bizarre finding was that two incompatible personalities could be simultaneously and independently self-aware within the same brain.

Human split-brain experiments complement the findings of clinical multiple personality and offer clues to the organization of information storage in the brain. The wide dispersal of related memories is surprising. Verbal memory, placed largely in the left cerebral hemisphere, is the key to analytic self-awareness and personal identity. Information stored without connections to verbal memory may control our behavior although outside our analytic awareness.

Our growing understanding of divided consciousness has social implications. The same abandonment of physical reality that allows the professional psychic to produce psi phenomena can also make him the undisciplined, amoral creature of his motivations. To satisfy himself, he must satisfy his clientele, and this he can do either by producing genuine ESP and PK or by simulating these phenomena by any means at his command. If it is PK the psychic has promised, he may imitate it by his own motor activity and we call him a fraud. But if he has promised only ESP and often produces false statements, these are regarded as permissible mistakes.

Similarly, some cases of fraud by experimenters may reasonably be assumed to involve multiple personality. This possibility should be examined in the larger context of the mechanisms by which criminals maintain their self-respect. The widespread occurrence of multiple personality raises questions of social policy in dealing with criminal acts.

Dissociation is a larger subject than clinical multiple personality because it occurs variously, every day, in everyone's life. There is reason to believe that many, and perhaps most, people shift frequently from one personality to another without gross discontinuity in memory. There may be a psychic factor in this that leads to mob action. I suspect that the study of these ideas will prove of great importance in the future science of sociology and will perhaps radically alter our concepts of moral responsibility.

History of the Research

From a historical perspective parapsychology can be divided into three periods. From 1882 to 1901, the founders of psychical research focused upon postmortem survival as a challenge of paramount importance. In the transitional period from 1901 to 1930, the investigation of spirit mediums reached its greatest refinement, even while new objectives, new attitudes, and new methods were taking over the field, which thereafter became known as parapsychology.

The early studies had shown that psi phenomena could be produced in a quasi-religious trance setting and that they also occurred spontaneously in sleeping and waking states. Recent compendia of spontaneous cases (L.E. Rhine, 1961; 1967; 1981) show how psi phenomena happen in a wide variety of forms to many ordinary people throughout all walks of life, but especially to a few persons who presumably have a favorable genetic endowment.

For a long time it has been thought important to know: To what extent can these phenomena be produced at will? The card-guessing of J.B. Rhine, begun at Duke University in 1930, ushered in an era of systematic laboratory experimentation as opposed to observation and clinical research. The new hope was to find the important variables that control the appearance of ESP. What was needed, above all, was a repeatable experiment so that the phenomena could be systematically investigated as in other fields of science.

Attempts to find controlling variables associated with the test subject's personality and beliefs and with the test environment (other than those invoking dissociation) have proved generally unsuccessful. Manipulation of such variables has occasionally yielded statistically significant correlations, but the final conclusion has always been that the variables under investigation have only a remote and weak relationship to psi (Kanthamani & Rao, 1971; 1972a; 1972b; Palmer, 1971; 1972).

The Methodological Milieu

With the rise of methodological self-awareness, brought on by the philosophic revolution caused by quantum physics and shown by the proliferation of philosophy-of-science programs in universities after World War II, a few working scientists in all fields came to a clearer understanding of their epistemological relationship to the physical world. They discovered to their dismay that they could never grasp reality in the way nineteenth-century scientists had believed possible but must be content with something much less satisfying to their intuition and emotions.

In the same period, parapsychologists began to wonder what was wrong with their approach that so much effort had produced so little understanding. In growing numbers they could guess what had been foolish in the hopes of earlier investigators, and they now rejected the kinds of philosophizing that had cluttered the literature of the field for many decades.

When Thomas Kuhn's analysis of scientific progress appeared in 1962, parapsychology was recognized as still in what he called the "preparadigm" stage. The problems of parapsychological research vis-a-vis establishment science were seen to be normal for a new field still lacking theory.

Thomas Kuhn divides science into two alternating phases: revolutionary and elaborational. The latter he calls "normal science" because it occupies most scientists for most of their lives. Scientists are trained not to welcome fundamentally new ideas and are embarrassed when they encounter observational data that contradict their expectations. Their philosophic stance might be compared to that of the Church of Rome in the sixteenth century.

The acceptance of psi phenomena is hindered by the fact that most scientists have never examined their own methodology except at the level of technique. With rare exceptions, scientists have not progressed beyond naive realism and are unaware of the limits to human understanding inherent in the use of models. Many scientists stoutly declare that there is no place in science for psi phenomena. That is hardly surprising because psi has been omitted as superfluous from our current models used to explain other phenomena. Similarly, there are no serious accounts of spontaneous psi in history because scholarly historians have left them out to avoid conflict with the Cartesian world view. (See Chapters 1, 5, 17, 18, 21.)

At the end of the nineteenth century many scientists were open-minded toward psi phenomena. Some of the greatest names in the history of psychology (William James, William McDougall, Sigmund Freud, V.M. Bekhterev) were convinced of the observational reality of these phenomena—without commitment, of course, as to their ultimate nature.

Experimenters in this field in the nineteenth century were men of intelligence, energy, and integrity. The doubts with which psychical research has been regarded arose, in part, from their use of dissociating subjects who sometimes resorted to fraud, but even more, perhaps, from the unwillingness of behaviorists and, later, neobehaviorists to examine the ever-growing accumulation of evidence for the reality of psi phenomena.

Because psi phenomena ordinarily appear in the laboratory only as sporadic, undependable effects and are usually hidden in the noise of chance, it has been customary to enhance them by statistical analysis whenever possible. Probability calculations alone cannot prove the occurrence of psi phenomena. At most, they can show with reasonable certainty that some causal (nonchance) factor was at work in the creation of the data. The further conclusion that psi was operating is an engineering judgment involving every aspect of the experiment.

Nevertheless, the web of spontaneous and experimental evidence was sufficiently extensive and tight long before 1930—some would say, well before 1900—that any competent and dedicated student of the literature could have had no doubt that psi phenomena of some kind do occur.

The search for understanding has been unceasing since Rhine began his quest for experimental control in 1930. Perhaps by 1940, and certainly by 1960, all rational criticisms of the laboratory procedures for demonstrating psi had been publicly met. The one remaining hurdle was, and is, to discover a way of producing these phenomena whenever they are desired.

GROSS PSYCHOKINESIS

Recurrent spontaneous psychokinesis is one of the most philosophically unsettling of the well established forms of psi. Apparently, the mind is capable of unleashing considerable amounts of physical energy. The prevailing speculation is that so-called poltergeist activity occurs in the presence of deeply frustrated individuals and represents a pathological breakthrough of psychic energy normally confined to the mind-brain interaction.

Experimental psychokinesis has been sought most often in the form of control of the final resting position of falling objects, but recently it has been tentatively demonstrated in many other modalities. In my judgment there is no remaining reasonable basis for doubting the willed psychokinetic movement of mechanical systems in stable equilibrium requiring power expenditures of not less than 10^{-4} watts.

PATTERNS IN THE DATA

The task of the scientist is to find dependable patterns in his observations. From these patterns, by induction, he creates theories, and these theories constitute our scientific understanding of the universe.

Without pattern there can be no progress in science. Persistent above-chance scoring in a card-guessing experiment may be a challenging anomaly, but until a relation between success at guessing and some condition of the experiment has been discovered, we cannot hope to understand extrasensory perception.

The first quantifiable patterns in parapsychology were not formally recognized until 1927, 45 years after the founding of the Society for Psychical Research. These were "task-structure effects" in which the scoring rate in repeated-trial experiments was found to depend upon the spatial or temporal position of the trial in the data-gathering format.

Another and presumably related effect is the avoidance of success by various mental stratagems that find analogies in Freud's concepts of repression, displacement, and reaction formation. These success-avoidance effects confirm Freud's belief that the mind is functionally multipartite and that the unconscious is a bad logician.

What may be a significant step toward understanding the brain mechanisms of psi was made by McConnell and Clark in 1979 and appeared in a privately published monograph (McConnell, 1982a) after rejection by the journals of parapsychology. In a repeated-trial falling-dice experiment these authors found two countervailing scoring trends which they ascribe to what they call an "organizing principle" and a "principle of ambivalence." In so doing, they may have provided the beginnings of a unified explanation for data-structure and success-avoidance effects.

According to the organizing principle, a psi effect becomes increasingly stable against short term (within about a minute) reversals of its sign if the experimental task is one that leads to increasing mental dissociation within the testing session.

Their intervening-variable interpretation of the principle of ambivalence postulates that psi expresses itself in a positive or negative sense by the unbalancing of two normally balanced channels
of affirmation and negation. While such unbalancing may presumably be brought about in various ways, their data showed that
positive psi occurred after brief (two-minute) rests within the testing session, while, at the same time, increasingly negative psi
occurred during the uninterrupted segments of the session so as
to cause a reversal of the sign of the moving-average score after
several minutes.

Brain-to-Brain PK

Another unifying research idea in parapsychology involves a relationship between hypnosis and psychokinesis. Although the fact
will be denied by both psychologists and parapsychologists, it now
seems clear from experiments involving hypnosis at a distance
(Vasiliev, 1962) that the principle of parsimony requires the postulate that psychokinesis exerted by the operator on his subject is the
essential element of hypnosis.

The best available conceptualization of psi phenomena is in
terms of ESP and PK as incoming and outgoing information/energy
relative to a human being. This model is deficient if for no other
reason than it fails to accomodate precognition. However, the defi-
ciency of this ESP/PK model will hardly provide an escape from
the ethical imperatives inherent in a redefinition of hypnosis as the
psychokinetic control of one brain by another.

Games Parapsychologists Play

At some level of consciousness, parapsychologists are aware that
the full acceptance of psi phenomena by orthodox science will
cause their field to be overrun by outsiders. At that point they will
face stiff professional competition and their heroic role as martyrs
of science will disappear.

To prevent this happening in their lifetimes, some parapsychologists have followed a policy of simultaneous right-wing and left-wing
appeasement. On the one hand, they have declined to challenge
blatant prejudice when shown by the scientific establishment. On
the other, they have earned the contempt of other scientists by
associating promiscuously with laymen who pretend to be scientists.

PHILOSOPHY AS PREJUDICE

As we have seen in Chapters 1, 4, 5, 17, 18, and 20–23, opposition to parapsychology has a deeper explanation than an inadequacy in the evidence. Epistemologists agree that we cannot fully represent reality by concatenating symbols representing elements of our experience. Because our models are inadequate, freedom to structure the world is constrained only by intelligent self-discipline. We can believe whatever pleases us, and for most of us there is neither pleasure nor short-term profit in using models that conform tightly to the outer world. To this must be added the mysterious empirical fact that, with rare exceptions, all of us, in passing from adolescence to adulthood, achieved mental stability and dedication to purpose by closing our minds to value change. Our prejudices are those beliefs to which we give unlimited commitment, and our philosophy of life is the sum of our prejudices.

25

TIME PRESENT

To what extent has parapsychology been accepted as a science? This question might be pursued by asking subsidiary questions: What do recognized scientific authorities say about parapsychology? Are the contents of its journals abstracted in some broader field of science? Do its experimental reports ever appear outside its own journals? How are psi phenomena treated in science textbooks? Is parapsychology taught as a separate subject in universities? Do its organizations interact with the other organizations of science? What is the level of training, the degree of commitment, and the geographical distribution of parapsychologists? As judged by opinion polls, do other scientists accept psi phenomena? Is the research financially well supported? I shall examine these questions sequentially.

To those seeking an authoritative opinion concerning the reality of psi phenomena, it must be said at once that none exists. Scientific authority rests upon a consensual web of judgment extending beyond a coterie of committed specialists. Such a consensus has not yet been reached regarding the reality of any psi phenomenon. Without it, only a limited and rather inconsequential degree of societal acceptance is possible. A "scientific authority" is someone whose statements on a subject are accepted without dispute by most other scientists from fields perceived as immediately related. Until there is an authoritative endorsement of parapsychological research by leading physicists and psychologists, there can be no hope of support for it from the nonscientific centers of power in our society—and the latter determine our national research priorities (McConnell, 1976b; 1977a).

Since 1950 more than 1500 parapsychological papers have been reviewed in *Psychological Abstracts,* which is the abstracting organ of the American Psychological Association. However, in the same period only a handful of original experimental papers on psi phenomena have appeared in American psychological journals and none at all in the journals of physics. Oddly enough, one important experimental paper was published in the *Proceedings of the Institute of Electrical and Electronics Engineers* (Puthoff & Targ, 1976).[1]

Although a few bold writers of psychology textbooks have been favorably mentioning parapsychology for several decades, a breakthrough in this direction first occurred when a widely used general psychology text by E.R. Hilgard and R.C. Atkinson devoted four pages to a friendly outline of the evidence favoring extrasensory perception and psychokinesis (Hilgard & Atkinson, 1967, pp. 241–244). Both authors are members of the U.S. National Academy of Sciences and are respected for their experimental and theoretical contributions to orthodox areas of psychology. Since textbook writing is a follow-the-leader game, as of today nearly all beginning textbooks of psychology give at least circumspectual treatment to extrasensory perception. There has been no corresponding recognition in physics textbooks of the idea that psychokinesis may be waiting in the wings to open a new era in our understanding of the physical universe.

Parapsychology is being taught for academic credit in about 50 U.S.A. colleges and universities. (This figure excludes general studies, extension, and community-college courses.) About half of the courses for credit are given in psychology departments, but these are almost entirely at smaller schools (ASPR, 1980).

In 1969, twelve years after its formation, the Parapsychological Association was favorably recommended by the Board of Directors of the American Association for the Advancement of Science for status as an affiliated society. This was approved by the National Council of the AAAS in formal assembly by a vote estimated as 165 to 30. Since then the Parapsychological Association has participated in programs at most of the annual meetings of the AAAS and at many of the conventions of the American Psychological Association.

The membership of the Parapsychological Association, as of December, 1981, was 285, of which 98 lived in 26 countries other than the U.S.A. Close to 57% hold doctoral degrees in science, medicine, or engineering, and about one third journal-published some

---

1. This work on "remote viewing ESP" has since been replicated by Dunne and Bisaha (1979) and by Schlitz and Gruber (1980; 1981).

observation of psi within a five-year period (McConnell & Clark, 1980). As of 1982, perhaps two dozen parapsychologists, world-wide, were devoting themselves to experimental research in the tradition of Western science.

In a self-selected sample of *New Scientist* readers (i.e., scientifically literate Englishmen), 67% accepted ESP as either an established fact or a likely possibility, while only 3% considered it an impossibility (Evans, 1973).

Similarly, in a 1973 survey of college faculty in the U.S.A., with a 49% response to 2400 questionnaires directed equally to five areas (the natural sciences, social sciences, humanities, arts, and education), 66% of the responders regarded ESP as an established fact or a likely possibility and only 4% regarded it as an impossibility. However, among the psychologists in that sample, only 34% were thus favorably disposed toward ESP; while another 34% considered it an impossibility (Wagner & Monnet, 1979).

In 1981, in his doctoral dissertation in sociology McClenon (1982) received a 69% response to a parapsychological questionnaire sent to 492 members of Section Committees and the Council of the American Association for the Advancement of Science. Of the responders, 29% considered ESP to be an established fact or a likely possibility, while 50% regarded ESP as either a remote possiblity or impossible. These scientists, drawn from a range of natural and social sciences, have in common their willingness to serve as the bureaucrats of the scientific establishment. Their attitudes are probably typical of the members of the committees that must decide—and with near unanimity—what scientific research will be financially supported in the U.S.A.

I know of no current financial grants for parapsychology from the U.S. Federal Government. For several parapsychologists, myself included, there has been quiet assistance from a handful of private foundations and individual donors (McConnell, 1976a). Nationally, there is no support commensurate with the potential importance of the field.

We can look at these few steps toward scientific acceptance and rightly believe that some progress has been made in the last 15 years. We should be deceiving ourselves, however, if we were to think that consensual scientific acceptance is imminent. The battle has not been joined. Orthodoxy has its legions ready in full array, but the opposing revolutionary forces are not yet gathered. Meanwhile, their exploring scouts are threatened, as the following example shows.

At the January, 1979, meeting of the American Association for the Advancement of Science in Houston, Texas, an illustrious nuclear physicist and member of the National Academy of Sciences, using as his title "Drive the Pseudos out of the Workshop of Science," said the following:

> With the decade of permissiveness now well past . . . the Council and the Board of Directors will serve science well to vote "parapsychology" out of the AAAS. . . . Nor is there in this proposal any intention to deny investigators full freedom of speech and a forum for their fribbles. There is forum enough already in a country that can afford 20,000 astrologers and only 2,000 astronomers. (Wheeler, 1979)

Anyone with a serious interest in the subject knows that parapsychology does not include astrology. Wheeler's willingness to damn by false association suggests the depth of revulsion that parapsychology commonly arouses in those physicists who have the insight to recognize it as a threat to their intellectual way of life.

If you have read the preceding chapters and glimpsed with me the future that awaits discovery, you will understand why I am pessimistic about quick acceptance by the leaders of science. Regardless of what Mother Nature has in store for us, we already know that she will destroy our present cosmic perspective. We shall pass from one intellectual watershed into another, where, in the sense of Jacques Monod (1971, Chap. 9), we shall continue to live as gypsies, at least for a long time to come. What we leave behind is the ascent of man from savagery as masterfully portrayed by Jacob Bronowski (1973). What we face is unknown.

THE ASCENT OF MAN

Bronowski's television series, *The Ascent of Man,* is undoubtedly the finest popular synthesis of scientific knowledge yet created. He was a mathematician with a background in physics and biology. He was also a poet, a scholar, and a wise and compassionate spectator of history. I have recently reread the book edition of his television series, hoping that it might throw light upon his blindness to the possibility of psi phenomena and that, through him, I might better understand the obstinate refusal of the best scientific minds of our time to examine the evidence for these phenomena.

There is much that he said that I could not have said better. In the *Introduction* to his book he wrote (Bronowski, 1973, p. 15):

> My ambition here has been . . . to create a philosophy for the twentieth century which shall be all of one piece . . . a philosophy of nature rather than of science. . . . The recent findings in human biology have given a new direction to scientific thought, a shift from the general to the individual, for the first time since the Renaissance opened the door into the natural world.
>
> There cannot be a philosophy, there cannot even be a decent science, without humanity. . . . For me, the understanding of nature has as its goal the understanding of human nature, and of the human condition within nature.

I can hear him in memory as he spoke of both man's glory and his limitations. In the last few minutes of this 13-hour series, looking into the future, he said (Bronowski, 1973, p. 437):

> I am infinitely saddened to find myself suddenly surrounded in the west by a sense of terrible loss of nerve, a retreat from knowledge into—into what? Into Zen Buddhism; into falsely profound questions about, Are we not really just animals at bottom; into extrasensory perception and mystery. They do not lie along the line of what we are now able to know if we devote ourselves to it: an understanding of man himself. . . . Knowledge is our destiny. Self-knowledge, at last bringing together the experience of the arts and the explanations of science, waits ahead of us.

This curious concatenation of ideas deserves analysis. What is the term "extrasensory perception" doing here? This phenomenon of parapsychology appears from nowhere, and only this once in the entire television series. To whom is Bronowski talking? What is his message? His demeanor suggests humility but displays the self-assurance of the elite that he represents. He speaks as the brahman of science to the untouchable layman. What does he say?

He denies parapsychology's claim to be an experimental science by the persuader's device of grouping it with an effete religion (Zen Buddhism) and a naive philosophy (Watsonian behaviorism). He then asserts with authority, but more in sadness than in anger, that these things cannot lead to an understanding of man. This is "word magic" at its finest. His is an assertion that brooks no answer—in the sense that Hitler's Big Lie allowed no denial. We are expected to believe that this unsupported statement would not have been uttered if it were not unquestionably true.

Are we to suppose that Bronowski forgot his earlier words:

> In every age there is a turning point, a new way of seeing and asserting the coherence of the world. . . . Each culture tries to fix its visionary moment, when it was transformed by a new conception either of nature or of man. (ibid., p. 20)
> Science is a very human form of knowledge. We are always at the brink of the known, we always feel forward for what is to be hoped. Every judgment in science stands on the edge of error, and is personal. Science is a tribute to what we can know although we are fallible. In the end the words were said by Oliver Cromwell: "I beseech you, in the bowels of Christ, think it possible you may be mistaken." (ibid., p. 374)

There is something here that cries out for attention. How could a man so great and good engage in intellectual legerdemain? Perhaps it was mere oversight, a moment of carelessness?

I hardly think so. This was his final message in a project that occupied three years at the end of his life. On the penultimate page of a 438-page work devoted to aspiration, one does not choose for condemnation a purported psychological phenomenon (ESP) unless one feels strongly about it. What Bronowski perceived and did not like, is that ESP reveals physics as an intellectual Alhambra, an incomparable work of art devoid of the human form. What he did not know—because he did not want to—is that parapsychology as practiced by its leaders is an experimental science and that the empirical evidence for ESP is such that any scientist of competence and integrity must accept it.

To know as much as he did about science in general, and to know it so well in preparing his television series, was a tour de force beyond the capability of any but a great intellect. But only the tiniest part of his knowledge was gained firsthand from nature. He was creative in his own areas—that was necessary if he was to understand the rest of knowledge. But nearly everything that he presents to us in his series of lectures was gathered from reading and from the foremost physicists of our time who were his friends. What he reflected was not his own judgment but the consensual judgment of scientists—not a new vision, but the essence of Western culture, rounded and smoothed as the collective wisdom of an age. We can admire him for what he was: a curator but not a harbinger.

The true measure of the opposition to parapsychology by physicists is to be found, not in Edward Condon's (1969) call for the public horsewhipping of those who teach ESP, nor in John Wheeler's (1979) plea to drive parapsychologists from the workshop of science, but in Bronowski's comforting congruity achieved by the manipulation of words without regard for reality.

I have spent this much time on a few words by Bronowski because his is a devious, quasi-mystical opposition to parapsychology that I have encountered repeatedly in my communications with leading physicists over the last 35 years. Concealed within this opposition (which seems to be especially typical of the Jewish tradition) is an insistence that matters of science and of the spirit must never be allowed to contaminate one another. This, of course, is Cartesian dualism. I am convinced that it is a nearly universal philosophy among academic physicists who are innately religious and who are intelligent enough to know intuitively that, whatever may be within the box marked "ESP," they will no longer be comfortable if they lift the lid.

It would be wrong to close with a melody suggesting that scientists as a class are especially prejudiced. The truth is more universal and more discouraging than that. As I have tried to convey several times in this series of essays, the avoidance of reality on every conceivable subject by all of us is the key to the human condition. If there is hope, it lies in a renaissance of the spirit in which self-awareness will be the leitmotiv.

26

THE LONG TOMORROW

FUTURE SCIENCE

With Apollo 17 we came to the close of the Age of Heroic Materialism. Like the Romans in the Dark Ages, soon we shall gaze upon the ruins of our great cities and wonder: How were these built?

"It was done with cheap energy," they will say. "And when that was gone, the end came quickly."

That will be only a half-truth. Western technology was a triumph of courage and self-deception—with the former supported by the latter. The Age of Reason decreed: There are no gods or devils. Nature is impersonal. Each human exhibits an isolated element of consciousness and communicates with the external world by sensorimotor means only. Mind is an impotent epiphenomenon of the brain. Each of us is alone forever.

With these assurances, religion could be dispensed with by philosophers and relegated to Sunday by the rest of us. These materialist beliefs about the nature of man were essential to the creation of science and industry. They freed the thinker from the constraints of superstition and gave him the courage to aspire to unlimited understanding. He could believe that the natural world, existing apart from mind, could be explained in terms of elemental mechanisms—as indeed it can, up to a point.

Belief in the isolation of man freed the entrepreneur to assume power over the destiny of others in order to create an industrial civilization. If evil done to individuals is not visited upon the whole, then the individual does not matter in so great an enterprise.

It is a cosmic irony that, at the historical instant when the faith of the West in itself is being overwhelmed by poverty and pollution, the science of the West should have discovered in parapsychology its own metaphysical flaw that led to this debacle.

As explained by Thomas Kuhn (1962), the power of scientific method lies in the ultimate destruction of every theory by the exposure of its limitations. Since no model can fully represent reality, every model must eventually fail as our understanding grows. By generalization, this principle applies as well to the entire framework of scientific belief.

As we begin now to apply the method of science to the study of

269

man's conscious self, what do we find? From the class of what Kuhn describes as the inviolable "rules of science," Cambridge philosopher C.D. Broad (1953, pp. 9–12), somewhat earlier had exhibited what he called the "basic limiting principles" that seem to be contradicted by the phenomena of parapsychology. In paraphrased form these are: (1) Causal connectivity must be preserved in space. (2) Causal sequence must be preserved in time. (3) Consciousness is unitary and can occur only in association with a single living brain. (4) Information about a physical event can be gained by consciousness only via sensory mechanisms of the brain. (5) Consciousness can act upon brain but not directly on other matter. If these rules are violated by psi phenomena, then the belief structure of science (but not its method) has been fractured.

Man is captured in a carnival house where he sees nothing but himself in mirrors that he can bend as he chooses. Among history's strange beliefs about the nature of underlying reality, none is so right or so wrong as our own. Our technical greatness was achieved by excluding from our scheme of things one-half of reality: the reality of mind in a nonphysical realm, capable of interacting directly with the contents of the space-time domain of physics.

When experiments performed according to the canons of science reveal by their anomalous outcome that nature is not encompassed by the physics of inanimate objects, what kind of a response might we expect from scientists? Resolute rejection, of course. But more than that, a desperate counterattack by all who are too old to accept the loss of a philosophy. That is what I believe faces parapsychology as it begins to attract the attention of our leaders.

For those few who are willing to accept reality upon its own terms, what encouragement is there? The world of the future will be different from the present in both metaphysics and technology. Our conceptions of interpersonal relationships, and therefore our morality, will be basically altered. It is reasonable to suppose, also, that there will be practical utilizations of psi. That is perhaps as far as one can predict at this moment.

Judging from the past, the prospect for mankind seems desperate. Looking forward to the Age of Mind, I find room for hope.

FUTURE MAN

If one is searching for clues to the possible social significance of parapsychology to future man, there may be no better starting place than the final chapter of anthropologist Ernest Becker's *Escape From Evil* (1975, pp. 146–170).

After a critical juxtaposition of ideas from Rousseau, Marx, Marcuse, Freud, Jung, Otto Rank, Norman O. Brown, Nietzsche, Lewis Mumford, A.M. Hocart, Levi-Strauss, and others, Becker concludes that the root cause of aggression and self-destruction is not directly innate in man nor does it lie in the social arrangements to which he is subjected. Instead, these behaviors are the misguided expression of a universal striving for immortality.

> Men have to keep from going mad by biting off [only] small pieces of reality. . . . This means that their noblest passions are played out in the most narrow and unreflective ways, and this is what undoes them. . . . Man may well prove to be . . . an impossible animal—one who, individually, needs for healthy action the very conduct that, on a general level, is destructive to him [p. 153]. . . . There are no particular leaders or special councils of elite to blame in all this [p. 160].

Becker acknowledges a long list of "maddening dilemmas," e.g.: "If men kill out of heroic joy, in what direction do we program for improvements in human nature? . . . What kind of child-rearing programs are we going to promote—with Fromm, Horney, et al.— . . . if aggression in the service of life is man's highest creative act?" (p. 155). A child matures into an adult by a neurotic twisting of his perceptions (p. 155). The ability to love requires susceptibility to illusion (p. 157). "Character" in man is the deception by which he obscures the painful contradictions of his animal-godlike nature (p. 163).

As an escape from these dilemmas Becker hopes for the recognition and acceptance of an already existing balance between conservative and radical perspectives. As a goal, he suggests universal self-understanding, achieved by the free flow of criticism of society's systems of heroic transcendance (p. 166–167).

Becker's analysis is brilliant but flawed. What hope he sees for the future of man rests upon the implications of the following statement: "But I also know that differences in talent are not so biological or hereditary as conservatives often want to make out." (p. 165) This is his metalanguage assertion that individual ability differences are not predominantly determined by heredity and that any who disagree with him on this point are ideologically motivated in their evaluation of the evidence. Becker's proposal is to eliminate by reasoned discourse the more dangerous and costly of the illusions by which mén live. But to do this may, in fact, require eugenics and more time than is available. (See Appendix G.)

It is at this point, I foresee that parapsychology might play a crucial role. It is conceivable that the study of psi phenomena could, in Becker's language, provide a cosmic heroism for the common man and do away with his need for self-abasement and displaced idealism.

I shall leave to others the elaboration of this theme. It must suffice here to say that parapsychology brings a new dimension to natural science through the experimental investigation of the direct relationship of consciousness to the physical world. This is a relationship whose consideration was formerly left to religion. As the core science for self-understanding, parapsychology might destroy what existentialists call "the guilt of being" and place man within an external system of meaning.

Appendix A

A BACKGROUND
FOR THE STUDY OF PARAPSYCHOLOGY

When we search for truth, we should listen to it whispering from the past and the future. Where is it that thoughtful persons think we have been—or are going—or ought to go? The following writings could serve as background for the study of parapsychology:

Arnold Toynbee:	*A Study of History.* (1946)
Elmer Pendell:	*Why Civilizations Self-Destruct.* (1977)
José Ortega y Gasset:	*The Revolt of the Masses.* (1930)
Aldous Huxley:	*Brave New World.* (1932)
B.F. Skinner:	*Walden II.* (1948)
George Orwell:	*1984.* (1949)
Ayn Rand:	*Atlas Shrugged.* (1957)
Robert G. Kaiser:	*Russia: The People and the Power.* (1976)
Hedrick Smith:	*The Russians.* (1976)
R.A. McConnell:	*Parapsychology, the Wild Card in a Stacked Deck: A Look at the Near Future of Mankind.* (1982c)
Raymond B. Cattell:	*A New Morality from Science: Beyondism.* (1972)
Gary Zukav:	*The Dancing Wu Li Masters.* (1979)

*　　*　　*　　*

In his *Study of History,* Toynbee (Somervell, 1946) examined the major civilizations of the past and found that political collapse was preceded by lowering of moral and intellectual standards. Toynbee, a deeply religious man, regarded the birth and death of civilizations as a spiritual problem—to be understood through scholarship and not by science. According to Toynbee, a civilization arises in response to a challenge in a situation of special difficulty; while the subsequent breakdown of that civilization results from the "failure of creative power in the governing elite."

Toynbee's implicit denial of causation does not detract from the excellence of his description of past events. It has remained, however, for scientists with a broader perspective and more biological knowledge to complete our understanding of history to a degree that might allow our civilization to control its destiny if we so desire.

In *Why Civilizations Self-Destruct,* Elmer Pendell (1977) has prepared for the educated nonscientist a highly readable explanation of the rhythm of history.

Physical anthropologists believe that man's innate intelligence has not appreciably changed since the end of the last ice age, 8000 years ago. From this premise, historians have concluded that the rise and fall of civilizations—whatever the causes—did not depend upon changes in intelligence. Pendell accepts the premise but not the conclusion.

Pendell points out that, although man's intellectual capacity as determined by skull size may not have changed in 8000 years, there are, nevertheless, tremendous variations in intelligence only slightly correlated with head size but strongly segregated by social class. This fact, and not Hitler's red herring of race, suggests a true explanation for the disappearance of civilizations.

Pendell examines various cultural mechanisms by which one social class will increase numerically relative to another and concludes that in every civilization the effective, genetically determined competence (of which intelligence is a major component) will inevitably grow and then substantially decline. This biological concept is a contribution to knowledge with conceivably far reaching implications.

Cro-Magnon man had a brain size 15 percent greater than modern Europeans. Pendell explains the disappearance of Cro-Magnon man at the start of an ice age about 26,000 years ago in terms of the same population dynamics that he believes have destroyed all civilizations in the last 8000 years. It is not too much to claim that Pendell has provided us with the first unified theory of history based upon biological and sociological principles. However, it appears that he does not emphasize sufficiently the morally debilitating effect of the comforts of civilization upon children even when they have good genetic endowment, i.e., upon the children of the leaders.

In the *Revolt of the Masses,* Ortega y Gasset gave us in 1930 a prescient sociological study of the present ending of European culture. This book has been compared in importance to Machiavelli's *The Prince,* Rousseau's *Social Contract,* and Marx's *Das Kapital.*

The next four books are modern utopias, of which the first three are well known. The fourth, *Atlas Shrugged* (Rand, 1957), explores the issue of elitism versus egalitarianism as it might trigger the collapse of industrial society. There have been many other utopias, beginning with Plato's *Republic,* but those antedating the age of mass communication have little relevance for us.[1]

The Soviet Union today is a dream come true, a utopia combining features from all four of those listed above. The Kaiser (1976) and Smith (1976) books (by *Washington Post* and *New York Times* correspondents, respectively) confirm and supplement each other in providing information about the USSR. The importance of these books, if we are trying to foretell or create the future, is threefold: (1) They tell us what to expect from the USSR economically and culturally (but not militarily). (2) They provide insights about our own society. The faulty social mechanisms they describe in the Soviet Union are also present at debilitating levels in Western industrial society. (3) By implication, Kaiser and Smith raise a question about our future. Given our history and temperament, it is not likely that we shall follow exactly the path of the Soviet Union. Will we grow into a stable, workable meritocracy, or are we doomed to anarchy unless there is an unforseen change in human nature?

In my essay, *Parapsychology, the Wild Card in a Stacked Deck* (1982c), I survey the challenge of the next twenty years, by which time I believe the die will be cast for or against civilized man. I close with some thoughts on a possible role for parapsychology in finding new social values based upon self-knowledge through science.

As the present book was in final editing, my attention was drawn to Raymond B. Cattell's *A New Morality from Science: Beyondism* (1972). Cattell's perceptions of social morality are so comprehensive and strikingly original as to deserve our considera-

---

1. For the nonfictional sequel to *1984,* see Bamford (1982).

tion. They may seem unassailable in the light of currently accepted scientific principles. How they will ultimately be altered by the findings of parapsychology, I cannot predict.

In his professional lifetime Cattell produced 30 books and 340 papers in technical branches of experimental, clinical, personality, social, and methodological-statistical areas of psychology. His scientific contributions place him among the dozen greatest psychologists of the last one hundred years.

Cattell's book is not a utopia but a study of utopian principles that might undergird man's continued existence. It should, in fact, bring an end to the writing of utopias: there can be no more until his conceptions have been assimilated.

Cattell's is not a practical work: it has no plan for implementation. Like the utopias it displaces, it merely says: "This is the way it ought to be." For example, he suggests as desirable future social reforms: the biochemical postponement of adolescent sexual activity, the eugenic guidance of reproduction, and a deliberately regressive income tax.

Beyondism rejects revealed religion as well as the secular religions of Communism, Humanism, and Existentialism. For the universalism of these he substitutes "cooperative competition" between cultures as an experimental procedure.

Because it is not possible to exhibit the Olympian scope of Cattell's book in a few words, I shall be content with several quotations selected to encourage my readers to go to the original.

> There has occurred through rationalist arguments an abdication of values in sexual morality, in everyday civil order, in the punishment of crime, in the defense of one's country, in relaxing what constitutes the harder, disciplined core of intellectual education . . . . Lacking the reality-testing procedures of science, the literary or political science intellectuals . . . take their departure . . . from entirely a priori postulates, e.g., that pleasure is the logical goal of life, that all men are equal, that rivalry between societies is bad, . . . that the natural ecology of existing species should never be disturbed, that if it is medically possible men should live forever, that education can always be pleasant, that man is naturally monogamous, and so on, ad infinitum, through the world of the "self-evident." (p. 50)

> It may turn out that man has only the choice of living by the laws of the universe, of which the evolutionary process is an inevitable part, or of refusing to live at all. (p. 78)

> [Let us lay aside] not only the pervasive passive resistance of narcism but also the rooted anthropocentrisms of Christianity . . . and, turn-

ing to the vistas of the astronomer and the biologist, frankly recognize the enormous magnitude of the adaptations to catastrophe that may at any moment be demanded collectively of mankind . . . . Maximally to reduce the chances of complete annihilation we have to recognize that there is no surplus of either resources or time. There is only one pace to increase basic knowledge and genetic progress—the fastest that well-organized societies can achieve. (pp. 277–278)

If we are right . . . that science is itself capable of deriving moral values, it may yet take years . . . to reach methodologically sound conclusions. During that time we should probably do well to lean temporarily on the ethical framework, though not the superstitions, provided by the deepest convictions of revealed religious authority. (p. 64)

Perhaps as much as 30–50% of the. . . . individual difference variance [in man's conscience is] due to heredity. . . . Whereas a strong [conscience] is advantageous to the group, it is obviously disadvantageous to the individual. . . . This we may call the principle of counteraction of within- and between-group natural selection. . . . There is little to prevent a genetic trend . . . in which the more altruistic and culture-oriented are sacrificed for the idle, the anti-social, the incompetent welfare-dependent type. (p. 251)

An ethics based on scientific evolutionary foundations leads to rules of [inter-cultural] conduct provocatively different from those somewhat unquestioningly assumed today to follow from revealed religions. [On the other hand,] the canons of [within-culture] morality so reached are remarkably close to Christian and other revealed ethics. (p. 295)

How surprised the environmentalist sociologists and economists will be when some of the "undeveloped countries" remain relatively "undeveloped" . . . after all has been done that foreign aid can do. . . . One must logically recognize that, if there can be behavior genetic differences between two individuals, such differences can also be statistically significant between groups. If people enter the room in pairs . . . and a receptionist assigns the more intelligent of each entering pair to the left of the room . . . it is extremely probable that the left and right groups will soon be very statistically different in their average intelligence. Nature has operated many times in the past as a receptionist. . . . Beyondism . . . demands as a first act of respect to the reality principle that human beings recognize equally the cultural and genetic origins of individual and group differences, and build an ethics of progress on that basis. (pp. 261–263)

The arresting conclusion from evolutionary law—and one difficult for many to digest—is that natural selection should be allowed and encouraged to act freely among [cultural] groups. (p. 178)

Outright transfer of [material] gains from one [cultural] group to another . . . constitutes, not an equivalent of "charity" between individuals but a pernicious and evil interruption of group evolution. (p. 216)

Euthanasia may [eventually] come for both individuals and races; for they need to fulfill their purpose and pass on. (p. 270)

Collectively, the foregoing writings by several authors portray a difficult and uncertain future. Can research into the nature of the human mind provide us with a new faith in ourselves that will avert the death of civilization? That question is the challenge that parapsychology might meet.

* * * *

Behind an enigmatic title, Gary Zukav has hidden a knowledgable, nonmathematical, and doggedly cute account of some of the findings and speculations of modern physics. It is written for nonphysicists who desire deeply to know the limits to our understanding of physical reality. This book may also be helpful to those whose doubts about psi phenomena arise from the following imaginary argument.

> The leaders of physics are men of the highest intellectual competence. They must be presumed to have learned open-mindedness from their own twentieth-century revolution. Yet, almost without exception, they oppose ESP and PK as impossible phenomena— even while admitting that these phenomena, if real, would be of profound importance to physics. How can an outsider—regardless of his proficiency in other areas—pit his opinion against the massed judgment of the leaders of physics? In short, physicists must be presumed to know more than others on any topic that they claim is within their jurisdiction.

If the myth of physicists' cosmic wisdom is not dissolved by the accounts of their prejudice related in Part III of the book you are reading, perhaps their opposition to psi as incompatible with physics can be laid aside on other grounds. In *The Dancing Wu Li Masters,* Zukav describes how, in the Einstein-Podolsky-Rosen Paradox (1935) the violations of "common sense" long accepted in subatomic quantum mechanics might be projected into our intuitively perceived macroscopic world, and how, since Freedman and Clauser's (1972) experiment relating to J.S. Bell's theorem, physicists must begin to consider epistemological anomalies that are as philosophically unexpected as those proposed by parapsychology. The "EPR controversy" is continuing actively on both theoretical and experimental levels (Robinson, 1983).

Appendix B

ON THE MALPRACTICE OF MEDICINE

To judge parapsychology, one must first judge the world that rejects it. Are our power-wielding elites worthy of the deference we give to their opinions? In my experience, the answer is *no*.

So broad a proposition cannot be briefly proved, but it can perhaps be illuminated by examples of untrustworthiness from within one of the professions. I have chosen the medical profession for this purpose for four reasons: (1) In the U.S.A., medicine is the most highly revered of all the professions. (2) Particularly through psychiatry, medicine has direct relevance for parapsychology. (3) Medicine is close enough to science that its mistakes can sometimes be documented. (4) Because all of us occasionally seek the help of a physician, we are able to understand and appreciate examples such as those given below.

PSYCHIATRY AND PARAPSYCHOLOGY

The competence of the psychiatric profession is important to parapsychology in at least three ways.

First, the psychiatric profession is the instrument by which society protects itself from those who "misperceive reality." Consequently, that profession is the arbiter of the reality of unusual mental phenomena. Although psychiatry takes no formal stand on psi phenomena, its silence on a matter of such fundamental psychiatric importance confirms the educated layman's belief that psi phenomena are misperceptions. Is this trusting interpretation justified?

Second, individuals frequently present themselves to parapsychologists and to psychiatrists, expressing fear that their psychic experiences indicate insanity. What guidance can such individuals (and parapsychologists) hope for from psychiatry on this question?

Third, the sanity of parapsychologists can be called into question in connection with possible or proven experimental fraud. What advice can be expected from psychiatry on this matter?

As a step toward answering these questions, it is desirable to gain some understanding of the limitations of psychiatry as a science and of how it interacts with the rest of the medical profession.

Schizophrenia

In this connection I recommend an article that appeared in *Science* under the title: "On Being Sane in Insane Places." (Rosenhan, 1973). This is a report of an experiment in which eight sane persons, by feigning illness, gained admission to 12 different U.S.A. psychiatric hospitals, including some of the best on the east and west coasts. The pseudopatients included three psychologists, a psychology graduate student, a psychiatrist, a pediatrician, a painter, and a housewife.

Each used a false name, a false vocation, and false employment. They all claimed to have the same, one symptom. In all other respects they were honest about themselves and their personal histories. As soon as they had been admitted as patients they said, when asked, that their symptom had gone and that they felt normal.

Their symptom was that they heard voices saying "empty," "hollow," or "thud."

All were admitted as patients without difficulty. In all but one case the diagnosis was "schizophrenia." At all times while they were in the hospital they acted and talked normally with the staff and with other patients. All of them openly spent a great deal of time taking notes about their hospital experiences. This was evidently considered a symptom of abnormality. It was up to each one to get out of the hospital as best he could by convincing the doctors that he no longer needed treatment. All but one of the pseudopatients desired to be discharged almost immediately after being admitted. Nevertheless, their stays ranged from 7 to 52 days. The average stay was 19 days. In no case was their sanity discovered by the attendants or doctors. When they were discharged, it was because their illness was said to be "in remission."

After the experiment was over, a research and teaching hospital heard about it and said it could not happen there. The hospital was then told that within the next three months one or more pseudopatients would attempt to gain admittance. All staff members whose duties required sustained contact with patients were asked by the hospital to rate every new patient on a scale of sanity to try to discover the pseudopatients.

Out of 193 patients admitted, "41 were alleged with high confidence to be pseudopatients by at least one member of the staff." In point of fact, no pseudopatient tried to get in.

In an interview (Greenberg, 1981) Rosenhan reported the existence of two unpublished replications by him of his 1973 study, with the same result. His *Science* paper is said to have been the most reprinted in the history of that journal. The adverse response from psychiatrists was massive—which would be expected from a profession whose basic competence had been questioned.

NEUROSIS

The problem of false psychiatric diagnosis is broader than might be supposed from the Rosenhan study described above. Medical students today are taught that more than half of all presenting patients require no treatment for organic disease. On the other hand, medical students are not given estimates of how many patients will have ailments whose diagnosis is beyond the power of the physician.

It is certain that there are still unrecognized diseases. The question is: How many? The layman tends to believe (1) that nearly all human diseases are known, and (2) that a person who "catches something" either gets well or dies. Medical doctors are beginning to suspect (1) that we have only scratched the surface of virus and genetic diseases, and (2) that the illness of such diseases typically may be of extended, rather than limited, duration. The medical scientist knows that our knowledge of biochemical malfunctioning in the body is but some tiny part of what is still to be learned.

These considerations lead one to suspect that a lot of organic disease is being diagnosed as neurosis. To discover what is actually taking place, one would need to know, among other things, how often, in their own minds and to their patients, physicians are willing to say: "I know too little to diagnose this case." Given the aura of omniscience that the medical profession has cultivated in its relations with the public, it seems probable that any physician who frequently admitted diagnostic bafflement would be regarded as incompetent and lose his clientele.[1]

For evidence on how medicine handles its diagnostic failures, one might go to the literature of a disease whose diagnosis is difficult and whose misdiagnosis can sometimes be proved. Brucellosis is a serious disease that usually appears in an easily diagnosed, acute phase but that can also persist as an obscure,

---

1. From what I find under "Symptoms of psychogenic origin" in textbooks of neural disease and from the experience of friends, I infer that neurologists are especially eager to preserve their image of competence by referring their difficult cases to psychiatrists.

chronic affliction which is sometimes resolved by finding live Brucella bacteria. This disease, transmitted to humans principally by cows, swine, and goats, is now rare in the U.S.A. but common in many other countries. Although treatable in the blood by antibiotics, it may live indefinitely in soft tissue anywhere in the body. To pick but one example from the literature, Yow, et al., (1961) at Baylor University reported the case of a farm worker who suffered chills, fever, night sweats, headache, and arthralgia for 25 years before diagnosis and excision of a badly abscessed spleen.

Dr. Alice Evans, a renowned bacteriologist, contracted brucellosis while studying the disease at the U.S. Public Health Laboratory. Her persisting illness went unrecognized for some years, while on the basis of her complaints she was diagnosed as neurotic. Subsequently, she wrote (1934, p. 667):

> I shall draw from my own experience certain conclusions as to the diagnosis that the patient with the chronic form of the disease generally receives. I have been consulted by a number of patients . . . who have been fortunate enough to receive, finally, the correct diagnosis. Usually there was a long delay before the correct diagnosis was given, and in the meantime the diagnosis was almost invariably neurosis. . . .
>
> It is a severe trial for the brucellosis patient, which contributes to the mental depression characteristic of the disease, that when he appeals for medical aid he is told that his illness is only imaginary and that all that is necessary for his recovery is that he should acquire the proper mental attitude.

Later she wrote: "The verdict of guilty of feigned illness unless proven innocent, or a diagnosis of neurosis, continues to be the common fate of patients suffering from chronic brucellosis." (1961, p. 942). She was referring to a Government sponsored study of 24 persons who had contracted brucellosis while working at the U.S. Army biological warfare laboratory.

Without much effort I have found eight medical authorities who warned of the danger of misdiagnosing brucellosis as neurosis. Three quotations suffice to show the range of opinion:

> The lot of [those with chronic brucellosis] is a sordid one. Individuals have dragged their way through many years of brucellosis, continually complaining of weakness, headache, pains in the muscles and joints. Without warning, there would be an acute episode extending over several days followed by the chronic state. Too frequently, those patients have been diagnosed as neurotic (Soule, 1950, p. 252).

>The longer brucellosis remains unrecognized and untreated, the more likely is the diagnosis to be confused with anxiety state, chronic nervous exhaustion, and psychoneurosis (Spink, 1956, p. 214).

>It is important to realize . . . that a diagnosis of neurotic illness may be made when the true cause is chronic brucellosis (Jamieson, 1975, p. 58).

For fifty years chronic brucellosis has been misdiagnosed as neurosis. It must be obvious that the same danger of misdiagnosis exists for all still unknown organic diseases causing chronic pain.

In such cases, if the symptoms are severe, a psychiatric referral will be made. The correct, current view in psychiatry is that everyone has neurotic tendencies. Can a profession that readily finds schizophrenia in normal individuals fail to find clinical neurosis in patients whose illness has been judged by the referring physician to be without probable organic cause? And what are the chances that an otherwise mentally sound person who consults a psychiatrist because of alarm over genuine psychic experiences will be diagnosed as psychotic? The "myth of mental illness" is not what Szasz supposes, but it nevertheless is very real.

THE PATIENT AT RISK

Forty years ago the author's wife was discovered to have advanced, bilaterial, pulmonary tuberculosis. After five years at Trudeau Sanatorium at Saranac Lake, New York, her diease was arrested by streptomycin and by the expedient of lung compression through the removal of six ribs on one side.

In 1978, after my wife's previous physician retired, she went to Dr. A, who was recommended as a competent internist specializing in lung disease. After examining my wife, Dr. A should have made sure that she knew that her remaining lung capacity would slowly decrease with age and that she was in constant danger of death from common lung infections. She should have been told the symptoms of congestive heart failure and what steps to take if she noticed an increased shortness of breath. Instead, she was left with the impression that her only concern was to live healthfully so as to avoid a recurrence of tuberculosis.

After her annual medical examination in June 1981, as in previous years, my wife was told by Dr. A that her pulmonary capacity was low but that she was in good health. In the following 12 months she noticed increased shortness of breath but was able to continue a normally active life—maintaining a home without out-side help, managing the family finances, selecting the family's news reading in the daily *Washington Post,* and giving regular volunteer service to a Pittsburgh hospital.

At her next annual examination by Dr. A on 3 June 1982, my wife traveled by taxi rather than by public bus because of general weakness. She complained to Dr. A of low energy, shortness of breath, and morning edema below one eye. On that date Dr. A gave her, as usual, a pulmonary function test, chest x-ray, urine analysis, and blood battery and dismissed her with the advice that she could come back in six months rather than a year if she wished.

As I later discovered, the pulmonary function test results, which were immediately available to Dr. A at the time of the examina-tion, showed a forced vital capacity of 0.63 liters (21% of her normal, and down 35% of her value of one year earlier) and a forced expiratory volume in one second of 0.46 liters (down 29% of her value a year ago). These drops indicated serious deteriora-tion of lung function, which should have been investigated at once.

Although on May 20 my wife had been able to walk two and one-half kilometers without difficulty, two weeks later on 3 June, after her examination by Dr. A, an eight-tenths kilometer walk from the bus stop to home left her exhausted. Evidently, some sudden change had occurred in her health.

In the following days she had a quarter-degree Centigrade fever and showed a pulse rate of 80–100, with blood pressure in the low-normal range. These measurements in themselves gave no cause for alarm. The above-mentioned swelling under one eye, I later learned was a sign of congestive heart failure. Her appetite was poor, and she lost a kilogram. She slept four extra hours per day, and was unable to do any household chores. She had no cough, but occasionally raised a little mucous.

Because my wife had just been examined by her physician, I felt no immediate concern. However, one week after her examination, when her condition had not improved, I telephoned Dr. A to ask his advice. He reported that Mrs. M's test results were now in hand and all were normal, but that her pulmonary capacity was extremely limited.

Since my wife was not in pain, I asked: "Should she wait a little longer to see if she has a virus that might go away, or should she be seen by you at once?" Dr. A said to call again in a week. I now know that an arterial blood-gases test should have been ordered immediately in view of my wife's symptoms as told to the doctor.

A week later, on Thursday, 17 June, I telephoned Dr. A to say that my wife could scarcely move about and that action was necessary. Dr. A said he would mail to her a request for an arterial blood-gases test on his prescription form, which she could take to a hospital conveniently near our home. This was a procedural error. Dr. A should have ordered the blood test by telephone without delay.

I received the blood test request on Friday evening. On Saturday morning I was told by the hospital to call the following Monday morning. In a telephone call shortly after 8 AM, Monday, I was told that my wife could be worked into the testing schedule if it were urgent. My wife and I arrived by car at the emergency entrance of the hospital at 9 AM, and she traveled by wheel chair to the pulmonary laboratory. However, when it was discovered that Dr. A's request called for a blood test before and, if possible, after a stress test (which would take some time), the testing was rescheduled for the next day at 8 AM. It is not clear why Dr. A asked for a stress test in view of my wife's pulmonary function test results and the fact that he had been told twice that she was seriously incapacitated.

On 22 June a blood sample was drawn and, before giving the stress test, an unscheduled pulmonary function test was done because of the patient's obvious distress. As I later learned, the blood-gases test results were: Oxygen, 42 mm (where normal is 75–100, and 55–60 is the danger point). Carbon dioxide, 61 mm (where 40 ± 4 is normal). Acidity, 7.31 (where 7.38–7.42 is normal). These results were telephoned to Dr. B, Dr. A's medical colleague (it being Dr. A's day off).

A hospital staff physician was called by the hospital technician. The staff physician told my wife that Dr. B had said to cancel the stress test. He explained that the patient's blood values were "borderline" and that a stress test might "push them into the abnormal range." The test results were, in fact, already seriously abnormal, although neither my wife nor I was told so. One presumable purpose of this misrepresentation was to protect the interest of the referring physician.

Not knowing that I ought to demand my wife's immediate admission to the hospital, I took her home and proceeded to my university office. There I telephoned Dr. A's office and reached another one of his colleagues, Dr. C. He said that he could not respond to questions about my wife's condition but that she could go to the emergency room of the hospital where Dr. A practices if she felt she was in danger and that, otherwise, she should telephone Dr. A at 9 AM the next morning. Immediately thereafter, Dr. C telephoned my wife to ask how she was. He told her that her voice sounded strong and that she should contact Dr. A the next morning. Evidently, he was disturbed by what he saw in her file.

At this point, alarmed by my wife's fading strength plus several cues (including the sudden solemnity of the pulmonary laboratory staff when my wife's pulmonary function tests appeared on the cathode-ray screen), I began searching the chapter on pulmonary illness in the *Merck Manual of Diagnosis and Therapy.*

The next morning, Wednesday, I telephoned Dr. A at 9 AM and learned the blood-gases test results as listed above. Dr. A said that, before he decided what course to pursue, he would like to have my wife seen by another physician, whose name he furnished.

I telephoned the other doctor at once and was able to arrange an emergency appointment for 11 AM the next day. At 4:30 PM I picked up an envelope of my wife's x-rays at Dr. A's office for delivery to the new doctor. At home, I opened the sealed envelope and found the pulmonary function test results for 6 June 1981 and 3 June 1982, from which I have quoted above.

No hospital bed was immediately available after the new doctor's examination on 24 June. My wife was admitted to the hospital on the following day, at which time she could walk only a few steps and her arterial oxygen pressure while resting was 30 mm.

My wife was diagnosed as suffering congestive heart failure caused by chronic pulmonary insufficiency plus a minor lung infection of unknown nature. After a week in the hospital she was discharged with her blood oxygen pressure above 60 mm while receiving oxygen by nasal cannula. We then learned that she has severe "restrictive and obstructive" lung disease and will require oxygen therapy for the rest of her life.

One may ask why Dr. A sent my wife to another physician when immediate hospitalization, oxygen therapy, diuresis, and a search for an infecting pathogen were clearly required. When he suggested that I obtain independent advice, he remembered the proposed consultant's first name as "Carl." When I asked how to spell it, he left the telephone and came back with the information that the first name was "John." The new physician, as it turned out, is a highly regarded pulmonary specialist, but evidently he is not a colleague with whom Dr. A has frequent dealings. Given all the circumstances, Dr. A must have known that the patient would not return to him. Perhaps he wanted to dispose of a difficult case.

I include this detailed case history in this book because it illustrates a universal principle. A public reputation for technical competence has as little meaning as the letter grades on a university student's transcript. One should not trust a person merely because he occupies a position of authority, be it medical, military[2], governmental[3], industrial, scientific, or religious. In this life, in the final analysis, we are on our own when it comes to ascertaining truth. Any other attitude implies a wish to be gulled.

Spokesmen for the medical profession would say that my wife's mistreatment was an isolated occurrence, not likely to happen often in the U.S.A. I believe, on the contrary, that competent, dedicated physicians form a very small minority of their profession. Perhaps because of my academic position, I have always received excellent medical care, but from the experience of close friends I could give a dozen cases of malpractice as detailed and clearcut as that of my wife's. This situation exists because a physician will not often offer criticism of a colleague to a layman. The system will not allow it. In theory, malpractice is corrected internally by the profession. In fact, it is not. This reflects the moral corruption of our time.

Those who believe that a medical doctor can be trusted just because he has a large practice and a prestigious hospital connection, will profit by reading *Heartsounds* (Lear, 1981), a professional writer's account of her physician-husband's treatment and death. This book was recommended to me by my physician.

FUTURE MEDICINE

Having gone this far in condemning physicians, perhaps, in fairness, I should say something about the responsibility of the patient.

---

2. After 16 years the story is slowly unfolding (Smith, 1982a; 1982b) of how the military in peacetime and the scientists of the Atomic Energy Commission concealed from a federal court that the death of 4000 sheep and the dangerous irradiation of more than 100,000 people had resulted from fall-out from Nevada bomb tests in 1953.

3. Ford (1982) has assembled from confidential Government documents a record of how for the last 20 years the safety of nuclear-reactor design and construction has been compromised by high-level bureaucratic and industrial treachery, the publication of which will surely hasten the end of the U.S. nuclear power industry.

In the U.S.A. at least 50% of all hospitalizations could have been avoided had the patient diligently pursued good health in the preceding years. Of the remainder, at least 90% are unavoidable only because of the poor genetic endowment of the patient. Therein lie two keys to a sound national economy in the Age of World Poverty that lies ahead (McConnell, 1982c).

The first natural rule of medical practice is that the primary responsibility for the health of the patient rests with the patient and not with his physician. When we must call upon a doctor to cure our disease, more often than not, that is an admission of our failure to live well. Future medicine will emphasize the prevention of disease rather than its cure. Under present social arrangements, only illness is profitable for the physician. That explains why we have so much of it.

In the future, competent physicians will decline to treat those who use alcohol, tobacco, or other harmful drugs. Those who do not respect their bodies will be encouraged to die—not explicitly by plan, but inevitably by the force of economic poverty. The concept of unearned entitlement will disappear, because it is contrary to natural law.

The layman is always at the mercy of the specialist. In the case of medicine, it is not hard to see how this can be changed. Beginning medicine is not a difficult subject to understand. Eventually, all secondary school students with above-average intelligence will be required to take courses in physics, chemistry, and biology. Hopefully, by 1990, all college students will take a 180 class-hour course in general medicine based upon the *Merck Manual of Diagnosis and Therapy* or its equivalent.

Meanwhile, self-respecting persons will own a *Merck Manual* and consult it about any medical condition that requires a visit to a doctor, and will have at hand a recent edition of the *Physician's Desk Reference,* to be consulted before taking any prescription drug. For most drugs, the manufacturer gives warnings of side effects and counter-indications. In my experience, competent physicians are pleased to deal with well informed patients.

Appendix C

SOME PERSONS OF PROMINENCE
IN THE HISTORY OF PARAPSYCHOLOGY
WHOSE WORK WAS PUBLISHED IN ENGLISH

Barrett, William (1844–1925)
Physicist. Member of the Royal Society. The leading sponsor of the founding of the Society for Psychical Research.

Broad, C.D. (1887–1971)
Eminent Cambridge philosopher. Proponent of psychical research. See his *Lectures on Psychical Research* (1962).

Forwald, Mr. Haakon (1897–1978)
Swedish high-voltage switching authority. In the 1950s, the foremost experimenter in psychokinesis.

Gurney, Edmund (1847–1888)
One of the five founding workers of the SPR. Co-author of *Phantasms of the Living* (1886).

Hodgson, Richard (1855–1905)
First great figure in American parapsychology. Best known for his study of Mrs. Piper.

Hyslop, James H. (1854–1920)
Columbia University philosopher. Second great figure in American parapsychology. Founded the second ASPR after Hodgson's death.

James, William (1842–1910)
American psychologist who was convinced of the reality of ESP, did much to encourage research, and conducted some of his own with the medium, Mrs. Piper.

McDougall, William (1871–1938)
British-American psychologist who supported J.B. and L.E. Rhine when they came to Duke University and later sponsored the founding of the *Journal of Parapsychology*.

Murphy, Gardner (1895–1979)
American psychologist who promoted and defended parapsychology throughout his life.

Myers, Frederic (1843–1901)
The theoretician among the five SPR founding workers. Author of *Human Personality and Its Survival of Bodily Death* (1903). Co-author of *Phantasms of the Living* (1886).

Podmore, Frank (1856–1910)
The junior and most skeptical of the five SPR founding workers. Author of *Modern Spiritualism* (1902). Co-author of *Phantasms of the Living* (1886).

Pratt, J.G. (1910–1979)
Parapsychologist. Received doctoral degree in experimental psychology, 1936. Co-worker with J.B. Rhine, 1937–1963. Psychiatry Department, University of Virginia, 1964–1976.

Price, H.H. (1899-   )
Eminent Oxford philosopher. Proponent of parapsychology.

Prince, Walter Franklin (1863–1934)
Third great figure in American Parapsychology. Best known for his study of the Doris case of multiple personality.

Rhine, J.B. (1895–1980)
The foremost experimenter in the first 100 years of parapsychology. His base of operations was Duke University from 1928 to 1965. Thereafter, he directed the Foundation for Research on the Nature of Man in Durham, N.C.

Rhine, L.E. (1891-   )
Wife of J.B. Rhine and a distinguished scientist in her own right.

Sidgwick, Eleanor (1845–1936)
From 1892 to 1910, the Principal of Newnham College, Cambridge. Wife of Henry Sidgwick and indefatiguable leader of the SPR from 1900 to 1932 as the last of the founding workers.

Sidgwick, Henry (1838–1900)
Cambridge philosopher. First president of the SPR.

Sinclair, Upton (1878–1971)
American socialist reformer who did picture-drawing experiments for three years with his wife as reported in *Mental Radio* (1930).

Tyrrell, G.N.M. (1879–1952)
Mathematician and physicist. Prominent British parapsychologist of the period 1920–1945. His two best known books: *Science & Psychical Phenomena* (1938) and *The Personality of Man* (1946).

Vasiliev, L.L. (1891–1966)
The Soviet Union's greatest parapsychologist. His most important research dealt with the hypnotic control of sleep from a distance.

Appendix D

CHRONOLOGY OF MAJOR, PROFESSIONALLY GUIDED CENTERS OF PARAPSYCHOLOGICAL RESEARCH IN THE U.S.A.

1882	Founding of the Society for Psychical Research in England.
1885	Founding of the first American Society for Psychical Research in Boston.
1890	The ASPR becomes a branch of the British SPR under Richard Hodgson in Boston.
1904	Incorporation of the American Institute for Scientific Research by James Hyslop.
1906	After the 1905 death of Hodgson, SPR folds its U.S.A. branch.
1906	Section *B* of the American Institute for Scientific Research becomes the American Society for Psychical Research under the direction of James Hyslop in New York City.
1922–3	Demise of the Institute for Scientific Research and the separate incorporation of the ASPR.
1923	Capture of the ASPR by Spiritualists whose purpose was to popularize psychical research.
1925	Resignation of Walter F. Prince from the ASPR and the formation of the Boston Society for Psychic Research.
1934	Death of W.F. Prince and suspension of Boston SPR activity.
1935	Creation of a Parapsychological Laboratory as a research organization independent of the Psychology Department at Duke University, Durham, North Carolina.
1937	Publication of the *Journal of Parapsychology* begun by the Duke University Press, under the editorship of William McDougall and J.B. Rhine.
1939	Editorship of *Journal of Parapsychology* transferred to Gardner Murphy and Bernard F. Riess in New York City.
1941	Reconstruction of the ASPR in New York City under the aegis of Gardner Murphy, including jointure with the Boston SPR.
1942	Editorship of *Journal of Parapsychology* returned to J.B. Rhine, *et al.*, at Duke University.
1952	Creation of the Parapsychology Foundation in New York City by the medium, Eileen Garrett. This nonprofessionally guided organization has published parapsychological monographs and

has served as an instrument for the exchange of information concerning activities among lay and professional groups.

1953   Beginning of a parapsychological research program in the Biophysics Department at the University of Pittsburgh, Pennsylvania. Directed by R.A. McConnell. Funded by the A.W. Mellon Educational and Charitable Trust. Currently in the Biological Sciences Department.

1957   Founding of the Parapsychological Association, a professional society for parapsychologists.

1960   Creation of the Psychical Research Foundation at Durham, North Carolina, under the direction of W.G. Roll for investigating the hypothesis of postmortem survival.

1962   Creation of the (parapsychological) Dream Laboratory in the Department of Psychiatry at Maimonides Medical Center in Brooklyn, New York, under the Director of the Department, M. Ullman. (Closed in 1978 with Dr. Ullman's retirement).

1962   Establishment in Durham, N.C. of the free-standing Foundation for Research on the Nature of Man and its operating arm, The Institute for Parapsychology, completed when Dr. J.B. Rhine retired from Duke University in 1965.

1968   Creation of a Division of Parapsychology under Dr. Ian Stevenson within the Psychiatry Department of the University of Virginia Medical School at Charlottesville, Virginia.

1969   Affiliation of the Parapsychological Association with the American Association for the Advancement of Science.

1972   Initiation of a research program in parapsychology at Stanford Research Institute at Menlo Park, California.

1974   Reorganization of the Mind Science Foundation of San Antonio, Texas, into a parapsychological research center.

1979   Psychophysical Research Laboratory established at the Princeton, New Jersey, Forrestal Center under the direction of Charles Honorton.

1980   Creation of the McDonnell Laboratory for Psychical Research at Washington University of St. Louis, Missouri, under the direction of physicist Peter Phillips.

1980   Initiation of a research program in parapsychology in the School of Computer and Information Science, Syracuse University, New York.

(No attempt has been made to list recent parapsychological activity in colleges and universities unless a program of research has been formally established with a staff of at least two professional investigators.)

Appendix E

GOVERNMENTAL ASSISTANCE TO A PRETHEORETICAL SCIENCE

When our Federal Government wants to convene a conference on a well established scientific subject, such as recombinant DNA or high-energy physics, it may uncover differences of opinion on important aspects of the subject, but at least it can be sure whose opinions are worth considering. Not so in parapsychology, where there are no authorities and all experts are self-designated. In any field still lacking a generally accepted theory, the true and the false, the trivial and the profound, are all inextricably mixed so that the outsider, and in particular the Federal Government, is not in a good position to be constructive. This is illustrated by an aborted attempt to promote parapsychology that occurred nine years ago. The situation is little different today.

In early 1973, apparently as a result of curiosity about parapsychology among scattered individuals in several government agencies, an exploratory memorandum was prepared by a "plans and process analyst" of the National Institute of Mental Health proposing a one-week state-of-the-art conference on "psychic research."

That memo was sent to more than a dozen individuals, scattered over the U.S.A., none of whom belonged to the Parapsychological Association. Three months later the same memorandum, along with some informal responses to it, was sent for comment, under new (HEW) aegis—this time to 20 individuals (including myself) who were engaged in parapsychological research or otherwise closely associated with the field.

The memo described tentative plans for a conference of "very 'blue ribbon' scientists and professionals across a wide range of disciplines to explore . . . and to recommend firmly developed . . . standards that can be used to identify . . . the potentials for advancing [parapsychological] knowledge and its *use*." [italics added]

There were to be "two days spent in examining the state of the art; another day devoted to identification of scientific and technical questions that need to be raised to identify the boundaries of the domain of inquiry; and finally a two- or three-day work session to develop specific statements of research that [would] be needed in order to establish psychic research and *development* as a legitimate field of scientific inquiry [italics added]. . . . [This] final portion of the conference [would] address itself to such questions as: What are the criteria of credibility? . . . What kinds of data and findings will establish credibility? . . . *What type of research work is worth doing?* [italics added] . . . How should it be undertaken?"

This example of bureaucratic ignorance of the nature of basic science posed a dilemma. On the one hand, an educational effort was (and is) needed so that interested Federal personnel could know how to go about identifying what to support in the way of applications for parapsychological research. On the other, a conference such as that proposed would almost certainly have brought discredit upon the sponsoring agencies and upon parapsychology (for reasons to be explained below).

The indications were that the inadequacies of the original proposal were suspected by its new sponsor. I presumed that his plan was to tack in a new direction that would satisfy the original sponsors and yet be creative rather than harmful. However, I did not see how that could be done.

Some of the preliminary responses received by the first agency that were sent to me along with the memorandum were more alarming than the memo itself. None of the authors was a parapsychologist. As a group they seemed to be professional idea brokers who by their avid amateur interest in parapsychology had achieved a certain visibility as authorities on the subject. Their advice was interesting, but skewed and in some respects misinformed. Their success in gaining attention in a major government agency suggested that, in the absence of authority figures who had won credentials in orthodox science, the field of parapsychology could be at the political mercy of fringe scientists, as was Soviet genetics for a different reason in the time of Lysenko.

My letter to HEW follows:

*   *   *   *

It is a pleasure to respond to your memorandum of 26 October 1973 requesting comment on an NIMH memorandum dated 13 July 1973 from Mr. W.—— exploring the possibility of a state-of-the-art conference on psychical research.

I am in full agreement with the educational objective behind Mr. W——'s memorandum. There is need for a continuing examination of parapsychology in order to allow a widening circle of scientists and science administrators to determine to their own satisfaction the evidential status and possible social importance of psi phenomena.

I must confess, however, that I have misgivings with regard to the conference as proposed. Rather than attempt a detailed critique, I would prefer to express my response in the form of the following disconnected propositions, which can be examined upon their merits and allowed to influence your planning to whatever extent they may prove useful.

The criteria of credibility in science are well known. One can point to non-repeatability and to the absence of theory as valid reasons for the general reluctance of scientists to accept the empirical evidence for the occurrence of psi phenomena. I suspect, however, that other barriers to credibility lie in psychological subtleties that are already understood by those who are familiar with the psychopathology of everyday life and with the history of science. In either case, I do not see how a government-sponsored endeavor to face the challenge of psi phenomena can generate scientific authority or credibility.

What other advantages might accrue from a gathering of scientists across a wide range of disciplines—assuming it were possible to get uncommitted scientists of stature to give of their time to such a dubious activity?

I do not believe that at the present early date, cross-fertilization between parapsychology and various sciences is likely to result from the short-term interdisciplinary conferring of groups of experts who have little knowledge of, let alone feeling for, parapsychological phenomena.

Cross-fertilization aside, in the light of my own experience I doubt whether attempting to depict in a cultivational conference the total possible scientific scope of parapsychology (defined as the study of psi phenomena) will encourage its friendly consideration by a competent scientist in an ostensibly distant field, such as physics, biology, sociology, anthropology, political science, or medicine, unless he should happen to have a prior personal interest.

For an established scientist in another field, parapsychology has typically been seen, first as absurd, next as irrelevant, later as a threat, and only after long consideration as a welcome opportunity. The intermediate-stage opposition of eminent scientists is likely to be concealed—typically by recommendations that we turn away from psi phenomena as an experimental field of endeavor and concentrate attention for the present on other problems "of greater importance to science and mankind."

For a conference in a pretheoretical field there is another special hazard that is not likely to be foreseen by those experienced only in the later stages of science. I refer to the difficulty of isolating the discipline—not from established fields of science toward which it should be leaning, but from its pretheoretical competitors who would sap its efforts.

There are many peripheral areas of psychology, biology, and even applied physics that are associated in the popular mind with parapsychology but that are not directly concerned with psi phenomena. For a conference intended to clarify the status of parapsychology, it would be a mistake, I think, to invite psychologists or biologists who are committed to the study of such areas as biofeedback, Kirlian photography, psychotropic drugs, biological rhythms, or the biological effects of physical energy fields.

Some of these peripheral activities are important in their own right. Some may find a theoretical basis in biochemistry. Some may prove to be of great value in the future development of parapsychology. But none of these areas has yet shown the conceptually revolutionary potential associated with psi phenomena. In this sense, none has as persuasive a claim to our special attention, much less a claim to be a part of parapsychology.

The foregoing deprecations can be restated positively as follows. A discipline must be allowed to define itself. Parapsychology is defined by its most respected practitioners as the study of extrasensory perception and psychokinesis in both natural and experimental settings. Under these two terms parapsychologists can readily encompass such widely divergent activities as card guessing and faith-healing, or a range of spontaneous effects from hunches to poltergeists. If order is to emerge from pretheoretical chaos, parapsychology must be allowed to impose *its* organizing principles upon *its* selection from the conceptually unassimilated mass of empirical fact. In a word, it must be allowed its attempt to become a distinct discipline. For government agencies to stir up the primordial stew of unexplained phenomena by calling emotionally incompatible protagonists into a joint, command performance would not contribute to governmental or to public understanding nor, indeed, to an enhancement of parapsychology's scientific image.

My positive contribution to your informational problem must primarily consist of the enclosed reprint, "Parapsychology and the Occult" (McConnell, 1973), and the enclosed manuscript, "Parapsychology: Its Future Organization and Support" (McConnell, 1974a). In a sense, these articles are a distillation of my own quarter-century effort to achieve the objectives of Mr. W——'s memorandum.

There are, however, many aspects of the problem of relating parapsychology to the Scientific Establishment and to society that I have not touched upon in the above cited papers. The following deserve special attention.

The state of our knowledge in parapsychology seems today to be changing more rapidly than at any time in its history. The most dramatic development is the emergence of gross psychokinetic effects on stable physical systems as a probable reality.

The possible implications of parapsychological findings are of two kinds: theoretical and technical. It would be premature to concern ourselves with specific possible technical developments at a time when the existence of psi phenomena has not yet been widely accepted by scientists and while we lack even a glimmer of theoretical understanding of these phenomena. I would suppose that everyone agrees it is impossible to preconceive a technology for which the basic scientific laws are still undiscovered—any more than electric lighting could have been predicted by the Greeks from a pith ball jumping to rubbed amber. A fortiori, it is impossible by the methods of the social sciences to anticipate how such a nonexistent technology will interact with society. I fear this will not deter some socially concerned thinkers from writing extensively on this topic without relating their words to the real world.

To promote parapsychology on the basis of imagined technical uses would be unjustified at this stage. To speak of research and development, as was done in the conference proposal, would most kindly be called naive. My position regarding parapsychology vis-a-vis the needs of society is this: Parapsychology will yield increased theoretical knowledge of man's inner nature. Nothing but good can come from self-understanding. For example, deeper insights into parapsychology may well lead to modifications of our present conceptions of good and evil so as to bring those conceptions into better conformity with nature. I regard the search for new human values as the most important psychological task we can undertake for survival. On this basis I urge parapsychology upon the attention of scientists.

I hope these hasty thoughts will help you in your planning. What impresses me as I look back through this letter is that the methodological ideas we are discussing are tremendously exciting, but that, as topics for elaboration, they are not primarily what is appropriate in a tutorial conference such as is needed within government agencies at this time.[1]

Sincerely yours,

R.A. McConnell

1. For whatever reasons, the proposed conference was never held.

Appendix F

ANALYSIS OF THE HONORTON-
SCIENCE CONTROVERSY, 1972–1975

(A summary prepared for classroom use)

When *Science,* the leading interdisciplinary scientific journal of the U.S.A. rejected an experimental paper on extrasensory perception and when the relevant referee-author-editor correspondence was published elsewhere with the paper (Honorton, Ramsey, & Cabbibo, 1975), it was possible for scientists everywhere to discover that the three referees who recommended against publication in *Science* had variously:

1. Claimed falsely that the authors had "violated a number of basic assumptions underlying" their statistical tests without revealing what the violations were (ibid., page 141, middle paragraph, line 2).

2. Stated that the authors' conclusion was "erroneous" without indicating the nature of the supposed error (page 141, middle paragraph, line 9).

3. Ridiculed the paper by name-calling and sarcasm (page 141, last three paragraphs).

4. Complained that the authors had failed to describe the detailed content of a questionnaire, claiming that it was the basis of "a major conclusion" of the paper (page 141, middle paragraph, line 4), when, in fact, the associated analysis of the questionnaire scores was only of minor interest (page 137) and could have been omitted from the paper. Under these circumstances a detailed description of the questionnaire would have been clearly inappropriate.

5. Failed to understand the secondary role of theory in relation to experiment in the exploration of a new phenomenon (page 142, second paragraph, lines 7–11).

6. Criticised the authors for failing to use a control group that would, in principle, have been impossible to create (page 147, paragraph No. 1, lines 1–3).

7. Falsely stated that failure to have proved a hypothesis (which the experimenters did not claim to have tested) cast doubt upon the hypothesis actually under test (page 147, paragraph No. 3).

8. Made unjustified assumptions about the nature of ESP and then invoked those assumptions as objections to the observed characteristics of the experimental data (page 148, paragraph No. 5).

9. Falsely criticised the authors for comparing their treated subjects with binomial chance expectation (page 147, paragraph No. 1, lines 4–5) when, in fact, the authors' experimental hypothesis was clearly stated to have been tested by a *t*-test between two differently treated groups (page 138, lines 2–4).

10. Falsely accused the authors of testing their hypothesis by comparing the means obtained by pooling all within-subject data (page 147, paragraph No. 2) when it was obvious from the number of degrees of freedom cited that the analysis was correctly performed using subject mean scores (page 138, lines 2–4).

11. Wrongly criticised the conclusion of the paper as having been based upon "unreliable" data because (in an incidental calculation to show the internal consistency of their data) the authors, in using a split-half reliability test, had obtained product-moment correlations (0.6 and 0.8) that were significantly different from zero but not extremely high. Two of the referees made this mistake. Evidently, they remembered from their study of elementary statistics that a correlation coefficient of 0.6 is not high enough to make reliable individual predictions (e.g., of John Doe's weight from his height). Encountering the word "reliability" in the name of the test was apparently enough to trigger the wrong program in their minds (page 141, middle paragraph, lines 8–9, and page 147, paragraph No. 4).

These criticisms are arranged more or less in the order of their increasing technical complexity. Each criticism is discussed in detail in the published correspondence. The student can determine whether these referees' oversights and mistakes are as inexcusable as they sound by consulting any teacher of statistics.

The reader who thoroughly understands elementary statistical method will judge this matter for himself, but he is likely to be left with a feeling of puzzlement. How does it happen that *Science* has pursued for many years an adverse policy toward parapsychology as typified by the Honorton affair and as described more broadly in Chapter 22 of this book?

On the basis of (1) my own correspondence with *Science*, (2) correspondence between the Parapsychological Association and *Science* of which I have been apprised, and (3) private statements from members of the editorial staff of *Science*, I am convinced that the policy of *Science* toward parapsychology directly reflects the attitude of its editor, Philip Abelson—a fact that I do not think he will wish to deny.

Dr. Abelson's opposition to parapsychology is interesting to me because he is a physical chemist, a member of the National Academy of Sciences, and a generally well informed scientist for whom I have profound respect. I think a good case could be made for the proposition that Abelson is the politically most influential scientist in the U.S.A.

It is the virulent opposition to parapsychology by men of the calibre of Jacob Bronowski (Chapter 25) and Philip Abelson that led me to say in my closing chapter that, as psi phenomena begin to attract the favorable attention of our leaders, we may expect a desperate counterattack upon this field by all those scientists who are too old to accept the loss of their philosophy. I shall be content if the book you are reading hastens the day when orthodoxy commits itself to an honest evaluation of these anomalous phenomena.

Appendix G

LISTENING GUIDE TO THE CONTROVERSY ABOUT THE RELATION OF INTELLIGENCE TO INHERITED BIOLOGICAL STRUCTURE

Purpose

This guide is intended to help the reader ask questions by which he can discover for himself who is searching for truth in this controversy and who wants to conceal it. The writer, R.A. McConnell, does not claim to be an authority—merely a student of authorities. The ideas presented must stand on their own in the light of the relevant scientific literature.[1]

The influence or lack of influence of inherited structure in determining intelligence is a biological matter and therefore absolute and permanent, and cannot be changed by legislation. For some who are trained in law but not in science, this may be a difficult principle to grasp.

The Challenge

A.R. Jensen (1981) and other scientists say that 70 to 80% of the variation of intelligence in the North American white population is determined by heredity.

Definition of Intelligence

Intelligence is most simply defined as the ability to grasp abstract relationships. Its best available measure is the well known Stanford-Binet Test, which yields a score called the intelligence quotient (IQ).

---

1. Those who are inclined to doubt that reputable individuals or institutions might wish to conceal truth in this controversy will profit by reading Herrnstein (1982) and Jensen (1982). The American Psychological Association, by a head-in-sand policy, has encouraged the misrepresentation and vilification by the popular press of those who study the genetics of human intelligence. A special 200-page issue (October, 1981) of the APA's *American Psychologist* (circulation, 62,000) was devoted to 20 invited papers defending mental testing as a rigorous, neo-behaviorist science. This journal issue was unusual in that it was directed, not to specialists in testing, but to "individuals not technically trained in testing who make policy decisions about the use of tests" (p. 998), as well as to others. The orientation was tacitly environmentalist throughout. The possibility that there might be a measureable biological basis of intelligence was dismissed in four pages of ridicule (p. 1176–1179).

How IQ Scores Scatter

In many areas of science, measurable characteristics whose size results from the addition of a number of chance causes of similar importance (e.g., by the summation of the effects of more than a few chance-assorted genes) usually scatter according to a mathematical equation called "the normal curve of error," which is drawn in Figure G.1. IQ scores have been found to follow this curve rather closely.

On the horizontal base line are numbers representing the measured characteristic (i.e., IQ score, increasing to the right). The vertical distance between any point on the base line and the curve is proportional to the number of scores of that size one would expect to find in a sample of the population represented. (For IQs, a score of 85 is only 60% as likely to occur as a score of 100.)

For convenience, the area under the entire curve is set equal to unity, so that the area beyond any given score (e.g., the cross-hatched area beyond 115) tells the probability of getting a score greater than the given score.

Everything You Need to Know About The Normal Curve of Error

The normal curve is bell-shaped. Its maximum occurs at the middle, or average, score. The width of the curve is measured by its "standard deviation." The standard deviation in the case of the normal curve is the distance along the horizontal base line from the middle score to the point where the curve reverses its curvature. In the measurement of IQ, the average score has been set to 100 and the standard deviation happens to be nearly 15.

For most practical purposes the normal curve reaches the base line at 3 standard deviations away from the middle. In other words, IQ scores above 145 and below 55 (aside from brain-damage cases) very rarely occur. Close to two-thirds of the area under any normal curve lies within a distance of one standard deviation from the middle score. Thus, only about 16% of the population has IQ scores greater than 115 (the cross-hatched area) and another 16% is below 85.

Some Ideas That Do Not Depend Upon Whether IQ is Inherited and Concerning Which There Is, or Should Be, General Agreement

1. High IQ is necessary in order to master natural science and engineering, upon which the economic well-being of our civiliza-

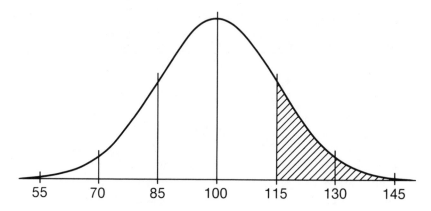

Figure G.1. The normal curve of error.

tion is dependent. Whether high IQ is necessary for success in other professions depends upon the criteria for success.

2. For whatever reason, a difference of about 40 IQ points separates the average unskilled laborer and the average medical doctor.

3. Those with an IQ of less than 85 are becoming increasingly unemployable as the complexity of civilization grows. More precisely, they are needed in ever decreasing proportion as mechanization advances. There is a problem here as fundamental as the energy, pollution, and population problems, and it may be more urgent than any of these.

4. Those with an IQ between 85 and 100 can usually find work if they are trained and willing, but they are second-class citizens because, as a rule, they do not understand the fundamentals of contract law, banking, physics, chemistry, and medicine, and consequently are preyed upon by those who sell technically complex goods and services.

5. As those with IQs below 100 become increasingly aware of their disadvantage in the modern world, and are told that this is "society's fault" and not dependent on the genes from their parents, they become increasingly angry.

6. Citizens with an IQ less than 115, i.e., perhaps 85% of the population, tend to do little serious reading that is not required to earn their living and they usually ignore those few educational TV programs that might partially substitute for reading. Except at a simplistic level they are cut off from the history of mankind, in-

cluding that great body of subtle and complex recorded experience that might allow them better to guide their own lives and to help preserve the nation. Their political opinions are determined mostly by those with whom they have personal contact and by the mass news media, with little critical reasoning by themselves. In an indirect but very real sense, they are the intellectual wards of the 15% whose brains are better biological thinking machines.

7. Most persons have little, intimate social interaction with others whose IQs differ from their own by more than 20 points. As a result, most Americans seriously misconceive the intellectual life-styles of other population segments. The consequences in misgovernment, misguided idealism, and misery are everywhere apparent.

8. IQ is the only personality trait that can be measured with technical adequacy at present. However, most hereditarians believe that all psychological as well as physical traits are largely determined by a person's genes. Everyone agrees that high IQ does not necessarily accompany other desirable traits and that intelligence without empathy and altruism will not solve mankind's problems.

Essence of the Controversy

IQ differences are admitted. The only important point of contention is whether they are more than 50% genetically determined or are almost entirely environmental in origin. No hereditarians with scientific training say that the "heritability" of IQ is greater than about 80%. Most are sure that it is at least 50% in the populations so far measured. Today, only a few environmentalists still say that the heritability of IQ is zero. Most say that it is unknown and negligibly small.

Social forces opposing resolution of the controversy

If heredity is the major determinant of IQ, the American dream that all persons are equally educable and that everyone can produce a comfortable living for self and family if given a chance and willing to work, is just that—a dream. The people of a nation who have lived with an illusion can be expected to resist desperately any effort to dispel it.

If IQ is largely determined by chance assortment of parental genes, the role of education will be more limited than otherwise. It is not surprising that from kindergarten to university, almost without exception, educators reject the importance of heredity.

It is understandable that the poor do not welcome the possibility that their chains are chromosomal. More puzzling is the emotional response this proposition evokes from egalitarian intellectuals. Could it be that they would be forced to trade their condescension toward the poor for the humility of noblesse oblige if they acknowledged that credit for their own success belonged primarily to their ancestors and to Lady Luck?

Propositions deserving public examination

What makes people different from animals is not love but the analytical power of the human brain. To deny the importance of intelligence is to deny the worth of mankind's distinguishing characteristic.

Legislation that attempts education beyond what is biologically feasible wastes money, alienates the intended beneficiaries, and, by lowering standards and wrecking morale, may, or will, destroy the quality of our educational institutions.[2]

If the hereditarians are right, poverty can be increased or decreased by selective breeding and legislation that raises the birthrate of the poor relative to that of the affluent is selective-breeding legislation—whether or not it is so called by its proponents. Perhaps it is time that we openly decide what kind of selective breeding we favor.[3]

---

2. Between 1972 and 1980, the number of U.S.A. 18-year-olds increased by 5% to 4.1 million, while the number of high school seniors taking the Educational Testing Service so-called *Scholastic Aptitude Test* dropped 3% to 991 thousand. Between these same years, the number of students with verbal scores over 650 dropped 46% to 29 thousand, while the number of math scores over 650 dropped 22% to 73 thousand. (Source: The College Entrance Examination Board)

These are our future leaders upon whom efficiency will depend in industry, commerce, science, education, and government. Supplementary studies and analyses have shown that these catastrophic declines cannot be artifacts resulting from a drifting examination or shifting relevance to college studies but are real effects representing loss in the intellectual skills of our youth. Whatever may be the specific causes, unless reversed, this educational debacle makes certain the quick end of the U.S.A. as a great nation.

3. Eysenck (1982) reports that Lipovechaja, et al., obtained a heritability for intelligence of 0.78 in a 1978 Moscow study of 144 pairs of monozygotic and dizygotic twins. The significance of this and similar Communist research is the interest it reveals. Because the USSR leadership is committed to elitism, it seems likely that they have recognized the importance of intelligence for survival and will try to breed for it. If they can succeed in discouraging procreation by the unfit

To solve our social problems, we need understanding as well as action. Our failures in social planning in the last half century suggest a lack of understanding. Can we afford to continue to deny the possibly hereditary basis of our problems?

and thus decrease the incidence of mental and physical disability, they will begin reaping economic benefits immediately. By selective breeding of the most intelligent, they may gain pre-eminence in science in one generation.

Appendix H

TWO INSTANCES OF SPONTANEOUS, PROBABLE ESP KNOWN FIRST-HAND TO THE AUTHOR

In 35 years of attention to parapsychology I have encountered first-hand only two instances of recognized, spontaneous, ostensible ESP—and these quite recently. The first occurred to me and the second to my wife.

I present these trivial instances (as they were recorded at the time) because I can vouch for them and because they convey the flavor of a vast number of cases recorded in the serious literature of spontaneous psi.

This literature raises a tantalyzing question: How often do psi phenomena go unrecognized because we fail to receive confirming information or because the incident is too trivial to hold our attention or, at most, seems like a chance coincidence?

On Tuesday, 27 September 1977, I traveled to the university athletic gymnasium for my customary noontime swim. Since the weather was threatening, I carried an umbrella. The next morning, when I noticed that the umbrella was missing, I telephoned the locker-room attendant to ask him to hold the umbrella until the following day if he found it.

On Thursday I went to the gymnasium, passed through the security gate, and entered the elevator with another passenger whom I did not recognize. In the usual way, as I reached for the "down" button, I looked back toward the security gate, 10 meters away, to see if anyone else was coming. A student-age stranger passed through the gate and called out: "Would you hold the umbrella for me—no, the elevator?" (This suddenly reminded me of my missing umbrella.)

No one else was moving our way. Seconds later, as he stepped into the elevator, I asked: "Have you any idea what made you say 'umbrella'?" His light-hearted reply: "A Freudian slip, I guess." Nothing else was said. I had noticed no umbrellas in the security lobby. The weather was pleasant outside, with the sun shining through broken clouds. The three of us got off the elevator, and I asked the attendant at the adjacent desk if my umbrella had been found. (I discovered later that it was missing from my office because I had taken it home the night before.)

The stranger's mistake in wording could have been a coincidence caused by some independent train of thought in his own mind. But anyone familiar with the laboratory evidence for ESP and with the literature of spontaneous psychic occurrences would be more inclined to suppose that it was a psychic flash. As often happens in such cases, the psychological circumstances seemed to "make sense." Some subconscious part of my brain was struggling to bring my conscious attention to the fact that in a few seconds it would be time to ask the attendant about my umbrella. Although my casual conscious attention toward the approaching stranger was one of polite waiting, subconsciously (because I am always in a hurry) I must have been telling him to hurry. He responded as though to a mixture of my two subconscious messages. The fact that his response made no sense to him shows that his attention was not directly upon what he was saying.

I offer the foregoing as only a probably psychic event. It suggests to me the following question: If psi phenomena are primarily spontaneous in occurrence and subconscious in their operation, and if they can be caught in the laboratory as a rule only by "looking the other way," is it surprising that Western science, to which they are philosophically repugnant, has not acknowledged and accepted them?

On Sunday, 14 March 1982 about 7:30 AM, as I was leaving our bedroom, my wife, still in bed, said she had had a disturbing dream, which she then briefly related. Later, shortly after 8:30 AM, she entered my home office and said she had just heard a national news report in which a recreational vehicle called a "van," crossing a railroad in the state of New York, was struck with many resulting fatalities.

At my request, she wrote at once a description of her dream, which agreed with what she had told me at 7:30. I have shortened and clarified it as follows:

> I dreamt of a railroad crossing gate attached to our front-yard corner fence post so as to control traffic from the street into our neighbor's wide walkway toward the rear of his house. The striped gate was in an upright position, very plain to be seen. Opposite it, was a post holding a standard, railroad double warning light. As I

looked from our front door in my dream and discovered these rail-road crossing devices, there was a rusty, open jeep standing in front of this neighbor's house and someone was climbing in, just ready to drive away. I became very disturbed and wondered when these sig-nalling devices had been installed and how we were going to get rid of them. I awakened at 6:45 AM.

At 8:30 AM, I listened to the Mutual Radio Network news. One item described a van accident at a railroad crossing in New York State in which many young people were killed.

Later in the day I saw a television account of the accident in which a striped crossing gate, warning lights, and the wreckage of the van were featured. According to a report issued nine months later by the U.S. National Transportation Safety Board, a Ford van occupied by nine teenage passengers and a teenage driver was struck by a railroad passenger train at 2:18 AM after driving around a lowered gate with flashing lights at a crossing at Mineola, New York. There were nine fatalities. The driver's body showed ethyl alcohol concentration at a level indicating impairment of driving ability under New York law. There was one witness in a car that had stopped behind the van.

The fragmentary and distorted information and the misguided emotion in my wife's ostensibly veridical dream of this accident are frequent characteristics of spontaneous extrasensory perception.

REFERENCES AND
SELECTED BIBLIOGRAPHY

Items preceded by *e* are publications since 1965 having unusual evidential interest regarding the reality of psi phenomena.

Items preceded by *s* are publications having unusual sociological interest in relation to parapsychology.

In brackets after each item are listed the chapters and appendixes in which the item is referred to.

Abbreviations:

SPR = Society for Psychical Research (London).

ASPR = American Society for Psychical Research.

Alvarado, C.S. (1980). Letter to the editor. *Journal of Parapsychology, 44,* 93–95. [16]

American Psychiatric Association (1968). *Diagnostic and Statistical Manual of Mental Disorders* (second edition). Washington, D.C. [4]

American Psychiatric Association (1980). *Diagnostic and Statistical Manual of Mental Disorders* (third edition). Washington, D.C. [4]

American Society for Psychical Research. (1980). *Courses and Other Study Opportunities in Parapsychology.* [25]

s   Bamford, J. (1982). *The Puzzle Palace.* Boston: Houghton Mifflin. [A]

Barber, T.X. (1965). Experimental analyses of "hyponotic" behavior. *J. Abnormal Psychology, 70,* 132–154. [6]

Barber, T.X. (1969). *Hypnosis: A Scientific Approach.* New York: Van Nostrand Reinhold. [6]

Barber, T.X., Spanos, N.P., Chaves, J.F. (1974). *Hypnosis, Imagination, and Human Potentialities.* New York: Pergamon Press. [6,15]

Barrington, M.R. (1974). Mrs. Albert's testimony: Observation or inference? *Proceedings of the SPR, 56,* 112–116. [19]

Becker, Ernest. (1975). *Escape From Evil.* New York: Free Press (Macmillan). [26]

s   Beloff, J. (1973). Belief and doubt. Pages 189–200 in W.G. Roll, R.L. Morris, and J.D. Morris (Eds.), *Research in Parapsychology—1972.* Metuchen, New Jersey: Scarecrow Press.

Beloff, J. (1974). Why I believe that Soal is innocent. *Proceedings of the SPR, 56,* 93–96. [19]

e   Braud, L.W., & Braud, W.G. (1974). Further studies of relaxation as a psi-conducive state. *Journal of the ASPR, 68,* 229–245. [7]

e   Braud, W.G., Wood, R., & Braud, L.W. (1975). Free response GESP performance during an experimental hypnogogic state induced by visual and acoustic Ganzfeld techniques: A replication and extension. *Journal of the ASPR, 69,* 105–113. [7]

Bridgman, P.W. (1927). *The Logic of Modern Physics.* Macmillan. [17]

Broad, C.D. (1938). Henry Sidgwick and psychical research. *Proceedings of the SPR, 45,* 131–161. [8,21]

Broad, C.D. (1953). *Religion, Philosophy and Psychical Research.* New York: Harcourt Brace & Co. [26]

Broad, C.D. (1962). *Lectures on Psychical Research*. London: Routledge & Kegan Paul. [C]

Bronowski, J. (1973). *The Ascent of Man*. Boston: Little Brown. [25]

Broughton, R.S. (1976). Brain hemisphere specialization and its possible effects on ESP performance. Pp. 98–102 in J.D. Morris, W.G. Roll, and R.L. Morris (Eds.), *Research in Parapsychology—1975*. Metuchen, New Jersey: Scarecrow Press. [7]

Broughton, R.S. (1977). Brain hemisphere differences in psi-influenced reaction time. Pages 86–88 in J.D. Morris, W.G. Roll, & R.L. Morris (Eds.), *Research in Parapsychology—1976*. Metuchen, New Jersey: Scarecrow Press. [7]

Cadoret, R., & Pratt, J.G. (1950). The consistent missing effect in ESP. *Journal of Parapsychology, 14*, 244–256. [13]

Carington, W. (1940). Experiments in the paranormal cognition of drawings, Part I. *Proceedings of the SPR, 46*, 34–151. [13,19]

Cattell, Raymond B. (1972). *A New Morality from Science: Beyondism*. Elmsford, New York: Pergamon Press. [A]

s   Condon, E.U. (1969). UFOs I have loved and lost. *Bulletin of the Atomic Scientists, 25*, 6–8. [21,25]

Cox, W.E. (1951). The effect of PK on the placement of falling objects. *Journal of Parapsychology, 15*, 40–48. [12]

Davis, J.W. (1975). Comments on the Levy affair. Pages 11–12 in J.D. Morris, W.G. Roll, and R.L. Morris (Eds.), *Research in Parapsychology—1974*. Metuchen, N.J.: Scarecrow Press. [19]

Davis, J.W. (1979). Psi in animals: A review of laboratory research. *Parapsychology Review. 10* (2), 1–9. [19]

Ducasse, C.J. (1961). *A Critical Examination of the Belief in a Life After Death*. Springfield, Illinois: C.C. Thomas. [8]

e   Dunne, B.J., & Bisaha, J.P. (1979). Precognitive remote viewing in the Chicago area. *Journal of Parapsychology, 43*, 17–30. [25]

Duval, P., & Montredon, E. (1968). ESP experiments with mice. *Journal of Parapsychology, 32*, 153–166. [19]

Einstein, A., Podolsky, B., & Rosen, N. (1935). Can quantum-mechanical descriptions of physical reality be considered complete? *Physical Review, 47*, 777–780. [A]

Eisenbud, J. (1967). *The World of Ted Serios*. New York: William Morrow & Co. [12]

s   Ellenberger, H.F. (1970). *The Discovery of the Unconscious*. New York: Basic Books. [9]

Estabrooks, G.H. (1927). *A Contribution to Experimental Telepathy, Bulletin No. 5*. Boston Society for Psychic Research. (Reprinted in the *Journal of Parapsychology, 25* [1961], 190–213.) [14]

Evans, A.C. (1934). Chronic brucellosis. *Journal of the American Medical Association, 103*, 665–667. [B]

Evans, A.C. (1961). Chronic brucellosis: The unreliability of diagnostic tests. *Journal of the American Medical Women's Association, 16*, 942–946. [B]

Evans, C. (1973). Parapsychology—what the questionnaire revealed. *New Scientist, 57*, 465. [25]

Eysenck, H.J. (1982). The sociology of psychological knowledge, the genetic interpretation of the IQ, and Marxist-Leninist ideology. *Bulletin of the British Psychological Society, 35*, 449–451. [G]

Ford, D. (1982). *The Cult of the Atom*. New York: Simon & Schuster. (Condensed in *The New Yorker*, October 25 and November 1, 1982.) [B]

Freedman, S.J., & Clauser, J.F. (1972). Experimental test of local hidden-variable theories. *Physical Review Letters, 28*, 938–941. [A]

Freud, S. (1901). *The Psychopathology of Everyday Life.* (Vol. 6 of his *Complete Psychological Works.*) London: Hogarth Press. [19]

Freud, S. (1921), Psychoanalysis and telepathy. Page 175–193 in J. Strachey (Ed.), *The Complete Psychological Works of Sigmund Freud, Volume 18,* London: Hogarth Press, 1955. [13]

Fukurai, T. (1931). *Clairvoyance and Thoughtography.* London: Rider & Co. [12]

s Gauld, Alan (1968). *The Founders of Psychical Research.* London: Routledge & Kegan Paul. [9]

Gazzaniga, M.S., & LeDoux, J.E. (1978). *The Integrated Mind.* New York: Plenum Press. [3,4,24]

Goldney, K.M. (1974). The Soal-Goldney experiments with Basil Shackleton: A personal account. *Proceedings of the SPR, 56,* 73–84. [19,21]

Goldney, K.M. (1978). Statement. *Proceedings of the SPR, 56,* 278. [19,21]

Grad, B. (1965). Some biological effects of the "laying on of hands": A review of experiments with animals and plants. *Journal of the ASPR, 59,* 95–129. [12]

Grad, B. (1967). The "laying on of hands": Implications for psychotherapy, gentling, and the placebo effect. *Journal of the ASPR, 61,* 286–305. [12]

Greenberg, J. (1981). An interview with David Rosenhan. *American Psychological Association Monitor, 12* (6–7), 4 ff. [B]

Gregory, Anita (1980). Why do scientists engage in fraud? *Parapsychology Review, 11* (6), 1–6. [19]

Griffen, D.R. (1976). *The Question of Animal Awareness.* New York: Rockefeller University Press. [8]

Gurney, E., Myers, F.W.H., & Podmore, F. (1886). *Phantasms of the Living* (in two volumes). London: Trubner & Co. A one-volume abridgment prepared by Eleanor Balfour Sidgwick was published in 1918 by Kegan Paul, Trench, Trubner & Co., Ltd., of London and republished in 1963 by University Books, Inc., as Volume 2 of a two-volume series of the same title. [9,C]

Hall, C.S. (1954). *A Primer of Freudian Psychology.* New York: New American Library. [13]

Hall, Radclyffe (1928). *The Well of Loneliness.* New York: Blue Ribbon Books. [2]

Hansel, C.E.M. (1966). *ESP: A Scientific Evaluation.* New York: Scribners. [22]

Haraldsson, E. (1980). Confirmation of the percipient-order effect in a plethysmographic study of ESP. *Journal of Parapsychology, 44,* 105–124.

Hasted, J.B. (1976). An experimental study of the validity of metal bending phenomena. *Journal of the SPR, 48,* 365–383. [12]

Hasted, J.B. (1977). Physical aspects of paranormal metal bending. *Journal of the SPR, 49,* 583–607. [12]

Hasted, J.B., & Robertson, D. (1979). The detail of paranormal metal bending. *Journal of the SPR, 50, 9–20. [12]*

Herrnstein, R.J. (1982). IQ testing and the media. *The Atlantic Monthly, 250,* August, 68–74. [G]

Heston, L.L. (1970). Genetics of Schizophrenic and Schizoid Disease. *Science, 167,* 249–256. [4]

Hilgard, E.R. (1965). *Hypnotic Susceptibility.* New York: Harcourt, Brace, & World. [6]

Hilgard, E.R. (1968). *The Experience of Hypnosis* (a shorter, paperbound version of *Hypnotic Susceptibility*). N.Y.: Harcourt, Brace, & World. [6,15]

Hilgard, E.R. (1973a). The domain of hypnosis. *American Psychologist, 28,* 972–892. [6]

Hilgard, E.R. (1973b). A neodissociation interpretation of pain reduction in hypnosis. *Psychological Review, 80,* 396–411. [6]

Hilgard, E.R. (1977). *Divided Consciousness: Multiple Controls in Human Thought and Action.* New York: John Wiley. [4,6]

Hilgard, E.R., & Atkinson, R.C. (1967). *Introduction to Psychology* (4th ed.). New York: Harcourt, Brace, World. [25]

e   Honorton, Charles (1971). Automated forced-choice precognition tests with a "sensitive." *Journal of the ASPR, 65,* 476–481.

Honorton, Charles (1974). ʻApparent psychokinesis on static objects by a "gifted" subject. Pp. 128–131 in W.G. Roll, R.L. Morris, and J.D. Morris (Eds.), *Research in Parapsychology—1973.* Metuchen, NJ: Scarecrow Press. [12]

e   Honorton, Charles (1977). Psi and internal attention states. Pp. 435–472 in B.B. Wolman (Ed.), *Handbook of Parapsychology.* New York: Van Nostrand Reinhold. [7]

s   Honorton, C., Ramsey, M., & Cabibbo, C. (1975). Experimenter effects in extrasensory perception. *Journal of the ASPR, 69,* 135–149. [7,20,22,F]

Huxley, Aldous (1932). *Brave New World.* New York: Doubleday, Doran & Co. [A]

Inglis, B. (1977). *Natural and Supernatural: A History of the Paranormal from Earliest Times to 1914.* London: Hodder & Stoughton. (Paperback from Sphere Books, Ltd., London, 1979.) [9]

James, William (1890). *Principles of Psychology, Vol. 1.* New York: Henry Holt. [5]

Jamieson, W.M. (1975). Diseases due to infection. (Pages 1–72 in W.N. Mann, Ed.) *Conybeare's Textbook of Medicine.* Edinburgh: Churchill-Livingstone. [B]

s   Jen, C.K. (1982). Some demonstrations of extraocular image in China. Pages 5–17 in R.A. McConnell (Ed.), *Parapsychology and Self-Deception in Science.* Pittsburgh, Pennsylvania: R.A. McConnell (1983). [9]

Jensen, A.R. (1981). *Straight Talk about Mental Tests.* New York: Free Press. [G]

Jensen, A.R. (1982). The debunking of scientific fossils and straw persons. (A review of S.J. Gould's *The Mismeasure of Man.*) *Contemporary Education Review, 1* (2), 121–135. (Published by the American Educational Research Association.) [G]

Jephson, I. (1928). Evidence for clairvoyance in card guesssing, *Proceedings of the SPR, 38,* 223–268. [14]

Johnson, J.M. (1927). Case of the will of James L. Chaffin. *Proceedings of the SPR, 36,* 517–524. [8]

Jones, W.T. (1965). *The Sciences and the Humanities: Conflict and Reconciliation.* Berkeley: University of California Press. [5]

Kaiser, R.G. (1976). *Russia, the People and the Power.* New York: Atheneum Publishers. [A]

Kanthamani, B.K. (H.), & Rao, K.R. (1971). Personality characteristics of ESP subjects: I. Primary personality characteristics and ESP. *Journal of Parapsychology, 35,* 189–207. [24]

Kanthamani, B.K. (H.), & Rao, K.R. (1972a). Personality characteristics of

ESP subjects: II. The combined personality measure (CPM) and ESP. *Journal of Parapsychology, 36,* 56–70. [24]

Kanthamani, B.K. (H.), & Rao, K.R. (1972b). Personality characteristics of ESP subjects: III. Extraversion and ESP. *Journal of Parapsychology, 36,* 198–212. [24]

Kanthamani, H., & Kelly, E.F. (1974a). Card experiments with a special subject: I. Single-card clairvoyance. *Journal of Parapsychology, 38,* 16–26. [22]

e Kanthamani, H., & Kelly, E.F. (1974b). Awareness of success in an exceptional subject. *Journal of Parapsychology, 38,* 355–382. [7,22]

Keil, J., & Fahler, J. (1976). Nina Kulagina: A strong case for PK involving directly observable movements of objects. *European Journal of Parapsychology, 1* (2), 36–44. [12]

Keil, J., Herbert, B., Ullman, M., & Pratt, J.G. (1976). Directly observable voluntary PK effects. *Proceedings of the SPR, 56,* 197–235. [12]

Kelly, E.F. (1979). Reply to Persi Diaconis. *Zetetic Scholar,* No. 5, 20–28. [22]

e Kelly, E.F., & Kanthamani, B.K. (H.) (1972). A subject's efforts toward voluntary control. *Journal of Parapsychology, 36,* 185–197. [22]

e Kelly, E.F., Kanthamani, H., Child I.L., & Young, F.W. (1975). On the relation between visual and ESP confusion structures in an exceptional ESP subject. *Journal of the ASPR, 69,* 1–31. [13]

e Krippner, S., Honorton, C., & Ullman, M. (1972). A second precognitive dream study with Malcolm Bessant. *Journal of the ASPR, 66,* 269–279. [7]

Kuhn, Thomas (1962). *The Structure of Scientific Revolutions.* Chicago: University of Chicago Press. First edition, 1962; second edition, 1970. [18,24,26]

Lakatos, I., & Musgrave, A. (Eds.). (1970). *Criticism and the Growth of Knowledge.* Cambridge University Press. [18]

Lang, Andrew. (1900). Discussion of the trance phenomena of Mrs. Piper, Part III. *Proceedings of the SPR, 15,* 39–52. [2]

Lear, M.W. (1980). *Heartsounds.* New York: Simon & Schuster. [B]

Leonard, Mrs. Gladys Osborne (1969). Obituaries. *Journal of the SPR, 45,* 95–115. [2]

Lodge, Oliver (1893). *Pioneers of Science.* Reprinted by Dover Publications, 1960. [18]

s Mackenzie, B., & Mackenzie, S.L. (1980). Whence the enchanted boundary?—sources and significance of the parapsychological tradition. *Journal of Parapsychology, 44,* 125–166.

Margenau, Henry (1950). *The Nature of Physical Reality.* New York: McGraw-Hill. [17]

Markwick, B. (1978). The Soal-Goldney experiments with Basil Shackleton: New evidence of data manipulation. *Proceedings of the SPR, 56,* 250–277. [19]

s Mauskopf, S.H., & McVaugh, M.R. (1980). *The Elusive Science: Origins of Experimental Psychical Research.* Baltimore: Johns Hopkins University Press. [9]

s McClenon, J. (1982). A survey of elite scientists: Their attitudes toward ESP and parapsychology. *Journal of Parapsychology, 46,* 127–152. [25]

McConnell, R.A. (1958). Further comment on "Wishing with dice." *Journal of Parapsychology, 22,* 210–216. [22]

McConnell, R.A. (1968). The structure of scientific revolutions: An epitome. *Journal of the ASPR, 62*, 321–327. [18]

s   McConnell, R.A. (1969). ESP and credibility in science. *American Psychologist, 24*, 531–538. [22]

s   McConnell, R.A. (1973). Parapsychology and the occult. *Journal of the ASPR, 67*, 225–243. [9,20,21,C]

s   McConnell, R.A. (1974a). Parapsychology: Its future organization and support. *Journal of the ASPR, 68*, 169–181. [9,C]

McConnell, R.A. (1974b). PK on stable systems: Some comments. Pp. 134–136 in W.G. Roll, R.L. Morris, and J.D. Morris (Eds.), *Research in Parapsychology—1973*. Metuchen, NJ: Scarecrow Press. [12]

s   McConnell, R.A. (1975a). Parapsychology in the USSR. *Journal of Parapsychology, 39*, 129–134.

s   McConnell, R.A. (1975b). The motivations of parapsychologists and other scientists. *Journal of the ASPR, 69*, 273–280. [19]

s   McConnell, R.A. (1976a). Foundation interest in parapsychology. *Journal of Parapsychology, 40*, 145–150. [25]

s   McConnell, R.A. (1976b). Areas of agreement between the parapsychologist and the skeptic. *Journal of the ASPR, 70*, 303–308. For the ensuing correspondence see *Journal of the ASPR, 71*, 223–229. [23,25]

s   McConnell, R.A. (1976c). Parapsychology and physicists. *Journal of Parapsychology, 40*, 228–239. [12,15,22]

s   McConnell, R.A. (1977a). The resolution of conflicting beliefs about the ESP evidence. *Journal of Parapsychology, 41*, 198–214. (This paper has been reprinted in R.A. McConnell, Ed., *Encounters With Parapsychology*.) [19,21,22,25]

McConnell, R.A. (1977b). A parapsychological dialogue. *Journal of the ASPR, 71*, 429–435.

s   McConnell, R.A. (1978). ESP and the credibility of critics. *Perceptual and Motor Skills, 47*, 875–878. [21]

s   McConnell, R.A. (Ed.) (1981). *Encounters with Parapsychology*. Pittsburgh, Pennsylvania: R.A. McConnell (1982). [Preface, 13]

es   McConnell, R.A. (Ed.) (1982a). *Parapsychology and Self-Deception in Science*. Pittsburgh, Pennsylvania: R.A. McConnell (1983). [Preface, 24]

e   McConnell, R.A. (1982b). Wishing with dice revisited. Pages 29–53 in R.A. McConnell (Ed.), *Parapsychology and Self-Deception in Science*. Pittsburgh, Pennsylvania: R.A. McConnell (1983). [14]

s   McConnell, R.A. (1982c). Parapsychology, the wild card in a stacked deck: A look at the near future of mankind. Pages 117–145 in R.A. McConnell (Ed.), *Parapsychology and Self-Deception in Science*. Pittsburgh, Pennsylvania: R.A. McConnell (1983). [20,A,B]

s   McConnell, R.A., & Clark, T.K. (1980). Training, belief, and mental conflict within the Parapsychological Association. *Journal of Parapsychology, 44*, 245–268. [9,25]

e   McConnell, R.A., & Clark, T.K. (1982a). Progressive organization and ambivalence within the psychokinetic testing session. Pages 55–70 in R.A. McConnell (Ed.), *Parapsychology and Self-Deception in Science*. Pittsburgh, Pennsylvania: R.A. McConnell (1983). [14]

s   McConnell, R.A., & Clark, T.K. (1982b). Guardians of orthodoxy: The sponsors of the Committee for the Scientific Investigation of Claims of the Paranormal. *Zetetic Scholar*, No. 10, 43–49. [22]

e   McConnell, R.A., & Forwald, H. (1967). Psychokinetic placement: I. A re-examination of the Forwald-Durham experiment. *Journal of Parapsychology, 31,* 51–69. [12]

McConnell, R.A., & Forwald, H. (1968). Psychokinetic placement: III. Cube-releasing devices. *Journal of Parapsychology, 32,* 9–38. [13]

s McConnell, R.A., & McConnell, Tron (1971). Occult books sold at the University of Pittsburgh. *Journal of the ASPR, 65,* 344–353. [9]

McConnell, R.A., Snowdon, R.J., & Powell, K.F. (1955). Wishing with dice. *Journal of Experimental Psychology, 50,* 269–275. [12,14,21,22]

McDougall, William (1907). The case of Sally Beauchamp. *Proceedings of the SPR, 19,* 410–431. [3]

Medical Economics Co. (1982). *Physicians' Desk Reference* (36th ed.). Oradell, New Jersey. [B]

Merck and Company, Inc. (1982). *The Merck Manual of Diagnosis and Therapy* (14th ed.). Rahway, New Jersey. [B]

Monod, Jacques (1971). *Chance and Necessity.* New York: Alfred Knopf. [25]

Moody, R.A. (1975). *Life After Life.* Covington, Georgia: Mockingbird Books (1975); New York: Bantam Books (1976). [8]

e Morris, R.L., Roll, W.G., Klein, J., & Wheeler, G. (1972). EEG patterns and ESP results in forced-choice experiments with Lalsingh Harribance. *Journal of the ASPR, 66,* 253–268.

Mundle, C.W. (1974). The Soal-Goldney experiments. *Proceedings of the SPR, 56,* 85–87. [19]

Murphy, Gardner (1935). Dr. Prince and the Doris case. Pages 66–81 in *Walter Franklin Prince, A Tribute to His Memory,* edited by the Boston Society for Psychic Research. Boston: Bruce Humphries, Inc. [3]

Murphy, Gardner (1945). Difficulties confronting the survival hypothesis. *Journal of the ASPR, 39,* 67–94. [8]

Murphy, J.M. (1976). Psychiatric labeling in cross-cultural perspective *Science, 191,* 1019–1028. [4,19]

e Musso, J.R., & Granero, M. (1973). An ESP drawing experiment with a high-scoring subject. *Journal of Parapsychology, 37,* 13–36.

e Musso, J.R., & Granero, M. (1981). *U*-effects in an ESP experiment with concealed drawings. *Journal of Parapsychology, 45,* 99–120.

Myers, Frederic (1886). On telepathic hypnotism and its relation to other forms of hypnotic suggestion. *Proceedings of the SPR, 4,* 127–188. [16]

Myers, Frederic (1903). *Human Personality and Its Survival of Bodily Death* (in two volumes). London: Longmans, Green & Co., reissued in 1954. A one-volume (470-page) condensation by his son was published in London by Longmans, Green & Co. in 1907. Another one-volume (416-page) abridgment appeared in 1961 from University Books, Inc., with all case material moved from the appendixes into the text. [9,C]

Nash, C.B. (1978). *Science of Psi.* Springfield, Illinois: C.C. Thomas.

Natsoulas, T. (1978). Consciousness. *American Psychologist, 33,* 906–914. [4]

Ortega y Gasset, José (1932). *The Revolt of the Masses* (authorized English translation). New York: W.W. Norton. [A]

Orwell, George (1949). *1984.* New York: Harcourt Brace & Co. [A]

Osis, K. (1961). *Deathbed Observations by Physicians and Nurses* (Monograph No. 3). New York: Parapsychology Foundation. [8]

Palmer, J. (1971). Scoring in ESP tests as a function of belief in ESP: Part I. The sheep-goat effect. *Journal of the ASPR, 65,* 373–408. [24]

Palmer, J. (1972). Scoring in ESP tests as a function of belief in ESP: Part II. Beyond the sheep-goat effect. *Journal of the ASPR, 66,* 1–26. [24]

Pearl, Raymond (1938). Tobacco smoking and longevity. *Science, 87,* 216–217. [21]

Pendell, Elmer (1977). *Why Civilizations Self-Destruct.* Cape Canaveral: Howard Allen. [A]

Pendery, M.L., Maltzman, I.M., & West, L.J. (1982). Controlled drinking by alcoholics? New findings and a reevaluation of a major affirmative study. *Science, 217,* 169–175. [19]

Pierce, H.W. (1973). RSPK phenomena observed by two families. *Journal of the ASPR, 67,* 86–101. [11]

Piper, Mrs. Leonora (1950). Obituary. *Journal of the SPR, 35,* 341–344. [2]

Podmore, Frank (1898). Discussion of the trance phenomena of Mrs. Piper, Part I. *Proceedings of the SPR, 14,* 50–78. [2]

Podmore, Frank (1902). *Modern Spiritualism: A History and Criticism.* (2 volumes) London: Methuen & Co. Republished under the title *Mediums of the 19th Century* (2 volumes). New York: University Books, 1963. [2,9,C]

Poincaré, H. (1903). *Science and Hypothesis.* New York: Dover (1952). [1]

Pratt, J.G., (1944). A reinvestigation of the quarter distribution of the (PK) page. *Journal of Parapsychology, 8,* 61–63. [13]

Pratt, J.G., (1947a). Target preference in PK tests with dice. *Journal of Parapsychology, 11,* 26–45. [13]

Pratt, J.G. (1947b). Rhythms of success in PK test data. *Journal of Parapsychology, 11,* 90–110. [13]

Pratt, J.G. (1947c). Restricted areas of success in PK tests. *Journal of Parapsychology, 11,* 191–207. [13]

Pratt, J.G., (1947d). Trial-by-trial grouping of success and failure in psi tests. *Journal of Parapsychology, 11,* 254–268. [13]

e   Pratt, J.G., (1973). A decade of research with a selected ESP subject: An overview and reappraisal of the work with Pavel Stepanek. *Proceedings of the ASPR, 30,* 1–78.

Pratt, J.G. (1974). Fresh light on the Scott and Haskell case against Soal. *Proceedings of the SPR, 56,* 97–111. [19]

Pratt, J.G. (1978a). Statement. *Proceedings of the SPR, 56,* 279–281. [19]

Pratt, J.G. (1978b). The Pearisburg poltergeist. Pp. 174–182 in W.G. Roll (Ed.), *Research in Parapsychology—1977.* Metuchen, New Jersey: Scarecrow Press. [11]

Pratt, J.G., & Forwald, H. (1958). Confirmation of the PK placement effect. *Journal of Parapsychology, 22,* 1–19. [12]

Pratt, J.G., & Keil, H.H.J. (1973). Firsthand observations of Nina S. Kulagina suggestive of PK upon static objects. *Journal of the ASPR, 67,* 381–390. [12]

Pratt, J.G., & Price, M.M. (1938). The experimenter-subject relationship in tests for ESP. *Journal of Parapsychology, 2,* 84–94. [7]

Pratt, J.G., Rhine, J.B., Smith, B.M., Stuart, C.E., & Greenwood, J.A. (1940). *Extrasensory Perception After Sixty Years.* New York: Henry Holt. [9,21]

Price, G.R. (1955). Science and the supernatural. *Science, 122,* 359–367. [22]

Prince, Morton (1901). The development and geneology of the Misses Beauchamp: A preliminary report of a case of multiple personality. *Proceedings of the SPR, 15,* 466–483. [3]

Prince, Morton (1905). *Dissociation of a Personality.* London: Longmans, Green & Co. (Reprinted, 1968, by Johnson Reprint Corp.) [3,4,19,24]

Prince, Morton (1929). *Clinical and Experimental Studies in Personality.* Cambridge, Massachusetts: Sci-Art. (Reprinted 1970, by Greenwood Press.) [3,4,24]

Prince, Morton (1855–1929). Obituary. *Journal of the SPR, 26* (1930), 42–43. [3]

Prince, Walter Franklin (1915). The Doris case of multiple personality, Part 1. *Proceedings of the ASPR, 9,* 1–700. [3,4,19,24]

Prince, Walter Franklin (1916). The Doris case of multiple personality, Part 2. *Proceedings of the ASPR, 10,* 701–1419. [3,4,19,24]

Prince, Walter Franklin. (1926). *The Psychic in the House.* Boston Society for Psychic Research. [3,4,6]

Prince, Walter Franklin (1928). *Noted Witnesses for Psychic Occurrences.* Boston Society for Psychic Research. [21]

Prince, Walter Franklin (1930). *The Enchanted Boundary.* Boston Society for Psychic Research. [21]

Prince, Walter Franklin (1863–1934). Obituary. *Proceedings of the SPR, 42* (1934), 289–291. [3]

Puthoff, H.E., & Targ, R. (1974). PK experiments with Uri Geller and Ingo Swann. Pp. 125–128 in W.G. Roll, R.L. Morris, and J.D. Morris (Eds.), *Research in Parapsychology—1973.* Metuchen, NJ: Scarecrow Press. [12]

e   Puthoff, H.E., & Targ, R. (1976). A perceptual channel for information transfer over kilometer distances: Historical perspective and recent research. *Proceedings of the Institute of Electrical and Electronics Engineers, 64,* 329–354. [25]

Radin, D.I. (1982). Mental influence on machine-generated random events: Six experiments. Pp. 141–142, in W.G. Roll, R.L. Morris, & R.A. White (Eds.), *Research in Parapsychology—1981.* Metuchen, New Jersey: Scarecrow Press.

Rand, Ayn (1957). *Atlas Shrugged.* New York: Random House. [A]

Randall, J.L. (1978). Letter. [19]

Rawlins, D. (1981). sTARBABY. *Fate, 34* (10), 67–99. [22]

Rhine, J.B. (1934). *Extrasensory Perception.* Originally published by the Boston Society for Psychic Research. Now available from Brandon Press. [9]

Rhine, J.B. (1967). Psychology and parapsychology. Pages 101–117 in R.A. McConnell (Ed.), *Encounters with Parapsychology.* Pittsburgh, Pennsylvania: R.A. McConnell (1981). [9]

Rhine, J.B. (1974). A new case of experimenter unreliability. *Journal of Parapsychology, 38,* 215–225. [19]

Rhine, J.B. (1975). Second report on a case of experimenter fraud. *Journal of Parapsychology, 39,* 306–325. [19]

Rhine, J.B., & Humphrey, B.M. (1944a). The PK effect: Special evidence from hit patterns. I. Quarter distributions of the page. *Journal of Parapsychology, 8,* 18–60. [13]

Rhine, J.B., & Humphrey, B.M. (1944b). The PK effect: Special evidence from hit patterns. II. Quarter distributions of the set. *Journal of Parapsychology, 8,* 254–271. [13]

Rhine, J.B., Humphrey, B.M., & Pratt, J.G. (1945). The PK effect: Special evidence from hit patterns. III. Quarter distributions of the half-set. *Journal of Parapsychology, 9,* 150–168. [13]

Rhine, L.E. (1961). *Hidden Channels of the Mind.* New York: William Sloane. [24]

Rhine, L.E. (1963). Spontaneous physical effects and the psi process. *Journal of Parapsychology, 27,* 84–122. [11]

Rhine, L.E. (1967). *ESP in Life and Lab.* New York: Collier-Macmillan. [24]

Rhine, L.E. (1970). Mind Over Matter: Psychokinesis. New York: Macmillan Co. [11,12]

Rhine, L.E. (1981). *The Invisible Picture: A Study of Psychic Experiences.* Jefferson, N.C.: McFarland & Co. [24]

Rhine, L.E., & Rhine, J.B. (1943). The psychokinetic effect: I. The first experiment. *Journal of Parapsychology, 7,* 20–43. [12]

Robinson, A.L. (1983). Loophole closed in quantum mechanics test. *Science, 219,* 40–41. [A]

s   Rockwell, T., Rockwell, R., & Rockwell, W.T. (1978). Irrational rationalists: A critique of *The Humanist*'s crusade against parapsychology. *Journal of the ASPR, 72,* 23–34. [22]

Roll, W.G. (1978). Understanding the poltergeist. Pp. 183–195, in W.G. Roll (Ed.), *Research In Parapsychology—1977.* Metuchen, New Jersey: Scarecrow Press. [11]

e   Roll, W.G., & Klein, J. (1972). Further forced-choice ESP experiments with Lalsingh Harribance. *Journal of the ASPR, 66,* 103–112.

Rosenhan, D.L. (1973). On being sane in insane places. *Science 179,* 250–258. [B]

Rush, J.H. (1977). Problems and methods in psychokinetic research. Pp. 15–78 in S. Krippner and R.A. White (Eds.), *Advances in Parapsychological Research: 1. Psychokinesis.* New York: Plenum Press. [11,12]

Ryzl, M. (1962). Training the psi faculty by hypnosis. *Journal of the SPR, 41,* 234–252. [7]

Sargent, C.L. (1980). *Exploring Psi in the Ganzfeld: Parapsychological Monograph No. 17.* New York: Parapsychology Foundation. [7]

Schechter, E.I. (1977). Nonintentional ESP: A review and replication. *Journal of the ASPR, 71,* 337–374.

Schiller, F.C.S. (1918). The Doris Fischer case of multiple personality (a review). *Proceedings of the SPR, 29,* 386–403. [3]

e   Schlitz, M., & Gruber, E. (1980). Transcontinental remote viewing. *Journal of Parapsychology, 44,* 305–317. [25]

e   Schlitz, M., & Gruber, E. (1981). Transcontinental remote viewing: A re-judging. *Journal of Parapsychology, 45,* 233–237. [25]

Schmeidler, G.R. (1973). PK effects upon continuously recorded temperature. *Journal of the ASPR, 67,* 325–340. [12]

e   Schmidt, Helmut (1969a). Precognition of a quantum process. *Journal of Parapsychology, 33,* 99–108. [10]

e   Schmidt, Helmut (1969b). Quantum process predicted? *New Scientist, 44,* 114–115. [10]

e   Schmidt, Helmut (1970). A PK test with electronic equipment. *Journal of Parapsychology, 34,* 175–181. [10]

e   Schmidt, Helmut (1973). PK tests with a high-speed random number generator. *Journal of Parapsychology, 37.* 105–118.

e   Schmidt, Helmut (1974). Comparison of PK action on two different random number generators. *Journal of Parapsychology, 38,* 47–55.

e   Schouten, S.A., & Kelly, E.F. (1978). On the experiment of Brugmans, Heymans, and Weinberg. *European Journal of Parapsychology, 2,* 247–290.

Schreiber, F.R. (1973). *Sybil.* New York: Warner Paperback Library. [3,19]

Scott, C. (1978). Letter. *Journal of the SPR, 49,* 969–970. [19]

Scott, C., & Haskell, P. (1974). Fresh light on the Shackleton experiments. *Proceedings of the SPR, 56,* 43–72. [19]

Shapere, D. (1971). The paradigm concept (a book review). *Science, 172,* 706–709. [18]

Shields, J. (1973). Heredity and psychological abnormality. Pp. 540–603 in H.J. Eysenck (Ed.) *Handbook of Abnormal Psychology.* London: Pitman & Sons (2d. ed.). [4]

Sidgwick, Eleanor Balfour (Mrs. Henry) (1900). Discussion of the trance phenomena of Mrs. Piper, Part II. *Proceedings of the SPR, 15,* 16–38. [6,7]

Sidgwick, Eleanor Balfour (Mrs. Henry) (1915). A contribution to the study of the psychology of Mrs. Piper's trance phenomena. *Proceedings of the SPR, 28,* xix + 657 pp. [2]

Sidgwick, E.B. (Mrs. Henry), Piddington, J.G., and deWolfe-Howe, M.A. (1907). Richard Hodgson: In memoriam. *Proceedings of the SPR, 19,* 356–372. [9]

Sinclair, Upton (1930). *Mental Radio.* Springfield, Illinois: C.C. Thomas, 1962. [7]

Sizemore, C.C., & Pittillo, E.S. (1977). *I'm Eve.* New York: Doubleday. New York: Harcourt Brace Jovanovich (paperbound). [3,4]

Skinner, B.F. (1948). *Walden Two.* New York: Macmillan. [A]

Smith, Hedrick (1976). *The Russians.* New York: Ballantine (paperbound). [A]

Smith, R.J. (1982a). Atom bomb tests leave infamous legacy. *Science, 218,* 266–269. [B]

Smith, R.J. (1982b). Scientists implicated in atom test deception. *Science, 218,* 545–547. [B]

Smythies, J.R. (1974). ESP fact or fiction: A sidelight on Soal. *Proceedings of the SPR, 56,* 130–131. [19]

Snow, C.P. (1959). *The Two Cultures and the Scientific Revolution.* Cambridge University Press. [5]

Soal, S.G. (1925). A report on some communications received through Mrs. Blanche Cooper. *Proceedings of the SPR, 35,* 471–594. [19]

Soal, S.G. (pseudonym: "Mr. V") (1929). Some automatic scripts purporting to be inspired by Margaret Veley, poet and novelist (1843–1887), Part II. *Proceedings of the SPR, 38,* 331–374. [19]

Soal, S.G. (1940). Fresh light on card guessing—Some new effects. *Proceedings of the SPR, 46,* 152–198. [19]

Soal, S.G., & Bateman, F. (1954). *Modern Experiments in Telepathy.* New Haven: Yale University Press. [19]

Soal, S.G., & Goldney, K.M. (1943). Experiments in precognitive telepathy. *Proceedings of the SPR, 47,* 21–150. [19]

Society for Psychical Research. (1882). Objects of the Society. *Proceedings of the SPR. 1.* 3–6. [15]

Somervell, D.C. (1946). *A Study of History* (an abridgment of Volumes I–VI of the work of Arnold J. Toynbee under the same title). Oxford University Press. [20,A]

Soule, M.H. (1950). A summary of present knowledge of brucellosis. (pp 247–255 in) *Brucellosis Symposium.* Washington, D.C.: American Association for the Advancement of Science. [B]

Sperry, R.W. (1980). Mind-brain interaction: Mentalism, yes, dualism, no. *Neuroscience, 5,* 195–206. [5]

Sperry, R.W. (1981). Changing priorities. Pp. 1–15 in W.M. Cowan, Z.W. Hall, & E.R. Kandel (Eds.) *Annual Review of Neuroscience, Volume 4.* Palo Alto, California: Annual Reviews, Inc. [5]

Sperry, R.W. (1982a). Some effects of disconnecting the cerebral hemispheres. *Science, 217,* 1223–1226. [3,5]

Sperry, R.W. (1982b). *Science and Moral Priority: Merging Mind, Brain, and Human Values.* New York: Columbia University Press. [5]

Spink, W.W. (1956). *The Nature of Brucellosis.* Minneapolis: University of Minnesota Press. [B]

e   Stanford, R.G., & Mayer, B. (1974). Relaxation as a psi-conducive state: A replication and exploration of parameters. *Journal of the ASPR, 68,* 182–191. [7]

Stevenson, I. (1966). *Twenty Cases Suggestive of Reincarnation (Proceedings of the ASPR, 26,* 1–362). [8]

Stevenson, I. (1974). The credibility of Mrs. Gretl Albert's testimony. *Proceedings of the SPR, 56,* 117–129. [19]

Szasz, T.S. (1961). *The Myth of Mental Illness.* New York: Harper-Hoeber. [4]

Taboas, A.M. (1980). The psychopathological model of poltergeist phenomena: Some criticisms and suggestions. *Parapsychology Review, 11* (2), 24–27. [11]

Tart, C.T., Palmer, J., & Redington, D.J. (1979). Effects of immediate feedback on ESP performance over short time periods. *Journal of the ASPR, 73,* 291–301.

e   Terry, J.C., & Honorton, C. (1976). Psi information retrieval in the Ganzfeld: Two confirmatory studies. *Journal of the ASPR, 70,* 207–217. [7]

Thigpen, C.H., & Cleckley, H.M. (1954). A case of multiple personality. *Journal of Abnormal and Social Psychology, 49,* 135–151. [3]

Thigpen, C.H., & Cleckley, H.M. (1957). *The Three Faces of Eve,* New York: McGraw-Hill. New York: Popular Library (paperback). [3,4]

Thouless, R.H. (1974). Some comments on "Fresh light on the Shackleton experiments." *Proceedings of the SPR, 56,* 88–92. [19]

Thouless, R.H. (1978). Letter. *Journal of the SPR, 49,* 965–968. [19]

Tietze, T.R. (1976). Ursa major: An impressionistic appreciation of Walter Franklin Prince. *Journal of the ASPR, 70,* 1–34. [9]

Toynbee, Arnold. *See* D.C. Somervell.

Troubridge, Una Vincenzo (Lady) (1961). *The Life of Radclyffe Hall.* New York: Citadel Press. [2]

Truzzi, Marcello (Ed.) (1982). Analysis and discussion of Rawlins (1981), *Zetetic Scholar,* No. 9, 33–83, and No. 10, 43–81. [22]

Tyrrell, G.N.M. (1938). *Science and Psychical Phenomena.* London: Harper & Brothers. [C]

Tyrrell, G.N.M. (1946). *The Personality of Man.* London: Penguin Books. [C]

e   Ullman, M., & Krippner, S. (1970). *Dream Studies and Telepathy: Parapsychological Monograph No. 12.* New York: Parapsychology Foundation. [7]

Van de Castle, R.L. (1977). Sleep and dreams. Pages 473–499 in B.B. Wolman (Ed.), *Handbook of Parapsychology.* New York: Van Nostrand Reinhold. [7]

Vasiliev, L.L. (1962). *Exsperimentalnie Issledovaniya Mislennogo Vnusheniya.* Leningrad: Zhdanov Leningrad State University. Translated to English as *Experiments in Mental Suggestion.* by the Institute for the Study of Mental Images, Hampshire, England, 1963, and as *Experimental Studies of Mental Suggestion* (Publication JPRS 59163) by the U.S. Joint Publications Research Service, Arlington, Virginia, 1973. [6,15,24]

s Wagner, M.W., & Monnet, M. (1979). Attitudes of college professors toward extrasensory perception. *Zetetic Scholar*, No. 5, 7–16. [25]

Watkins, G.K., & Watkins, A.M. (1974). Apparent psychokinesis on static objects by a "gifted" subject: A laboratory demonstration. Pp. 132–134 in W.G. Roll, R.L. Morris, and J.D. Morris (Eds.), *Research in Parapsychology—1973*. Metuchen, N.J.: Scarecrow Press. [12]

Weinberg, A.M. (1972). Social institutions and nuclear energy. *Science, 177*, 27–34. [21]

s Wheeler, J.A. (1979). Press release distributed at the AAAS annual meeting in Houston, Texas and published for the AAAS in R. G. Jahn (Ed.) *The Role of Consciousness in the Physical World*. Boulder, Colorado: Westview Press (1981). [25]

Whyte, L.L. (1974). The unconscious in history. *Contemporary Psychoanalysis, 10*, 379–386. [5]

Wolman, B.B. (1977). *Handbook of Parapsychology*. New York: Van Nostrand.

Worcester, E. (1935). Recent developments in the Doris case of multiple personality. Pages 82–88 in *Walter Franklin Prince, A Tribute to His Memory*, edited by the Boston Society for Psychic Research. Boston: Bruce Humphries, Inc. [4]

Young, P.C. (1952). Antisocial uses of Hypnosis. Pages 376–409 in L.M. Lecron (Ed.), *Experimental Hypnosis*. New York: Macmillan. [6]

Yow, E.M., Brennan, J.C., Nathan, M.H., & Israel, L. (1961). Calcified granulomata of the spleen in long-standing brucellar infection. *Annals of Internal Medicine, 55*, 307–317. [B]

Zorab, G. (1976). Parapsychological Developments in the Netherlands. *European Journal of Parapsychology, 1* (3), 57–82. [1]

Zukav, Gary (1979). *The Dancing Wu Li Masters*. New York: William Morrow & Co. [A]

NAME INDEX

Persons, Books, and Journals

("f" means "and on the following page")

Abelson, Philip, 301
Alvarado, C.S., 172
American Journal of Physics, 233, 243f
American Psychologist, 170, 244–248
Anthony, Susan B., 228
Aristotle, 172, 199f
Ascent of Man (Bronowski), 265
Atkinson, R.C., 245, 263
Atlas Shrugged (Rand), 273, 275

Balfour, Arthur, 86, 228
Bamford, J., 275
Barber, T.X., 59, 154, 162, 165–167, 169
Barrett, Sir William, 86, 289
Barrington, M.R., 209
Bateman, F., 209
"Beauchamp, Sally," 26–30, 37f, 40, 68, 255
Becker, Ernest, 271
Bekhterev, V.M., 257
Belasco, David, 228
Bell, J.S., 278
Beloff, J., 209, 311
Bisaha, J.P., 263n
Blavatsky, Helena P., 18, 87
Brahe, Tycho, 32, 207
Braud, L.W., 66f
Braud, W.G., 66f
Brave New World (Huxley), 273
Bridgman, Percy W., 184n, 222
Broad, C.D., 79, 230, 270, 289
Bronowski, Jacob, 265–268, 301
Broughton, R.S., 68
Browning, Robert, 228
Buchwald, A.M., 169
Burbank, Luther, 228
Butcher, S.H., 77

Cabibbo, C., 71, 217, 299
Cadoret, R., 135
Cardan, Jerome, 228
Carington, Whately, 135, 208
Cattell, Raymond B., 273, 275–278
Chance and Necessity (Monod), 265
Chauvin, Rémy, 210
Child, I.L., 135
Clark, T.K., xiv, 90, 145–153, 241, 259, 264
Clauser, J.F., 278
Cleckley, H.M., 27, 32, 38
Clemens, Samuel (Mark Twain), 228
Condon, E.U., 232, 267
Cox, W.E., 122

Crandon, Margery, 19, 89
Cromwell, Oliver, 267
Crookes, Sir William, 86

Dancing Wu Li Masters (Zukav), 273, 278
Das Kapital (Marx), 275
Davis, J.W., 211
Delmore, Bill, 68
Depew, Chauncey, 228
Descartes, René, 49f, 200
Diagnostic and Statistical Manual of Mental Disorders, 37
Dickens, Charles, 228
Discovery of the Unconscious (Ellenberger), 97
Dissociation of a Personality (M. Prince), 27
"Doris," *see* "Fischer, Doris"
"Dorsett, Sybil," 27, 33, 37f, 68
Doyle, Sir Arthur Conan, 96
du Maurier, George, 58
Dubrovsky, A.V., 59, 154ff
Ducasse, C.J., 81
Dunne, B.J., 263n
Duval, P., 210

Einstein, Albert, 200, 278
Eisenbud, J., 126
Ellenberger, H.F., 85, 97
Elusive Science, The, (Mauskopf & McVaugh), 85
Enchanted Boundary (W. Prince), 228
Encounters with Parapsychology (McConnell), xiv, 163
Escape from Evil (Becker), 271
Esdaille, James, 228
Estabrooks, G.H., 139
Estes, W.K., 168
Evans, Alice C., 282
Evans, C., 264
Experiments in Mental Suggestion (Vasiliev), 154–160
Extrasensory Perception (J.B. Rhine), 89
Eysenck, H.J., 306

Fahler, J., 128
Faraday, Michael, 228
"Feda," 17
"Fischer, Doris," 26, 30–32, 35n, 37f, 68
Fleming, Alice Kipling, 19
Ford, D., 287

324

SUBJECT INDEX

("f" means "and on the following page")